Bilingual
Education

Bilingual Education

A Reappraisal of Federal Policy

Edited by
Keith A. Baker
Adriana A. de Kanter
Department of Education

LexingtonBooks
D.C. Heath and Company
Lexington, Massachusetts
Toronto

Library of Congress Cataloging in Publication Data

Main entry under title:

Bilingual education.

    Includes bibliographical references.
    1. Education, Bilingual—Government policy—United States—Addresses,
essays, lectures. I. Baker, Keith. II. De Kanter, Adriana A.
LC3731.B546 1982   371.97′0973   82-48040
ISBN 0-699-05885-8

Copyright © 1983 by D.C. Heath and Company

Published simultaneously in Canada

Printed in the United States of America

International Standard Book Number: 0-669-05885-8

Library of Congress Catalog Card Number: 82-48040

Contents

Available for Eliminating Past Educational
Practices Ruled Unlawful under *Lau* **v.** *Nichols*
Office for Civil Rights   213

Appendix C   **The Proposed Regulations, August 1980**   223

              Index   239

              About the Contributors   241

              About the Editors   245

Acknowledgments

We are grateful for the support and assistance we received in conducting these studies from the management of the Office of Planning, Budget, and Evaluation during both the Reagan and Carter administrations. Gary Jones, Emerson Elliott, Bruce Barr, William Fischer, and Thom Rhue made the resources available to carry out this work and, more important, told us to charge ahead when the politics got hot.

Thanks also should be given for the help and comments we received from Marshall Smith, Charles Cooke, Lynette Ferrara, and staff members of the bilingual offices of Title VII, Office for Civil Rights, and the National Institute of Education.

Special thanks go to our secretary, Sandra Richardson, and to our families and friends who put up with the disruptions on the home front.

This book is based on a policy review of the U.S. Department of Education's programs for the education of language-minority students carried out by the Office of Technical and Analytic Services, Office of Planning, Budget, and Evaluation, in the U.S. Department of Education. Some of the analyses were made by staff members of the Office of Technical and Analytic Services and others by independent consulting firms under contract with the Office of Planning, Budget, and Evaluation. In all cases, the views expressed in this book are those of the authors and do not necessarily represent either the policy or the position of the U.S. Department of Education.

Introduction: Addressing the Needs of Language-Minority Children

Beatrice F. Birman and
Alan L. Ginsburg

The chapters in this book were prepared by the Office of Planning, Budget, and Evaluation (OPBE) of the U.S. Department of Education. The studies reported in them were designed to provide a factual basis for analyzing the issues that the federal government must address in developing educational policies for language-minority children. The studies were undertaken in August 1980 in response to a request by the Regulatory Analysis Review Group of the Council on Wage and Price Stability for an analysis of the proposed rule for Title VI of the Civil Rights Act. In essence, the proposed rule adopted transitional bilingual education (TBE) as the required approach for complying with federal civil-rights guarantees. TBE means using the student's native language to teach subject matter until he or she achieves English proficiency. It differs from English-as-a-second-language (ESL) programs, which provide supplemental instruction in the English language to students who are otherwise enrolled in a regular instructional program and from structured immersion.

Although the proposed rule was withdrawn in February 1981, federal civil-rights activities and support programs continue to emphasize TBE, generally discouraging the use of other forms of assistance to language-minority children. More than five-hundred school districts have signed compliance agreements with the Office for Civil Rights (OCR) that provide for TBE as the major method of instruction. The OCR rarely permits other programs to help language-minority children. And Title VII of the Elementary and Secondary Education Act, which concerns bilingual education, has not funded alternative approaches to TBE. Because many language-minority children have severe educational needs that merit special programs and because of the continued federal pressure for TBE to the exclusion of other approaches, it was felt that educational programs for language-minority children need reexamination.

Background

Data collected by the federal government and by private civil-rights and educational organizations in the late 1960s revealed substantial evidence of discrimination against language-minority students, especially Hispanics, in the nation's public elementary and secondary schools. Statistics on academic achievement and school retention clearly documented that hundreds of thousands of language-minority students suffered severe academic retardation and exceptionally high dropout rates.

While conducting compliance reviews, the OCR discovered a number of common practices that had the effect of denying equal educational opportunities to language-minority students. These practices related to the way in which schools responded to the deficiencies in English-language skills characteristic of many language-minority students.

On the basis of this evidence, the OCR, using its authority under Title VI of the Civil Rights Act, sent a memorandum to school superintendents on May 25, 1970, "to clarify DHEW [Department of Health, Education and Welfare] policy on issues concerning the responsibility of school districts to provide equal educational opportunity to national origin/minority group children deficient in English language skills." Schools were required to rectify the "language deficiency in order to open its instructional program to these students." They could not use English-language ability as a basis for assigning national origin-minority group students to classes for the mentally retarded or deny these students access to college preparatory courses "on a basis directly related to the failure of the school system to inculcate English language skills." Furthermore, "any ability grouping or tracing system employed by the school system to deal with the special language skill needs of national origin/minority group children must be designed to meet such language skill needs as soon as possible and must not operate as an educational dead-end or permanent tract." And finally, school districts must notify the parents of such students of the school activities that are called to the attention of other parents. The notice, to be adequate, must be in a language they can understand.

The Lau Decision

The OCR memorandum was affirmed by the Supreme Court in its 1974 decision in the case of *Lau* v. *Nichols*. *Lau* was a class-action suit against the San Francisco Public School District that alleged that the district's failure to provide special educational services to non-English-speaking Chinese students violated both the equal-protection-clause of the Fourteenth Amendment and Title VI of the Civil Rights Act of 1964.

The Court reviewed the California Education Code and concluded:

> Under these State-imposed standards there is no equality of treatment merely by providing students with the same facilities, textbooks,

teachers, and curriculum; for students who do not understand English are effectively foreclosed from any meaningful education.

Basic English skills are at the very core of what these public schools teach. Imposition of a requirement that before a child can effectively participate in the educational program, he must already have acquired those basic skills is to make a mockery of public education. We know that those who do not understand English are certain to find classroom experiences wholly incomprehensible and in no way meaningful.

It seems obvious that the Chinese-speaking minority receives less benefits than the English-speaking majority from respondents' school system which denies them a meaningful opportunity to participate in the educational program—all earmarks of the discrimination banned by the Regulations.

The Court declined to rule on the constitutionality of the school district's program, focusing instead on the statutory prohibition against national-origin discrimination set out in Title VI of the Civil Rights Act of 1964. Accordingly, the Supreme Court found the San Francisco Public School District to be in violation of Title VI. However, the Court declined to prescribe a specific program that would provide equal educational benefits, stating, "Teaching English to the students of Chinese ancestry is one choice. Giving instruction to this group in Chinese is another. There may be others."

The Supreme Court's *Lau* decision in effect outlawed submersion programs, defined as those in which language-minority children are placed into an ordinary English-speaking classroom with no special program to help them overcome the language problem. Three other methods of instruction are alternative ways of helping the language-minority child:

1. English as a Second Language. Language-minority students are placed in regular instruction for most of the day. During some part of the day, however, the curriculum differs from that of the regular classroom in giving extra instruction in mastering English. Generally, this extra help is based on a special curriculum designed to teach English as a second rather than a first language. The home language may or may not be used in ESL instruction.
2. Transitional Bilingual Education. Subject matter is taught at least partially in the home language of minority children until their English is good enough to enable them to participate successfully in the regular classroom. To help minimize the time children spend in mastering English, ESL is often a part of TBE. It is also generally held that learning to read in the home language facilitates learning to read in English. Sometimes home-language instruction is gradually phased out and regular English instruction gradually phased in; other times, the change

is more abrupt, with the student being mainstreamed out of the home-language program. The ultimate goal of TBE is to move the student into the all-English program. TBE is differentiated from submersion and ESL by the use of the home language for instruction.

3.   Structured Immersion. Almost all instruction is given in English. There are, however, important differences between immersion and submersion. First, immersion teachers are fully bilingual. Second, although students can ask questions of the teacher in the home language, an immersion teacher generally replies only in English. Further, the curriculum is structured so that no prior knowledge of English is assumed when subject areas are taught. No content is introduced except in a way that can be understood by the student. The student in effect learns English and content simultaneously. Structured immersion programs may include home language arts classes.

Lau *Remedies*

Following the Supreme Court's decision in *Lau*, DHEW asked a group of experts to develop informal policy guidelines concerning the remedial responsibilities of school districts that failed to comply with Title VI and the principles enunciated in *Lau*. This group produced a document titled, "Task Force Findings Specifying Remedies Available for Eliminating Past Educational Practices Ruled Unlawful Under *Lau* v. *Nichols*," better known as the *Lau* Remedies.

The *Lau* Remedies outlined the major elements that should be included in school districts' plans to remedy Title VI *Lau* violations:

Identification of students with a primary or home language other than English.

Assessment of the relative proficiency of such students in English and in their native language.

Instruction of elementary students through their strongest language until the students are able to participate effectively in a classroom where instruction is given exclusively in English.

Provision of special language instruction and compensatory educational services to language-minority students who are underachieving academically in secondary schools.

Because the *Lau* Remedies were never published as proposed regulations, their underlying assumption that TBE was the best, if not the only, way to satisfy the civil-rights requirements was never opened to public debate.

A cover letter transmitting the *Lau* Remedies to school officials explained the document's legal application. In part it stated:

> Voluntary compliance plans which set forth educational strategies consistent with the approaches outlined in this document and which contain the other elements specified therein, will be accepted by this office. School districts submitting voluntary compliance plans to this office which are not consistent with the outlined approaches or with other required plan elements must demonstrate affirmatively, at time of submission, that such plans, at a minimum, will be equally effective in ensuring equal educational opportunity.

Thus the federal government placed the burden of proof on the schools to demonstrate that an alternative to TBE was effective, even though the government had never shown TBE to be effective.

Although DHEW used the *Lau* Remedies to negotiate numerous voluntary-compliance plans, the document's legal authority was challenged in a 1978 federal court suit, *Northwest Arctic* v. *Califano.* As a result of the suit, DHEW agreed to publish its Title VI *Lau* compliance standards in the *Federal Register* for public comment. In keeping with the court-approved agreement, the Department of Education published a Notice of Proposed Rulemaking on August 5, 1980.

The standard proposed in the notice required that TBE be used to meet the needs of all language-minority students identified as eligible for services. Although it called for special instruction to encourage fluency in English, content areas of the curriculum would be taught in the child's home language until that child mastered English well enough to succeed with all instruction in English. Following an extended period of public comment on the proposed regulations, the notice was formally withdrawn February 2, 1981.

Title VII of the Elementary and Secondary Education Act

In addition to mandating TBE through its civil-rights policy, the Education Department has directly funded the development of bilingual-education programs. The Bilingual Education Act, passed in 1968 as Title VII of the Elementary and Secondary Education Act, is designed to "build the capacity" of local grantees to maintain programs of bilingual education when federal funding is reduced or no longer available. The act also provides funds for teacher training, development and dissemination of bilingual instructional materials, and the maintenance of a technical-assistance network. Funded at $7.5 million in 1969, the Title VII program received more than $157 million in appropriations in 1981.

The Title VII program provides resources to help school districts meet the needs of language-minority children. Programs funded under Title VII are, by law, programs in which instruction is given in English and, to the extent necessary, in the native or dominant language of the student in order to allow the student to achieve competence in the English language. Coupled with the program requirements embodied in the *Lau* Remedies, the Title VII constraints have increased incentives for districts to choose TBE over other possible approaches.

Examination of the TBE Approach

Although the proposed rule was withdrawn, the question of the appropriateness and effectiveness of TBE is still important, for several reasons.

1. The Department of Education may still be under a consent decree requiring that the *Lau* Remedies be replaced with formal regulations, so new regulations may have to be drafted. If a particular instructional approach can be justified, mandating it would be one option considered in the development of new regulations.
2. While the *Lau* Remedies are no longer being enforced by the Education Department, compliance agreements between school districts and OCR remain in effect. From 1975, OCR negotiated more than five hundred compliance agreements on the basis of the *Lau* Remedies, which stressed TBE. Many districts continue to rely on TBE exclusively, perhaps without investigating other methods that might better meet the needs of their students.
3. Other Department of Education policies and programs have emphasized TBE to the exclusion of other approaches. The department's approach to the problems of language-minority children over the past decade has been based on an assumption that TBE is the only acceptable approach. Thus federal funds have not been spent to improve methods for other forms of assistance.
4. Federal policy has formed the basis for bilingual programs and legislation in several states. When states follow the federal lead, both the states and the federal government need to be sure that the path taken by federal policy is justified.

The needs of language-minority children for special educational assistance cannot be disputed. In the process of justifying federal support of bilingual education, however, too little attention has been paid to identifying which children need services, which types of services would benefit them the most, and what constraints local school districts face in providing such services.

Federal-Policy Assumptions for Language-Minority Children

Federal policy has been based on several assumptions that warrant reexamination:

1. Approximately 3.6 million children need bilingual-education services.
2. If children from non-English-speaking backgrounds are not performing well in school, it is because of their dependence on the home language.
3. TBE is the appropriate remedy for addressing the educational needs of language-minority children.
4. Federal policy can ignore local constraints such as the shortage of bilingual teachers, program costs, and the lack of language-proficiency tests.

Although fundamental questions about federal policy have been raised before (Epstein 1977), recent studies provide empirical evidence that questions the assumptions on which federal policy is based.

Number of Language-Minority Children

The Department of Education has supported its annual budget request for bilingual education by citing estimates of 3.6 million children who are in need of bilingual-education services. The OCR has used the same figure to document the need for promulgating the *Lau* Remedies. As Robert Barnes shows in chapter 1, 16 percent of all children included in this figure use English as their only language, and another 40 percent use English as their usual language. If children not enrolled in school and children making no usual use of a language other than English are excluded, the number of children who might need some type of language assistance is between 1 million and 1.5 million. This new estimate much more closely approximates OCR's statistics on service rates for language-minority children, as Ann Milne and Jan Gombert show in chapter 4.

Factors other than Home-Language Dependence

While students from non-English-speaking homes may have severe educational needs, these difficulties may not result from a dependence on a language other than English. These students, in fact, may be more competent in English than in their home language, and some may have severe limitations in both languages. Recent research, for example, indicates that many Hispanic children in California who are limited in their English-speaking ability may be just as limited in Spanish (Dulay and Burt 1980).

The proportion of language-minority children who are either superior in English or limited in both English and the home language is unknown and the subject of considerable controversy (De Avila and Ulibarri 1981).

Factors other than home-language background have been ignored as a source of educational problems of language-minority children. Alvin S. Rosenthal and colleagues, whose work is reported in chapter 3 to this book, examined achievement and home-background data on a nationally representative study of about 15,000 students, about 1,850 of them from non-English-speaking home backgrounds. Their results indicate that a student's socio-economic status is responsible for much of the effect on student achievement that had been attributed previously to home-language background.

To overlook factors such as poverty or the child's own language proficiency has narrowed the range of strategies considered by federal policy-makers to address the needs of language-minority students. If students are as limited in their native language as they are in English, the value of teaching them in two languages could be challenged. If children's educational needs are poverty based, language programs may be only partial solutions. From the perspective of the federal government, if students receive services that do not match their needs, federal funds are dissipated.

Effectiveness of TBE

Federal civil-rights and funding policies have persisted in promoting TBE without adequate evidence of its effectiveness. In chapter 2, Keith Baker and Adriana de Kanter discuss their review of three-hundred documents on the effectiveness of bilingual education. They found that only thirty-nine of these both addressed the question of effectiveness in promoting the learning of English or subject matter, such as mathematics, and met minimal methodological standards. The authors used these thirty-nine studies to compare the effectiveness of alternative instructional approaches and found that the case for the effectiveness of TBE is not overwhelming and should not warrant sole reliance on this approach to the exclusion of others.

Constraints on the Provision of Services by School Districts

To some extent, federal civil-rights approaches have been justified in not recognizing financial constraints as legitimate reasons for continuing discriminatory practices. But when policies require instructional practices, then any constraints on states' and districts' abilities to develop effective programs must be acknowledged as a serious problem.

Bilingual-education programs are certainly costly, although the study by Margaret Carpenter-Huffman and Marta Samulon, reported in chapter 5, shows great variability in the cost of providing special services to language-minority children. These costs range from about $200 per child for in-class programs to about $700 per child for pull-out programs. If 1.2 million children require bilingual services, the cost would be between $240 million and $840 million. Although the Title VII program contributes money to offset these costs, the amount is relatively small, so school districts and states must bear a substantial portion of this burden.

Two other constraints seriously affect the ability of school districts to meet the needs of language-minority children: the lack of fully qualified personnel and the lack of test instruments to assess students' language proficiency. In chapter 6, Elizabeth Reisner documents a shortage of 13,000 qualified bilingual-education teachers. The use of teachers of English as a second language might alleviate this shortage, but ESL may not be the optimal instructional approach for many language-minority children. And structured immersion, which shows promising results in some cases, requires teachers who understand the student's home language. The distribution of qualified teachers also poses a major problem, especially in areas with a great diversity of language groups. The city of Chicago alone serves children from more than twenty-five major language backgrounds.

The lack of adequate tests constrains the ability of schools to determine student needs. For many languages, there are no instruments to assess children's proficiency (Rosansky 1981). The lack of test instruments increases the possibility that the educational needs of many children could be misdiagnosed, and ineffective services delivered.

Efforts must be directed toward increasing the pool of qualified teachers and assessing the needs of language-minority children. Federal policy cannot require services that presume adequate funding, teachers, and tests when they do not exist.

Policy Implications

A major theme of OPBE's studies is that the problems of language-minority children are too complex to lend themselves to one nationally mandated instructional approach. The needs of such students vary with a host of factors: socioeconomic status, language group, family reliance on a language other than English, and, more important, the child's own language proficiency. Past policies may have misidentified and provided an inappropriate language treatment for some language-minority children, especially those who are more dependent on English than on their home language (even if their English proficiency is low). Moreover, a program that is suitable in a district with a high proportion of students from one language-minority group may not be appropriate in a district educating children from ten or fifteen home-language backgrounds. The prescription of TBE as the sole approach has not taken into account the complex sources of language problems and the diversity of settings in which treatments must be applied. OPBE's studies have highlighted some lessons for future federal policy toward language-minority children.

Transitional bilingual education should not be the sole approach encouraged by federal policy. For children to receive the instruction required by the *Lau* decision does not necessarily mean that they must be taught all subjects in their home language. Indeed, many language-minority children may not benefit more from instruction in their home language than they would from instruction in English. If language and subject matter are taught in English, then special provisions should be made for children who have difficulty understanding the English language. Such provisions might include specially structured English-language curriculums, or the availability of personnel who are proficient in the students' home language, or both.

Furthermore, educational policymakers should recognize the complexity of the needs of language-minority children. The source of their educational difficulties may warrant the types of approaches that have been developed in compensatory-education programs, such as more individual attention or a more structured curriculum, for other children from economically disadvantaged backgrounds. The federal focus on Title VII bilingual programs may have limited the development of compensatory-education strategies specifically suited to the needs of language-minority children under Title I of the Elementary and Secondary Education Act, (now chapter 1 of the Education Consolidation and Improvement Act) the largest federal formula grant program.

States and school districts should have greater discretion to decide which type of special program is most appropriate for their unique settings. The educational needs of language-minority children and the ability of school districts to meet these needs vary tremendously. States and districts are in a good position to identify their needs and to select appropriate strategies. In the past, when local school districts have wanted to use an approach other than TBE, the federal government has placed the burden of proof for program effectiveness on the local districts, despite the fact that evidence for the effectiveness of TBE is not overwhelming. Although the federal government might wish to set general guidelines requiring special programs that would allow children to participate fully in English-language educational settings, the burden of proof should be on the federal government, rather than the states and school districts, to demonstrate that particular approaches will or will not succeed.

The constraints facing states and districts in providing services to language-minority children cannot be ignored. When a policy hinges on providing effective educational services, as bilingual-education policy does, constraints will seriously affect students. The provision of services to language-minority students is seriously hampered by inadequate funds, a poor supply of well-qualified teachers, and test instruments that cannot adequately determine students' relative language proficiency.

A policy that ignores such constraints can sometimes result in programs that meet the letter of the law despite questionable quality. Facing the fact that shortages of personnel and funds limit the options that school districts have would encourage a greater focus on special programs for the most-needy students, those who are denied access to an education because they cannot understand the English language. To acknowledge these constraints might also allow for a broadening of existing compensatory programs to meet the needs of students who have some knowledge of English but who need additional assistance to catch up with their peers.

Improved bilingual research and program evaluations are needed. More and better research and improved program evaluations in bilingual education are necessary if the needs of language-minority children are to be met adequately. A vast resource is lost when evaluations of Title VII programs are unusable because of their poor methodological quality. We need better evaluations of program effectiveness, as well as more descriptive information about the number of children currently being served, how long they remain in bilingual programs, staffing patterns, teacher qualifications, and the like.

Unfortunately, when Congress reauthorized the bilingual-education legislation in the Education Amendments of 1978, it limited research to examining TBE specifically rather than all pedagogical methods for students with limited English proficiency. As a result, federal research has been skewed to focus on one method. Areas for redirected research should include the following:

1. A study of the divergent educational needs of language-minority children in the United States to include the examination of how these children's language deficiencies differ in their home language and English.
2. Examination of the effectiveness of alternative instructional approaches and how these approaches might meet the needs of language-minority children.
3. A reexamination of the theory of TBE, which was designed for monolingual speakers of a home language other than English and which may not be directly relevant to many of the language-minority students in the United States.
4. Examination of bilingual-education teacher qualifications and the degree of fluency such teachers have in both languages.

The Future

The studies in this book highlight the need to assess children's home-language proficiency. Methods for screening children for both their home background and their English proficiency are inadequate at present; many children who lack proficiency in their home language are not accurately identified. The studies also indicate the usefulness of exploring alternative approaches to TBE. If the federal government becomes more flexible in its approach, states and local school districts will be able to examine the range of possible alternatives and to determine which approach best suits their resources, personnel, and student needs.

Some proposals to change federal policies for language-minority children have been introduced recently. For instance, the Reagan administration has proposed legislation that would authorize the funding of a broadened range of instructional approaches for serving children of limited English proficiency and target funding on projects that serve children whose usual language is not English.

The need for strategies to assist language-minority children is growing as these children become a larger proportion of the school-age population. Recent influxes of immigrant groups have increased the urgency of developing workable strategies. State and local governments bear most of this burden. The studies presented in this book have important implications for states and local school districts, as well as for federal policy.

Organization of the Book

Underlying this book is the assumption that the ultimate goals of bilingual-education programs are that the students learn English and keep up with English-speaking peers in subject matter. Although bilingualism is a laudable and worthwhile outcome, we judge benefit in terms of English-language acquisition and subject-matter learning. The 1978 amendments to the Elementary and Secondary Education Act embodied an emphasis on English-language education.

The chapters in this book describe the studies initiated by the OPBE to examine various policy aspects of bilingual education in the United States. The chapters have been divided into two parts. Part I presents four chapters directly bearing on the issues that grew out of the promulgation of the proposed regulations for the education of language-minority children. Part II addresses issues of more-immediate interest to local school districts: cost and personnel needs.

The appendixes reprint the three key federal-policy documents leading to this analysis: the Supreme Court's *Lau* decision, the *Lau* Remedies developed by OCR following the *Lau* decision, and the regulations proposed by the Department of Education in 1980 to replace the *Lau* Remedies.

References

Dulay, H., and Burt, M. 1980. "The Relative Language Proficiency of Limited English Proficient Students." In J.D. Alatis, ed., *Current Issues in Bilingual Education*. Washington, D.C.: Georgetown University Press.

De Avila, E., and Ulibarri, D. 1981. Letter to the editor. *NABE News* 4 (January).

Denham, C., and Lieberman, A. 1980. *Time to Learn*. Washington, D.C.: National Institute of Education, May.

Epstein, N. 1977. *Language, Ethnicity and the Schools: Policy Alternatives for Bilingual-Bicultural Education*. Washington, D.C.: Institute for Educational Leadership.

Gray, T. 1981. "Challenge to USOE Final Evaluation of the Impact of ESEA Title VII Spanish/English Bilingual Education Programs." Arlington, Va.: Center for Applied Linguistics.

O'Malley, M. 1978. "Review of the Evaluation of the Impact of ESEA Title VII Spanish/English Bilingual Education Program." *Bilingual Resources* 1:6-10.

Rosansky, E. 1981. "NIE Report on the Testing and Assessment Implications of the Title VI Language Minority Proposed Rules." Paper prepared for Briefing Book on Civil Rights Language Minority. NPRM, U.S. Department of Education. January.

U.S. Department of Education. 1980. "Preliminary Cost Estimate of Title VII Language Minority Rulemaking." August 11.

Part I
Federal-Policy Issues

1

The Size of the Eligible Language-Minority Population

Robert E. Barnes
with the assistance of
Ann M. Milne

An accurate estimate of the number of children who require special language services is critical to the development of effective federal policies toward language-minority children. The study described in this chapter was initially undertaken to assess the cost and service requirements under the Department of Education's proposed rules issued to protect the civil rights of language-minority children under Title VI of the Civil Rights Act, based on the Supreme Court's decision in the *Lau* case.

Although these rules were eventually withdrawn, the size of the target population remains a major issue. The department is still in the process of defining appropriate remedies under *Lau*, and the impact of any new rules also will have to be determined. Moreover, accurate knowledge of the size of the population at risk is critical to assessing the adequacy of federal civil-rights guarantees. Finally, the number of children who need special language assistance is essential information for developing the annual appropriation for the federal bilingual education program (Title VII of the Elementary and Secondary Education Act, ESEA). This program provides funds to help districts develop their capacity to provide bilingual instruction.

When this study was initiated, the Department of Education believed that 3.6 million children were potentially entitled to special remedies under *Lau*. This figure was also used in estimating the number of children that might require services under Title VII (Department of Education 1980a). The estimate of 3.6 million, derived from the Children's English and Services Study (CESS) (O'Malley 1981), represented the number of school-age language-minority children who had limited English proficiency. The relevance of this estimate for federal policy is by no means clear, however, because the population in question was defined to include children not enrolled in school, children making no significant use of a language other than English, and others clearly able to benefit from standard instruction in English.

We estimate that the target population of children who have serious difficulty in school because of dependence on a language other than English is in the range of 700,000 to 1.3 million, or about one-third of the 3.6 million figure estimated by CESS. These estimates are based on figures derived

3

from studies conducted prior to the recent wave of Indochinese, Cuban, and Haitian refugees. If this population were included, we would estimate another 250,000 children (U.S. Department of Education 1980b).

Our results are obtained from two sources: a reanalysis of the CESS data to correct for some of its definitional deficiencies and an analysis of home-language and reading-achievement data on a national sample of public elementary pupils from the 1977 Sustaining Effects Study.[1] We compared the results of these two sources with data collected from the 1978 Office of Civil Rights (OCR) survey of public schools and with data for selected states.

Definitional Issues

Since the *Lau* case, legislators and government officials have struggled to develop a set of definitions that would lend themselves to practical remedies. At the heart of the *Lau* decision is the recognition that language barriers can have the effect of denying children a meaningful opportunity to benefit from public education. In such cases, public-school systems have an obligation to provide special instruction designed to overcome these barriers (under Title VI of the 1964 Civil Rights Act), and the Department of Education (as a federal agency extending financial assistance to public-school systems) has an obligation (under the same law) to protect the rights of such children.

While the language-barrier concept is clear enough in the extreme case of children totally dependent on a language other than English, we know that language barriers are often a matter of degree. Most children with a non-English-language background attending public schools have some comprehension of English, and most of them do not rely exclusively on a language other than English outside the school. Accordingly, there are two interrelated problems: defining what constitutes sufficient limitation in English, and defining dependence on a non-English language. Assuming that practical criteria are developed for making these two determinations, we also must define the base population—that is, the most inclusive set of children to whom these criteria should be applied in arriving at a determination of children eligible for special remedies. Two major statements of federal policy are germane to these definitional issues.

Title VII of the Bilingual Education Act

This program is intended to provide federal resources to help schools develop their capacity to provide bilingual instruction. Thus, national estimates of eligible children are of interest for evaluating appropriation levels for this program, while local or regional estimates can contribute to a more-equitable apportionment of available funds, based on differences in relative needs.

The 1974 education amendments, which contained a mandate to count the eligible population, offered the following definition:

The terms limited English-speaking ability when used with reference to an individual, means—

(a)   individuals who were not born in the United States or whose native language is a language other than English; and

(b)   individuals who come from environments where a language other than English is dominant . . . and by reason thereof, have difficulty speaking and understanding instruction in the English language. Section 703 (a)(1)

This definition employs *limited English-speaking ability* as an umbrella concept that subsumes non-English-language background, dependence on a language other than English, and limitations in English. The definition offers no guidance on the question of what constitutes sufficient difficulty, but at least it specifies the language skills at issue (speaking and understanding) and the relevant context (instruction).

Concerning the issue of dependence on a non-English language, three possible factors are identified: (1) whether an individual's first (or native) language is other than English, (2) whether the individual comes "from environments where a language other than English is dominant," and (3) whether the individual's difficulty with English is "by reason thereof." As applied to children (not otherwise defined), the base population would appear to be all those with any sort of language-minority background by virtue of birth, first language, or home environment. For purposes of the Title VII program, enrollment in an elementary or secondary school might be construed as a further restriction on the base population.

Although the definition just quoted constituted the original mandate for the CESS, Congress further amplified its definition in the 1978 education amendments while the study was in progress. The principal changes were broadening the language skills at issue to include reading and writing (in addition to speaking and understanding) and amplifying the meaning of *difficulty*. Difficulty with English was now defined as "sufficient . . . to deny such individuals the opportunity to learn successfully in classrooms where the language of instruction is English." Along with these changes, references to limited English proficiency supplanted the term *limited English-speaking ability*.

These changes are important to all three of the definitional issues. First, "sufficient difficulty" is now defined in terms of opportunity to benefit from classroom instruction. Second, the factor of dependence on a non-English language is strengthened by requiring that this difficulty always be by reason of the child's non-English-language background (the 1974 definition had not stipulated this condition for children born outside the United States and individuals whose first language was other than English). Finally, the explicit focus on learning in classrooms strengthens the view that the base population should be restricted to children in school.

Proposed Title VI Rules

In contrast to the Title VII definitions, where the chief purpose being served was estimating aggregate need, the rules proposed in 1980 would have determined the eligibility of individual children to receive special language instruction, usually bilingual education (Federal Register, August 5, 1980). These rules also have a special significance for the present study, since our original charge was to estimate the number of public-school children who would qualify for service under the definitions proposed. We begin our examination of the proposed rules by describing how they dealt with each of the three definitional issues.

The Base Population: The rules required districts to assess the English-language proficiency and relative language proficiency of all children who qualified as having a primary language other than English. This determination was to be based on information supplied by all students or, for those students below the ninth grade, by their parents. Thus there is some question as to whether the base population was all students in the public schools or the much-smaller number of students found to have a primary language other than English.

Since the rules never went into effect, it is a matter of speculation what procedures schools would have followed in identifying potentially eligible children. We suspect, however, that many schools would have started with an intermediate population: children with a non-English-language background, defined as children from homes where some use is made of a language other than English. Relative to this population, the schools could have implemented the proposed definition of "primary language other than English" by asking parents whether the child's first language was the non-English home language or whether the non-English home language is a language the student normally uses. A "yes" to either question would qualify the child as having a "primary language other than English."

Sufficient Difficulty with English: Formally administered tests were to provide the basis for this determination, with oral-proficiency tests permitted at all grade levels and standard reading-achievement tests authorized for children in grades 2 and above. In interpreting the results of these tests, school districts were permitted to select among three standards: (1) the performance of other local students (excluding minorities), (2) the performance of all students statewide, or (3) national performance standards. Subject to these choices, sufficient difficulty to warrant *initiating* bilingual instruction was defined as performance below the fortieth percentile, and sufficient difficulty to warrant *continuing* bilingual instruction beyond two years was defined as performance below the thirtieth percentile.

Dependence on a Non-English Language: The rules would have required formal assessment of each candidate-child's relative language proficiency by documented procedures of the district's own choosing. These assessments were expected to discriminate reliably between students who were superior in the non-English home language ("primary-language-superior") and students who were superior in English. Students who did not clearly fall into either of these categories (and who were also found to be "limited-English-proficient") were to be classified as "Comparably Limited." Under alternative A of the proposed rules, only Primary-Language-Superior students found to be limited in English were entitled to bilingual instruction, while under alternative B, Comparably Limited children were also to be served.

Problems with National Estimates

Any estimation of the eligible population must deal with three groups:

1. The *base population.*
2. That part of the base population that can be defined as having limited English proficiency.
3. That part of the base population that demonstrates dependence on another language.

The difficulty with developing national estimates is the lack of direct measures of the variables. The estimate of the base population should be sufficiently inclusive to capture those children who may require or be entitled to services, without being so broad that costly screening procedures are required for children with no potential eligibility whatsoever.

Another question about the size of the base population is whether to include children not in school at all and children in private school. Children not in school are probably outside the province of federal education policy-makers and therefore should be excluded from the base population. Chil-

dren in private schools are not covered by Title VI of the Civil Rights Act
and accordingly are not in the realm of OCR responsibility. They may,
however, be entitled to bilingual-education services under Title VII of
ESEA.

Thus, the decision on how to define the base population hinges on practical and policy issues, as well as on measurement problems. Federal policy
has generally required some reasonable link to a language other than
English, such as birth in another country or the use of another language in
the child's home environment.

Estimates of English-language proficiency and of dependence on (dominance of) another language are more seriously hampered by measurement
problems. Norm-referenced standardized tests, such as those of reading
comprehension, can be and have been used to measure English-language
proficiency, even though it is understood that the results may be confounded with other effects related to ability, socioeconomic status, and the
like. Criterion-based measures are often advocated as a substitute for norm-
referenced tests, but in the absence of national norms it is difficult to
evaluate standards of proficiency. Tests of relative language proficiency or
of dependence on another language are still in their infancy.

Given these difficulties, it is understandable that different studies have
produced different national estimates of the various populations. This is
almost always a consequence of different definitions and different measures
of the critical variables. In the study described here, therefore, we attempted to reanalyze two major national data bases in a way that reconciles
these differences and to verify our estimates with two other data sources.

Our basic approach was to reanalyze the CESS data base, to use the
Sustaining Effects Study (SES) for nationally normed achievement (missing
in the CESS), to compare estimates from both sources for the same base
population (language-minority children in grades 1 through 6 of public
school), and to extrapolate these estimates to the total school population
using data from the Survey of Income and Education (SIE). The estimates
were then compared with an independent population estimate from the 1978
OCR survey of schools and with estimates for selected states.

Throughout these analyses, we have been sensitive to the fact that the
data sources differ in their purposes, methodology, and definitions of and
procedures for identifying language-minority children limited in English.
Where possible, our analyses adjust for these differences. Specifically we
have attempted to adjust the data bases to estimate the population of children in school who have sufficient dependence on a language other than
English to interfere with their ability to benefit from classroom instruction
given in English. It is our contention that this is the group of major concern
for federal education policy. We also attempt to differentiate the public-
school population from the private-school population. Where data limita-

tions do not allow us to estimate directly the number of private-school children, we adjust by their national proportion of total school enrollment, or approximately 10 percent.

Estimates of Eligible Children Based on the CESS

Description of the Study

The 1974 amendments to the Bilingual Education Act directed the commissioner of education to submit a report to Congress on the condition of bilingual education; this report was to include an assessment of the educational needs of children of limited English-speaking ability and an estimate of their numbers. The CESS was undertaken to provide this estimate. The work was performed by a consortium of contractors, under the direction of the National Institute of Education, with support from the National Center for Education Statistics and the Office of Education.

The CESS proceeded in three steps: the development of special tests designed to measure English-language proficiency (and provide a basis for classifying children as "limited" or "not limited"); the conduct of a household survey in which the newly developed tests were administered to a small, national sample of language-minority children in the spring of 1978; and the development of national estimates using earlier findings from the much lager SIE. Although we rely heavily on the CESS report (O'Malley 1981) for our description of the development of the English-proficiency measures, all the estimates and quantitative assessments presented here are based on our own analysis of the CESS survey file.

Development of the Tests and Establishment of Cutoffs: Based on the recommendations of a panel of experts, the CESS staff developed thirty-minute tests that interviewers could administer in the home. Tests were developed for each single year of age from 5 through 14, with the choice of test items being designed to reflect the increasing demands that English-language instruction makes of children at higher grade levels. Types of skills included oral and written comprehension, vocabulary, idiomatic expressions, and a variety of writing skills, such as punctuation, capitalization, and phrase and word sequence. Final selection of test items and establishment of cutoff scores were based on the performance of criterion groups furnished by a small number of schools judged to be using adequate methods of language assessment.

For each single year of age, these schools identified two groups of about thirty-five students each: a fluent group of native-English-speaking students making normal progress in school (defined in the instructions to these schools as within one-half a standard deviation of the mean) and a limited group made up of students representing a variety of non-English-language backgrounds who were judged to be having significant difficulties with English instruction. Individual test items that failed to discriminate between these two groups were discarded, and cutoff scores on proficiency were selected so that the maximum number of fluent students and the smallest possible number of limited students would be rated proficient. Overall, for the 691 students in the criterion groups in all ten ages, these procedures produced agreement in 88 percent of the cases, with 95 percent of the fluent students scoring above the cutoffs on the tests, and 81 percent of the limited students scoring below the cutoffs.

The 1978 Sample Survey: Design of the CESS sample was complicated by two facts: only about one household in thirty-five could be expected to contain an eligible child (children ages 5 through 14 in homes where a language other than English was spoken), and for the basic sampling frame it was necessary to use data from the 1970 census. As a result, a large number of households had to be screened in the field to obtain the final sample of 1,909 tested children, and the weights associated with these children are extremely variable, ranging from a low of 123 to a high of 65,000. The response rate in eligible households exceeded 90 percent for the questionnaire and 85 percent for the tests. Overall, 71 percent of the sample children scored below the preestablished cutoffs, but since these children tended to have lower-than-average weights, the estimated proportion of children with limited English proficiency in the total age groups 5 through 14 was 63 percent—about 2.4 million of the 3.8 million language-minority children.

Uses Made of the 1976 SIE: The SIE, which was a much larger survey containing detailed information on use of languages other than English, employed the same identification questions as did the CESS:

1. What language do the people in the household usually speak here at home?
2. What other language do the people in the household often speak at home?

A language other than English in response to either question qualified the child as language minority. Given the identity in definitions, CESS was able to use the SIE results to adjust the weights of its sample. Thus, estimates from the two studies are not entirely independent.

CESS also used the SIE data to arrive at the widely cited figure of 3.6 million school-age children with limited English proficiency. Since the SIE covered children of all ages, it was possible to estimate the number of language-minority children ages 4 through 18. This figure was close to 5.8

million, and by straight-line extrapolation from the CESS estimates for children ages 5 through 14, the figure of 3.6 million school-age children with limited English proficiency was obtained.

Evaluation and Reanalysis of the CESS

We believe that the CESS identifies excessive numbers of children in need of bilingual education. Our reexamination of the study identified two types of sources of potential overestimation:

1. Technical issues of methodology that may have artificially inflated the estimates of limited-English-proficient children.
2. Inclusion in the needy group of two categories of children who may not in fact require bilingual services: those who scored below the CESS English proficiency test cutoffs but may not be dependent on another language and those not enrolled in school.

Technical Issues: The major concern with the technical quality of the CESS estimates relates to the adequacy of the cutoff scores on the CESS test of English proficiency. The value of the CESS data is critically dependent on the merits of the CESS definition of limited English proficiency. In the absence of the test data, there would be no reason to use CESS since the SIE offers more-reliable and complete estimates of the base population (language-minority children) and their composition by categories of dependence on a language other than English. Unfortunately, there are a number of reasons to question the adequacy of the test data and the derived proficiency cutoff scores.[2]

First, there is no independent (objective, nationally normed) estimate of the actual school performance of the students in the fluent criterion groups. Such measures would have allowed us to judge how well the study's instructions (to identify students making normal progress) were carried out and whether the schools furnishing these criterion groups were nationally representative in terms of standards of student progress. This is critical, for the available independent estimates suggest that the cutoff scores are too high, with the result that excessive numbers of children were identified as limited English proficient.

These independent estimates come from two sources; a follow-up study of the CESS sample, which obtained teacher estimates of language proficiency and reported reading achievement, and a comparison of CESS test results with reading proficiency scores from another study.

The CESS staff attempted to collect school follow-up data on all students who were enrolled, but because of a lack of school district cooperation, they were able to collect data on only about half this group.[3] Although this means that children covered in the follow-up data are not necessarily representative, there is evidence of serious discrepancies between their performance on the CESS proficiency test and reported reading achievement or oral proficiency in English as rated by the children's teachers. For example, 65 percent of the children who scored below the proficient cutoffs on the CESS tests were judged by their teachers to have English proficiency that was adequate or better. In addition, of children reported in the school follow-up to be reading at least a half-year above grade level, 36 percent scored below the proficiency cutoffs on the CESS tests. When combined with the fact that only 5 percent of the students in the original fluent groups scored below the test proficiency cutoffs and that all of them should have been reading at grade level, these results lead us to conclude that the fluent groups were from exceptionally good schools (or from schools with exceptionally high standards) or that the selection of fluent students may have had an upward bias, or both. Thus the CESS cutoffs for proficiency may have been set too high, which would tend to inflate the estimates of numbers of limited-English-proficient students.

A further consequence of the lack of independent measures on the criterion groups and of the small number of fluent children (about thirty-five) at each age is a potential lack of comparability of proficiency standards across ages. In fact, an examination of age-specific proportions of children found to be limited English proficient bears out this concern; for example, only 56 percent of the 11-year-olds in the sample were found to be limited-English-proficient, compared with 83 percent of the 10-year-olds and 73 percent of the 12-year-olds. This unevenness carries over to the estimates of the total population, where it is exacerbated by disproportionate weights—different in some cases by a factor of 20 or 30—applied to individual test results.

Reanalysis of CESS Data to Exclude Nonrelevant Populations: The CESS's own estimate of the number of children ages 5 through 14 with limited English proficiency is 2.4 million. This estimate may be artificially inflated, based on excessively high cutoff scores on the CESS English-language proficiency test and on the inclusion of nonrelevant populations. The next section discusses our use of normed tests to develop appropriate cutoffs for the eligible population. This section shows how we can use information present within the CESS file to disaggregate the 2.4 million children whose test scores showed them to be limited in English by categories of relative dependence on a language other than English. It is our contention that a child who is not dependent on a language other than English, regardless of the child's limitations in English, should not require and would not benefit from services provided in the other language.

Table 1-1 presents estimates that reduce the 2.4 million children into successively smaller subsets defined at each step by progressively stronger evidence of dependence on a language other than English. As the table demonstrates, a large number of these children should not be classified as having sufficient dependence on a language other than English to warrant bilingual instruction. Sixteen percent of the total group speak English exclusively, and more than half (56 percent) usually speak English. It is likely that the 1.1 million estimate on line 4 is the one most relevant to our definition of limited-English-proficient children with a sufficiently strong dependence on another language to warrant bilingual instruction.

We can further refine this estimate, which includes all children regardless of their school enrollment (in or out of school, public or private), but only those ages 5 through 14, by limiting it to children in public schools and expanding it to include kindergarten through grades 12. Of the 2.4 million children in the 5 through 14 age group estimated by CESS to have limited English proficiency, 85 percent are enrolled in public school, 10 percent in private school, and 5 percent (mostly 5 year olds) are not attending school. Using the SIE data and the straight-line extrapolation method, we estimate that the 3.6 million children with limited proficiency in English in the age group 4 through 18 would include about 700,000 children not attending school and another 300,000 in private schools, leaving about 2.6 million (or 72 percent of the total) in the public schools.

Table 1-1
Estimates of Limited-English-Proficient Children, 1978

Progressively Restrictive Categories of Dependence on a Non-English Language	Number of Children Ages 5-14 (in 000s)	Proportion of Total
1. Children from homes where English is not the only language spoken	2,409	1.00
2. And the child does not speak English exclusively	2,022	.84
3. And the usual home language is not English	1,590[a]	.66
4. And the child's usual language is not English	1,072[a]	.44
5. And the child does not speak English or does not speak it well	283[a]	.12
6. And the child is *reported* to not speak English or to speak it less than well	147	.06

Source: CESS.

[a]Includes 136,000 children for whom information is missing. In other words, all subtractions are based on affirmative reports.

Summary: Thus, from our further analysis of the CESS data, we can estimate the size of the needy group of greatest relevance for federal policy. Table 1-2 summarizes our approximations to successively greater dependence on a language other than English (down the rows) and to the public-school population (kindergarten through grade 12) (across the columns). In this way, we disaggregate the CESS figure of 3.6 million English-limited children to find 1.2 million children who are dependent on a language other than English and who are in the public schools.

Estimates of Eligible Children Based on the SES

Description of the Study

The SES represents the largest evaluation effort ever undertaken in connection with a federal education program. The purpose of this study was to evaluate the effectiveness of compensatory-education services provided by local schools under Title I of ESEA. Most of the work was carried out over a four-year period by System Development Corporation under contract with the evaluation unit of the U.S. Office of Education, commencing in 1975. In addition to the SES participant file, on which our estimates rely, major products include three volumes of documentation (Hoepfner et al. 1977; Hemenway et al. 1978; System Development Corporation 1979) and numerous analytic reports by the System Development Corporation and by Decima Research, along with a growing number of studies by independent investigators.

Table 1-2
Estimated Number of English-Limited Children, 1978
(in millions)

Progressively Restrictive Categories of Dependence on a Non-English Language	Alternative Definitions of the Base Population		
	All Children Ages 4-18	All Children Enrolled in School, K-12	All Children Enrolled in Public School, K-12
1. Children from homes where English is not the only language spoken	3.6	2.9	2.6
2. And the usual home language is not English	2.4	2.2	1.8
3. And the child's usual language is not English	1.6	1.3	1.2

Source: CESS.

The SES Participant Sample Survey: The SES used a multistage procedure to arrive at a sample of 243 public schools offering instruction in grades 1 through 6. In the first stage, the 62,000 public schools were assigned to 90 strata, defined by 3 categories of enrollment size, 3 of poverty status, and 10 geographic areas. Schools in each stratum were weighted by their total enrollments in grades 1 through 6 and sampled at rates designed to yield equal numbers of children. This procedure, coupled with the choice of cutting points on proportions of children in poverty, resulted in a significant overrepresentation of poor children in the initial sample of 5,000 schools. Questionnaires sent to the principals of these schools provided current information on enrollments, grade span, and special programs offered. Using this information plus information supplied by state coordinators of the Title I program, three purposive samples were selected, which together make up the 243-school SES participant sample.

Two points about this selection process need to be mentioned: schools (and students) not participating in the Title I program were adequately represented, but 28 of the original 5,000 schools were excluded from consideration on the basis of reports that most of their students were in special language programs (bilingual or English as a second language) and would have difficulty with the study's English-language instruments.

On its face, this second decision introduced a bias in the procedures that produced the participant sample, since one or two of these twenty-eight schools would otherwise have been selected. The most serious effect of this bias, for the uses we make of the sample data, would be to underrepresent children who are heavily dependent on a language other than English, and thereby to underestimate the relative disadvantagement of language-minority children. This possibility cannot be dismissed, but comparisons with the CESS and the SIE are reassuring in two respects: the SES participant sample yields larger estimates overall of language-minority children enrolled in public school grades 1 through 6 and includes higher proportions of children from homes where English is not regularly spoken.

Fieldwork began with the 1976-1977 school year. For purposes of norming, reading and math tests were administered to all 81,000 elementary students in the 243 schools. Our focus in this study, however, is on the 15,579 children (an approximate one-fifth sample) for whom household data, including home-language use, are available. The home interviews were conducted early in 1977. These yielded information on languages regularly spoken at home for all but 136 of the 15,579 children and served to identify 1,856 children with home languages other than English in the sample. Language use was identified by a series of language-specific questions, starting with "Is English regularly spoken in your home?" and going on to ask the same question about Spanish, Portuguese, Chinese, Japanese, Italian, and other languages.

In homes where a language other than English was regularly spoken, parents were also asked what use they made of English and the other home language in helping the child with school work. Used in conjunction with the language-specific questions, this question about homework permits us to distinguish three categories of language-minority children with differential dependence on a language other than English. These three categories can be roughly equated with categories of parent and child language use from the SIE:

1. Children from homes where English is regularly spoken and homework help is given exclusively in English.
2. A middle group of children from homes where English is regularly spoken who receive homework help in both English and the home language.
3. Children from homes where English is not regularly spoken or help is given only in the non-English home language.

The Measure of Reading Achievement: Since reading and math skills constituted the principal focus of the study, much care was taken in the selection, administration, and scoring of test instruments. Reading and math subscales of six different batteries of the McGraw-Hill Comprehensive Tests of Basic Skills were eventually selected, but these were renormed and percentile scores derived. Total testing time ranged from 67 to 107 minutes (depending on the level) with reading accounting for slightly more than half of the 75 to 158 multiple-choice items.

Reading Achievement of Language-Minority Children

Table 1-3 presents population estimates from the SES participant file for three categories of language-minority children (plus a residual category). Also presented are estimates of the numbers and proportions scoring below the fortieth and twenty-fifth percentiles in reading. These percentiles are based on norms for all children in public school grades 1 through 6 in the 243 nationally representative schools. These two cutoffs were selected to represent, respectively, relatively liberal and relatively stringent definitions of limited English proficiency.[4] Within the limits of the questions asked and the sample size, table 1-3 represents about as much as the SES participant file can tell about the performance of language-minority children relative to these two cutoffs on reading achievement.

Using these cutoffs as alternative definitions of limited English proficiency, we note that proportions of "limited" children under each cutoff increase quite regularly with increasing dependence on a language other than

Table 1-3
Population Estimates of Reading Achievement of Language-Minority Children in Public Schools, Grades 1-6, by Language Group and Home Situation: SES, Spring 1977

Language Group and Home Language Situation	Size of Total Group[b]	Cutoffs on Reading Achievement			
		No. below 40th[b]	No. below 25th[b]	Proportion below 40th	Proportion below 25th
Spanish home language	1,418	940	684	0.66	0.48
1. English regularly spoken and all homework help in English	834	490	322	.59	.39
2. Homework help in English and home language	47	33	26	.70	.55
3. English not regularly spoken or all help given in home language	360	303	251	.84	.70
4. No help with homework or missing information[a]	(177)	(114)	(85)	(.64)	(.48)
Other non-English home language	851	290	152	.34	.18
5. English regularly spoken and all homework help in English	691	229	110	.33	.16
6. Homework help in English and home language	15	5	5	.32	.31
7. English not regularly spoken or all help given in home language	39	20	13	.51	.34
8. No help with homework or missing information[a]	(106)	(36)	(24)	(.34)	(.23)
Total, Spanish, and other	2,269	1,230	836	.54	.37
9. English regularly spoken and all homework help in English	1,525	719	432	.47	.28
10. Homework help in English and home language	63	38	31	.60	.49
11. English not regularly spoken or all help given in home language	399	323	264	.81	.66
12. No help with homework or missing information[a]	(283)	(150)	(109)	(.53)	(.39)

Source: SES participant file.
[a]Residual categories not used in our later analyses.
[b]In thousands.

English in the child's home. For example, language-minority children from homes with the most dependence on a non-English language are more than twice as likely to score below the twenty-fifth percentile as those from homes with the least dependence (line 11 versus line 9, or 66 percent versus

28 percent). The contrast between these two groups, however, results in part from their language composition. About 90 percent of the children in the most-dependent category are Spanish speaking, while substantial numbers of non-Spanish speaking children are in the least-dependent category.[5]

Development of Estimates of Eligible Children
in the Public Schools

Table 1-3 represents our starting point. As with CESS, the principal value of the SES is the test data—nationally normed measures of the ability of language-minority children to read English at their grade level. We developed our estimates by applying proportions of children limited in English under each of the two percentile cutoffs to figures from the SIE for the public-school population, kindergarten through grade 12. This procedure involves three critical assumptions:

1. That the SES sample is adequately representative of language-minority children in public school, grades 1 through 6.
2. That the SES and SIE categories of dependence on a language other than English can be meaningfully related.
3. That it is reasonable to extrapolate from evidence on reading performance in the elementary grades to all grade levels.

Sample Representativeness of SES: The SES estimate of 2,269,000 children from homes where a language other than English is used is about 13 percent higher than the CESS and SIE estimates. The difference in the questions used to identify use of a language other than English in the home may have contributed to this, but the SES estimate is higher primarily because an inflated figure of 21 million was used in weighting the sample. As of the spring of 1977 (the SES reference date), about 19.5 million children were enrolled in grades 1 through 6 in public schools. Correcting for this difference reduces the SES estimate for language-minority children to 2,107,000, or about 5 percent higher than the SIE and CESS estimates for the same population.

The critical question for our final estimates is whether children with the greatest need (those from homes where English is not regularly spoken) are underrepresented in the SES sample. A potential bias was introduced into this 243-school sample by the elimination of 28 schools with high proportions of students with limited English from the first-stage sample of 5,000 schools. Clearly, if children with the greatest need are underrepresented, then our estimates of proportions of reading-limited students may be too low.

Using estimates from CESS as our standard of comparison, we find in table 1-4 that the overall picture is reassuring, although there are some problems. For the group as a whole, the SES yields higher numbers and proportions of children in homes that appear to be wholly dependent on a language other than English. When the totals are broken down by language group, however, the results are mixed. Although non-Spanish-language-minority children are distinctly underrepresented (by a ratio of one to four) in the SES data, the high-need Spanish children appear to be substantially overrepresented, using the CESS data as our criterion.

This evidence persuades us that although high-need children are adequately represented in the totals, it is not feasible to develop separate estimates of eligible children by language group with these data. Accordingly, we turn to the task of relating the SES and SIE categories of dependence on a language other than English for both groups combined.

Relationship between SES and CESS-SIE Categories: We would like to be able to relate the three SES categories of increasing dependence on a non-English language to the three SIE categories of parent-child usual language. If this can be done, the rates of limited English proficiency as defined by performance of the SES group below the twenty-fifth or fortieth percentile can be applied to the numbers of children grades 1 through 6 in the parallel SIE language-dependence categories. We can then inflate these figures to

Table 1-4
Comparison of Numbers and Proportions of High-Need Language-Minority Children Enrolled in Public Schools, Grades 1-6, in Weighted Samples of SES and CESS

Source and Definition of High Need	Total	Spanish	All Other
1. SES: Number of children in homes where English is not regularly spoken	255,000[a]	241,000[a]	14,000[a]
2. SES: Line 1 as a proportion of all language-minority children	.121	.183	.018
3. CESS: Number of children in homes where English is neither the usual nor a second ("often spoken") language	154,000	103,000	51,000
4. CESS: Line 3 as a proportion of all language-minority children	.073	.080	.071

Source: SES and CESS.

[a]These figures represent estimates for a population of 19.5 million (all children enrolled in public-school grades 1 through 6 in the spring of 1977). This means that weights for a population of 21 million have been reduced by about 7 percent.

represent English-limited children as measured by reading scores in the public-school population, kindergarten through grade 12.

The three operational language-dependence categories for the two data bases are shown in table 1-5, along with the estimated proportions of children (grades 1 through 6) from each source who fall within each language-use category.

As table 1-5 indicates, there are appreciable differences in the relative proportions associated with the categories.[6] However, since our primary purpose in using the categories is to apply the rates of limited English proficiency developed under the SES categories to the numbers of children in the SIE categories, the match need not be exact. We must be certain only that our approach applies reasonable rates of limited English proficiency to the SIE categories. Referring to table 1-3, we note that the rates derived for the SES language-use groups are well ordered; that is, rates of limited English proficiency increase regularly with increasing dependance on a language other than English. Thus, we will apply the rates in table 1-3 for each SES category directly to the corresponding SIE categories. Because our major concern is with the third category of children (those most dependent on a language other than English), we are reassured that the SES and SIE proportions correspond closely there. The fact that there is a high observed rate of 81 percent of children in this category falling below the fortieth percentile gives us confidence that we will not be significantly underestimating the number of eligible children.

Table 1-5
Comparison of Three Language-Use Categories for SES and SIE, Grades 1-6

Language-Use Category: SES	Proportion of Children in Each Category	Language-Use Category: SIE	Proportion of Children in Each Category
1. English regularly spoken in the home, and all homework help given in English	0.77	Both parents and student usually speak English	0.55
2. English regularly spoken in the home, homework help in both English and the home language	.03	Only parents usually speak the language other than English; student's usual language is English	.21
3. English not regularly spoken in the home or all homework help in other than English	.20	Both parents and child usually speak language other than English	.24

Source: SES and SIE.

Extrapolating the Reading-Limited Rates: Our final estimates attribute to children in kindergarten and grades 7 through 12 the same proficiency rates calculated for children in grades 1 through 6. Doing this might appear to entail the assumption that children make no gains in English proficiency as they progress through the grades, but this is not strictly the case for two reasons. First, our reading measures of English limitations are based entirely on norms so they will reflect only gains achieved relative to the rest of the norming group, as opposed to absolute gains. Second, our procedure takes into account grade-level differences in the distribution of children across language-dependency categories with age. Table 1-6 shows that the proportion of language-minority children who usually speak a language other than English declines with advancing grade level. Thus, while we postulate the same proportion of reading-limited children within each category of language dependence, the average proportions of reading-limited children are lower for the higher grades.

Final Estimates of Children: Having evaluated and found support for our three assumptions, we can now apply the reading-limited SES rates to the SIE public-school population. The estimates of the total number within each category of progressive dependence on a non-English language are presented in column 1 of table 1-7. Applying the SES rates from table 1-3 (lines 9 through 11) to these figures, we arrive at public-school population estimates, kindergarten through grade 12, of reading-limited children—those below the fortieth percentile (column 2 of table 1-7) and

Table 1-6
Composition of Language-Minority Children in Public School by Grade Level, Language Group, and Parent-Student Usual Language, 1976

Language Group and Parent-Student Usual Language	Percentage of Children in Each Category		
	Kindergarten	*Grades 1-6*	*Grades 7-12*
Spanish			
Both usually speak the non-English language	40	30	23
Only parents usually speak the non-English language	15	23	26
Both usually speak English	45	47	51
Other Non-English languages			
Both usually speak the non-English language	20	13	11
Only parents usually speak the non-English language	17	17	15
Both usually speak English	63	70	73

Source: SIE.

Table 1-7
Estimates of Number of Reading-Limited Language-Minority Children Enrolled in Public Schools, K-12, 1976
(in thousands)

	(1) Size of Total Group	Number of Reading-Limited Children	
Parent-Student Usual Language		(2) Based on Reading Achievement below 40th Percentile	(3) below 25th Percentile
1. Both usually speak English	2,378	1,118	666
2. Only parents usually speak the non-English language	882	529	432
3. Both usually speak the non-English language	906	734	598
Total language minority	4,166	2,381	1,696

Source: SIE and SES.

those below the twenty-fifth percentile (column 3)—in each of the three categories.

In columns 3 and 4 of table 1-8, we summarize and aggregate these figures across categories to provide estimates of the potentially eligible population. Line 3 represents categories 2 and 3 of language dependence: those children whose usual language is English (but whose parents' usual language is not) and those children whose usual language is not English. We believe this category is too inclusive to represent the eligible population. Line 4 corresponds to those children whose usual language is not English, and who are thus most in need of bilingual education. (Line 5 adds 10 percent for the private-school population, who may be entitled to services under Title VII of ESEA.) For comparison purposes, we present two other estimates. Those in column 1 are developed by extrapolation of the CESS estimates of children ages 5 through 14 to the public-school population, kindergarten through grade 12. Those in column 2 are derived by applying CESS-observed proportions of reading-limited children in each of the three language categories for grades 1 through 6 to the entire public-school population. The CESS proportions are 0.46 (both usually speak English), 0.76 (only parent usually speaks a language other than English), and 0.86 (both usually speak a language other than English).

Summary

The SES, despite some problems, offers an important alternative source of data for the development of national estimates of children eligible for special

Table 1-8
Estimated Number of Children with Limited English Proficiency under Three Definitions, by Enrollment in Public School and Dependence on a Non-English Language, 1976
(in millions)

	(1) CESS: Straight-Line Extrapolation	(2) CESS: Component Method[b]	(3) SES: Below 40th Percentile on Reading Achievement, Component Method[b]	(4) SES: Below 25th Percentile on Reading Achievement Component Method[b]
1. All children, ages 4 to 18	3.6			
2. Enrolled in public school, K-12	2.6[a]	2.5	2.4	1.7
3. Usual parent (home) language is not English	1.8[a]	1.5	1.3	1.0
4. Child's usual language is not English	1.2[a]	.8	.7	.6
5. Line 4 plus 10 percent addition for private schools	1.3	.9	.8	.7

[a]These estimates represent test results for all children ages 5 through 14 inflated by the ratio of language-minority students in public school (4,167,000 from the SIE) to the CESS total (3,812,000) or 1.093.

[b]The component method applies estimated proportions of limited-English-proficient children in the three categories of language use for public-school children, grades 1 through 6, to SIE estimates of the same three categories for the entire public-school population. The SES proportions are given in table 1-3; the CESS proportions are, respectively, 0.46 (both usually speak English), 0.76 (only the parent usually speaks the non-English language), and 0.86 (both usually speak a non-English language).

instruction under Title VI of the Civil Rights Act. Its primary advantage is that it provides rigorously developed and normed measures of reading achievement, along with a means of distinguishing differences in the extent of reliance on a language other than English among language-minority homes. Using these normed measures and a definition of need that corresponds to the greatest dependence of the child on a language other than English, we would thus estimate that between 600,000 and 700,000 children (depending on the choice of the twenty-fifth or fortieth percentile) may be in the eligible public-school population. Including private-school students could raise these estimates to between 700,000 and 800,000 eligible children.

As for the SES defects, we have attempted to evaluate their potential impact and to adjust for them wherever possible. In this connection, our reliance on the much larger SIE serves to set reassuring bounds on the contribution of the SES data to our final estimates.

Comparison of Estimates from Other Sources

This section presents evidence from two other sources: the 1978 Survey of Elementary and Secondary Schools by the OCR and data from selected states. Again, we contend with sources that use different definitions and different methodologies. This is particularly true of data collected by states on their own student populations because the procedures vary widely both across and within states. Nevertheless, for those states for which we have relatively comparable data from a number of sources, it is clear that the discrepancies among our adjusted estimates, the OCR data, and the states' own data are far smaller than the discrepancy between any of these and the disaggregated CESS estimates.

Estimates of Eligible Children Based on
the 1978 OCR Survey

The OCR has conducted an annual or biennial Elementary and Secondary School Civil Rights Survey since the 1968-1969 school year. In the even-numbered years, the surveys sampled approximately half the public-school districts with enrollments larger than 300 within the fifty states and the District of Columbia and canvassed all schools within the sampled districts. Two forms were used: the 101 form, which is a school-district summary, and the 102 form, which is an individual school report. Data reported here are from the 102 form for the 1978-1979 school year. The analyses were conducted by AUI Policy Research under contract to the Office of Planning, Budget, and Evaluation and are further discussed in chapter 4.

The data requested in the survey reflect OCR responsibilities for school-district compliance with Title VI of the Civil Rights Act. The OCR survey asked school personnel to estimate the number of students within given racial/ethnic groups whose usual language is not English. Specifically, within the designated racial/ethnic groups—American Indian or Alaskan native, Asian or Pacific Islander, Hispanic, black (not of Hispanic origin), and white (not of Hispanic origin)—school personnel were asked to estimate numbers of "pupils in membership who speak or use a language other than English more often than English."

The survey is thus school based, and its estimates (provided by school personnel) are those of the child's relative language usage. Since no estimates of English-language proficiency are called for in the OCR questionnaire, some of the children counted in the OCR figures could be proficient in English, and the OCR figures could overestimate the English-limited population. Nor do we know what types of evidence—school records, children's performance, and the like—were used by school personnel to make the determination of the usual language. If they tended to attribute a language other than English to children of given ethnic backgrounds who were not performing well in school, possibly the figures are overestimates. Finally, it is possible that school personnel perceive the OCR survey as a compliance tool, and as a result they may underreport the number of children making limited use of English. Nevertheless, on their face, the OCR reports represent estimates of public-school children who are dependent on a language other than English.

Based on our analysis of the OCR survey file, 934,000 children in the public schools have a usual language other than English.[7] This is close to the estimates in table 1-8 of the number of children whose usual language is not English and who have limited English proficiency—1.2 million (CESS straight-line extrapolation), 0.8 million (CESS component method), and 0.7 million (SES fortieth percentile).

Because the OCR survey is conducted to collect data that could be used to monitor compliance, it has been suggested that school personnel may underestimate the number of English-limited children. A comparison of the OCR survey with the logically equivalent SIE study, however, indicates that these school-based estimates tend to be higher than those obtained in household surveys. Thus, the OCR school survey estimates 934,000 (or 953,000) such students nationally; the SIE study (which asks household respondents, "What language does . . . usually speak?" and "What language does . . . usually speak with . . . best friends?") found 906,200 such students in the public schools, kindergarten through grade 12, or about 3 to 5 percent fewer than the OCR figures.

The similarity of the OCR estimates to the other estimates is highly encouraging because the OCR data base is the largest sample available, using 5,654 school districts (roughly half the districts in the United States with enrollments over 300), all 54,082 schools within those districts, and 30 million children (approximately 72 percent of the public school enrollment in school year 1978-1979). Moreover, the sample may be the most-relevant national estimate in that it is an aggregate of experience and judgment at the local level—the level to which we must ultimately look for practical remedies.

State Education Agency Estimates

It has been suggested that states that conduct their own surveys of language-minority populations might have estimates that could be used to refine the more-global state-level estimates derived from national samples. In an effort to ascertain states' estimates and their procedures for arriving at these, we conducted a telephone survey of twelve states known from other data to have large language-minority populations.[8] Representatives in each state's bilingual-education office were first asked for their most-accurate estimates of the student minority-language population and the criteria used to define this population. Second, they were asked to describe state requirements concerning local school district identification and assessment procedures.

The states surveyed differ significantly both in the definition of language-minority population and in the extent of discretion permitted local school districts in formulating identification and assessment methods. States with bilingual-education programs tend to exhibit a more-consistent approach to defining and counting language-minority students, but again there are exceptions. Some states have altered their education funding mechanisms from categorical to block grants, which has loosened local school district reporting requirements. Other states that have passed bilingual-education legislation but have no specified school-district reporting procedures are moving toward greater uniformity. Overall it appears that little consistency exists among states. Because the estimates are so varied and the definitions so different across states, we present here only the figures for the three largest states: California, Texas, and New York.

California: Spring 1980 figures for limited-English-speaking and non-English-speaking students of kindergarten through grade 12 were 188,879 and 136,869, respectively, for a total of 325,748. The state requires that each student be administered a state developed home-language survey. If the student's home language or primary language is other than English, the student must be given an oral-proficiency exam. Students who qualify as limited or non-English speaking on the oral exam must be tested further for reading proficiency. Schools may select any state-approved testing instrument. For 1981, the Bilingual Syntax 1 and 2 and Language Assessment Scales 1 and 2 are the permitted evaluation instruments.

New York: The New York Office of Bilingual Education estimates that approximately 132,000 students with limited English proficiency are enrolled in the public-school system. (A recent call to that office to verify these figures met with a refusal to respond to other than a written request for information.) New York has recently released guidelines to school districts specifying a recommended level of identification procedures, but it is unclear whether state law requires districts to follow these guidelines. School districts are required to report their enrollment by ethnic group each year to the state education agency, and a comprehensive statewide system exists for this annual ethnicity count. The state bilingual-education program was formerly funded by discretionary grants, but beginning in 1981, it was funded according to a formula based on the number of students with limited English proficiency. Participation by local school districts is voluntary.

Texas: A total of 227,120 students in 1979-1980 from kindergarten through grade 12 were identified as limited English proficient. Of this total, 133,556 were served in full bilingual-education programs, and another 50,000 were placed in English-as-a-second-language programs. The state requires local school districts to identify eligible students according to the following procedures. First, all students must be administered a home-language survey. If either the primary home language or the student's primary language is other than English, a test for English proficiency must be given. The local school district may choose one or more of five state-approved assessment instruments. Students who score below grade level are then evaluated by a locally appointed language-proficiency assessment committee. The committee, in turn, prescribes either English as a second language, bilingual education, or regular program placement. It also reviews the student's progress every year.

Beginning in 1981, all Hispanics were administered a language-dominance instrument whose results are reviewed by the language-proficiency assessment committee.

Comparisons of Various Estimates for Three States

Table 1-9 presents estimates from four data sources for the three states. The state counts and CESS estimates are for children classified as having limited English proficiency (based on the definitions used by the state education agencies and by CESS, respectively), while the OCR and SIE estimates are for children who usually use a language other than English (based on the definitions used by OCR and on our reanalysis of the SIE figures, respectively).

The estimates in table 1-9 are thus for populations variously defined as being eligible for bilingual services. With some qualifications, it can be stated that all the estimates, with the exception of the CESS estimates, are easily within the same range; these CESS estimates are two to three times as large as the other estimates.

Because the SES data base is not large enough to be disaggregated by categories of language dependence and by state, we have derived the estimate on line 2 by multiplying the SIE estimates of numbers of these language-dependent children by 0.81, or the proportion of SES children with greatest dependence on a language other than English who are below the fortieth percentile. While this is clearly an oversimplification, it pro-

Table 1-9
Comparison of Selected Estimates of English-Limited Children in Public Schools in Three States, 1980
(in thousands)

Source	California	New York	Texas
SES/SIE			
1. Parent's and child's usual (home) language not English[a]	165	161	276
2. Limited English proficiency (0.81 times line 1)[b]	134	130	224
State education authority counts			
3. Limited English proficiency	326[c]	132	227
4. Non-English speaking	137	—	—
OCR			
5. Child's usual language not English	257	117	257
CESS			
6. Limited English proficiency (K-12)	649	512	479

[a]State share of SIE estimates of children from homes where the parents' and the child's usual language is not English.
[b]Estimates derived by multiplying SIE estimates (line 1) by the SES proportion of children scoring below fortieth percentile (0.81) on the reading-proficiency test.
[c]Includes 189,000 children described in the California reports as limited English proficient, plus the 137,000 children shown separately on line 4.

vides estimates that are remarkably similar to those provided by the states themselves (line 3). The major discrepancy is within the state of California, where the total limited population (limited English speaking plus non-English speaking) as estimated by the state is considerably higher than the SES-SIE estimate and somewhat higher than the OCR estimate. In fact, the subset of non-English-speaking students (line 4) in California appears to be closer to our SES-SIE estimate of eligible children. This may reflect the fact that California tests all language-minority children for oral English proficiency and defines as limited all who fall below specified cutoffs on the approved tests. Those who score lowest are then defined as non-English speaking, even though they may score higher than zero on the test. Thus, it is possible that the California estimate of the total limited population is overly generous as an estimate of children dependent on a language other than English.

In this connection, a study by Dulay and Burt (1980) of Hispanic students in seven California school districts demonstrates that for many children classified as limited English speaking, English may nevertheless be their strongest language. That is, they are just as limited in Spanish, if not more so, and they are not dependent on the non-English language.[9]

Regardless of the interpretation one applies to the California figures, they are still not nearly so high as the CESS estimates. It is interesting that the New York and Texas counts are 82 to 83 percent of the SIE estimates (line 1)—nearly identical with the 81 percent of the SIE group we estimate as limited by applying the SES fortieth-percentile cutoff (line 2).

In general, we are reassured about the level of our reestimates by their concordance with all other sources except CESS. It is interesting that the state education agency estimates are not closer to the CESS estimates, as both profess to relate to children who have limited English proficiency, rather than the (presumably) more-restrictive category represented by OCR and OPBE-SIE definitions of children dependent on a language other than English. It may be that state or local personnel are actually closer to the school-related needs of the children involved and define language limitation accordingly. This would also explain the general correspondence between state counts and OCR estimates, which are also based on information provided by school-level personnel.

Conclusions

We believe that the number of children whose opportunities to benefit from education are curtailed by dependence on a language other than English is almost certainly not more than 1.5 million and possibly less than 1 million. This range of estimates allows for appreciable errors in the national and locally reported data we have examined, as well as possible changes since the 1976-1978 period represented by our principal sources, including the influx of 200,000 to 300,000 refugee children from Indochina, Cuba, and Haiti. Even making these allowances, our figures are substantially below the original CESS estimates, which are two to three times any of our estimated numbers.

We are confident that our figures are in the correct range, for we have used four separate sets of figures to triangulate. That is, our reanalysis of the categories of children covered by the CESS data base and our use of norms of reading achievement from the SES study provide numbers that closely correspond to OCR data and to data from individual states.

Moreover, we believe our estimates reflect much closer correspondence with definitions of eligible children contained in legislation and in departmental rules and guidelines. That is, we believe the CESS estimate is too high because it includes children with little or no dependence on a language other than English, children not enrolled in school, and children who, while scoring below the "proficient" cutoffs on the CESS tests, are nevertheless performing satisfactorily in school.

For all of its defects, CESS represents a major pioneering effort in the field of language measurement, and further studies may substantially enhance the value of these data. A major study soon to be conducted for the Department of Education by the Census Bureau will contribute to this end by administering the CESS tests to national samples of all children, including native-English-speaking children, thus making it possible to establish realistic and comparable standards of proficiency at each age.

In the future, we can anticipate new challenges and opportunities in the field of population estimates for English-limited children. The Department of Education is still in the process of defining appropriate remedies for such children, and new data will shortly become available from the 1980 census.

While estimates of eligible children undoubtedly will change in response to new information and policy guidelines, we believe future estimates must continue to reflect the central concerns of the present study: the application of specific tests of dependence on a language other than English and appropriately normed measures to determine the child's English-language limitations.

Notes

1. Both sources also rely on data from a third major survey, the 1976 Survey of Income and Education (SIE). This survey of 155,000 households provides detailed information on language background for the entire school-age population. Thus, CESS generated the 3.6 million estimate for 4- to 18-year-olds by using the SIE data to extrapolate from the results of its study of children ages 5 to 14. Similarly, the SIE data are essential in estimating the reading-achievement performance of language-minority students in all grades of public school (kindergarten through grade 12) since the Sustaining Effects Study data pertain exclusively to children in grades 1 through 6.

2. Internal memorandums at the Bureau of the Census also question the adequacy of the procedures used in establishing cutoff scores on the CESS tests, based on reviews conducted in the bureau's Center for Human Factors Research and Statistical Methods Division.

3. For a description of these coverage problems and the basic tabulations on which our analysis of the follow-up results relies, see L. Miranda and Associates (1979).

4. Before the proposed Title VI rules were issued, serious consideration was given to identifying these two cutoffs as alternatives for public comment. Even after a decision was reached in favor of the fortieth-percentile cutoff, it was still necessary to estimate the smaller number of

children who would qualify for service under the lower cutoff, since an analysis of costs associated with "alternatives considered and rejected in the rulemaking process" was explicitly required as part of the department's impact analysis under President Carter's executive order 12044.

5. In general, smaller proportions of the non-Spanish-language group than of the Spanish-language group are limited in their reading skill.

6. The proportions shown for the SES categories are based only on those cases for which we have complete information on the language(s) used for homework help. The residual group is not included. To allot the cases with missing data to one or another category could bias our results.

7. The figure published by OCR is 953,000 (Office for Civil Rights 1979). It is not clear whether the discrepancy reflects an adjustment for Chicago (where usable survey data could not be collected) or OCR's failure to use the published state adjustment factors (some of which are less than 1).

8. The states surveyed were Arizona, California, Connecticut, Florida, Illinois, Louisiana, Massachusetts, New Jersey, New Mexico, New York, Texas, and Washington.

9. Dulay and Burt also note that the proportions who can be called English superior might rise dramatically if tests of reading and writing proficiency were added to the tests of oral proficiency, for "preliminary data . . . indicate that most Hispanic students reading below grade level in English read substantially less well in Spanish" (Dulay and Burt 1980:187).

References

Dulay, Heidi, and Burt, Marina. 1980. "The Relative Proficiency of Limited English Proficient Students." In Alatis, J.E., ed. *Current Issues in Bilingual Education.* Washington, D.C.: Georgetown University Press.

Federal Register. 1980. "Nondiscrimination under Programs Receiving Federal Assistance through the Department of Education: Effectuation of Title VI of the Civil Rights Act of 1964." Vol. 45, no. 152, August 5, pp. 52052-52075.

Hemenway, Judith A., et al. 1978. *The Measures and Variables in the Sustaining Effects Study.* Santa Monica, Calif.: System Development Corporation.

Hoepfner, Ralph, et al. 1977. *The Sample for the Sustaining Effects Study and Projections of its Characteristics to the National Population.* Santa Monica, Calif.: System Development Corporation.

L. Miranda and Associates. 1979. *Children's English and Services Study: Technical Report on Collection and Analysis of Pupil Survey Responses.* Bethesda, Md.: L. Miranda and Associates.

Office for Civil Rights. 1979. *Directory of Elementary and Secondary Districts and Schools in Selected School Districts: School Year 1978-1979,* vol. 1, pp. xiv-xxi. U.S. Department of Education, Washington, D.C.

O'Malley, J. Michael. 1981. *Children's English and Services Study: Language Minority Children with Limited English Proficiency in the United States.* Rosslyn, Va.: InterAmerica Associates.

System Development Corporation. 1979. *A Compilation of the Sustaining Effects Study Instruments.* Santa Monica, Calif.: System Development Corporation.

U.S. Department of Education. 1980a. *Justification of Appropriation Estimates for Committee on Appropriations, Fiscal Year 1981,* vol. 1. U.S. Department of Education, Washington, D.C.

_____ . 1980b. "Preliminary Cost Estimates of Title VI Language Minority Rulemaking." Paper submitted to the Council on Wage and Price Controls, August 11.

2

Federal Policy and the Effectiveness of Bilingual Education

Keith A. Baker and
Adriana A. de Kanter

This chapter considers whether the federal government's emphasis on transitional bilingual education (TBE), as virtually the only allowable instructional method to be used with language-minority children, is justified in the light of what is known about the effects of bilingual education. It presents the results of a review of the existing literature.[1]

This investigation grew out of a request from the White House Regulatory Analysis and Review Group for an assessment of the effectiveness of TBE, which was put forth in the proposed language-minority regulations issued in August 1980. Although the proposed rules have been withdrawn, the question of the effectiveness of TBE is nevertheless an important issue.

The review focused on two questions derived from the principal intent of federal policy toward language-minority students:

1. Does TBE lead to better performance in English?
2. Does TBE lead to better performance in nonlanguage subject areas?

Although a number of other goals are often recognized for bilingual education, including reduced dropout rates, improved self-image and attitude toward school, preservation of the primary language and culture, and lower absenteeism, the review was limited to these two overriding questions. Few of the studies reviewed addressed the accomplishment of other goals. Thus, a systematic assessment of the success or failure of these goals could not be made.

Since the issue underlying the study was whether the federal government was justified in proposing a legal requirement of TBE (as well as the de facto mandate of TBE found in Office for Civil Rights and Title VII policy) the specific questions addressed by the review were these:

1. Is there a sufficiently strong case for the effectiveness of TBE for learning English and nonlanguage subjects to justify a legal mandate for TBE?
2. Are there any effective alternatives to TBE? That is, should one particular method be exclusively required if other methods also are effective?

The review did not directly include all the evaluations of bilingual programs that have been completed. The Office of Bilingual Education (Title VII program) failed to provide copies of its pre-1978 evaluations, so most of them are not included in the review except insofar as we were able to locate them through other sources. However, since Zappert and Cruz (1977) reviewed and rejected as methodologically unsound most of the pre-1978 Title VII evaluations, we are unlikely to have lost any significant information by their omission. We have included here those studies Zappert and Cruz found to be methodologically sound.

The focus of our assessment was TBE. Although our limited time and resources prohibited an equally comprehensive coverage of alternative methods, we believe we have covered the major studies addressing the effectiveness of alternative methods.

Consideration of the literature and federal policy led to the identification of three basic instructional alternatives, in addition to the alternative of doing nothing for the language-minority child (also known as submersion):

1. Submersion: Language-minority children are placed in an ordinary classroom where English is spoken. There is no special program to help them overcome the language problem. Submersion is aptly described as "sink or swim." The minority home language (L1) is not used at all in the classroom.[2] In *Lau* v. *Nichols* the Supreme Court found that the submersion approach violated the civil rights of language-minority students and that schools had to make an extra effort to help overcome the language problems of these students.
2. English as a Second Language (ESL): ESL students are placed in regular submersion instruction for most of the day. During part of the day, however, these students receive extra instruction in English. This extra help is based on a special curriculum designed to teach English as a second language. L1 may or may not be used in conjunction with ESL instruction.
3. Structured Immersion: Instruction is in the second language (L2), as in the case of submersion, but there are important differences. The immersion teacher understands L1, and students can address the teacher in L1; the immersion teacher, however, generally replies only in L2. Furthermore, the curriculum is structured so that prior knowledge of L2 is not assumed as subjects are taught. Content is introduced in a way that can be understood by the students. The students in effect learn L2 and content simultaneously. Most immersion programs also teach L1 language arts for thirty to sixty minutes a day. Structured immersion differs from TBE in that L1 is rarely used by the teacher (except where it is a subject) and subject-area instruction is given in L2 from the beginning of the program.

4. TBE: Reading is initially taught in both the home language and English. Subject matter is taught in L1 until the students' second language (English) is good enough for them to participate successfully in a regular classroom. ESL is often used to help minimize the time needed to master English. L1 instruction is phased out as regular English instruction is gradually phased in. TBE is differentiated from submersion and ESL by the use of L1 for instruction in nonlanguage subject areas and by the teaching of L1 literacy as a school subject.

These three instructional types sometimes shade into one another; for example, most TBE programs include an ESL component. In addition, each type has a range of activities. Moreover, experts in the field differ in their definitions of bilingual education; as a result, many will argue with the definitions just provided. Nevertheless, the typology is real and important. If the types are thought of as representing different philosophies for addressing the needs of students with limited English proficiency, it is immediately apparent that the different philosophies lead to different classroom practices, which can be identified in actual settings.

The differences among the three methods also can be illustrated by a brief outline of the arguments used to support each method as a successful solution for the problems of language-minority children:

1. TBE: While children are learning English, they should be taught other subjects in their home language so their academic progress will not be retarded by their limited knowledge of English. It is easier to learn to read in the home language than in the second language, and reading in the home language will facilitate second-language reading.
2. ESL: Concentrated additional instruction in English-language skills will keep students from falling behind in the other subject areas.
3. Structured immersion: The solution to developing English proficiency and progressing in other subjects is to teach all subjects in English at a level understood by the students. Although the curriculum assumes no prior knowledge of English, language-minority students in effect learn English as they learn math, and learn math through English instruction that is understandable at their level of English proficiency. In short, practice makes perfect, and English is best learned by using it as much as possible throughout the school day.

This chapter first discusses our approach in assessing the literature, then presents the results of the review, and finally considers the implications for federal policy and local schools. Appendix 2A discusses how robust the findings of the review are. Appendixes 2B and 2C summarize the findings of applicable studies and the reasons for rejecting specific studies.

Methodological Approach

In reviewing a body of research to determine the effectiveness of a particular instructional program, three fundamental questions are asked:

1. Does the study present data relevant to the issues of interest?
2. Does the design of the study permit any plausible alternative explanation for the results other than that the program worked?
3. How widely can the results of the studies be generalized?

Each study was assessed to determine if it addressed the relevant questions through a methodologically sound design.[3] The following characteristics generally led to rejection of a study:

1. The study did not address our issues.
2. The study used nonrandom assignment with no effort to control for possible initial differences between control and program groups.
3. The study did not apply appropriate statistical tests.
4. The study used the norm-referenced design.
5. The study examined gains over the school year without a control group.
6. The study used grade-equivalent scores.

Reasons for Rejecting Studies

Failure to Address the Issues under Consideration: Although many of the studies reviewed examined several outcome measures, we are concerned here only with the effect of bilingual education on performance in English and nonlanguage subject areas. Our decision to concentrate on English and subject-matter acquisition stems from the basic federal-policy concerns that recognize the need to prepare language-minority children to function successfully in an English-speaking nation.

A program that produces mediocre English performance while maintaining the home-language skills will be judged a worse program than one that produces better second-language performance while ignoring home-language skills. The justification for this viewpoint is that in the United States, any successful education program must prepare the students to participate in an English-speaking society. Therefore the overriding concern in evaluating instruction for bilingual students is how well they learn English.

Nonrandom Assignment with No Effort to Control for Between-Group Differences: If students were not randomly assigned to the treatment and comparison groups and nothing was done to control for possible initial differences between the groups, the study was rejected. Any differences in achievement found between the students in the special program and the group not in the special program could have been due to preexisting differences between the two groups.

Among the factors affecting the performance of language-minority children in school, especially in learning English, are the following: age (Krashen 1979; Asher and Garcia 1969; Giles, 1971; Izzo 1981); differences in learning between oral and written language skills (Cummins 1978; Fishman 1965); socioeconomic status (Moore and Parr 1978; Veltman 1980; Rosenthal et al. 1981; De Avila 1981; Izzo 1981); ethnicity (Rosenthal et al. 1981; Matthews 1979; Veltman 1980; Balasubramonian et al. 1973; Baker and de Kanter 1981); student's motivation and self-concept (Christian 1976; Modiano 1973; Zirkel 1972; van Maltitz 1975; Del Buono 1971; Skoczylas 1972; Izzo 1981); parental support for the educational program (Lambert and Tucker 1972; Del Buono 1971; Izzo 1981); characteristics of the community (Lambert and Sidoti 1980; Lambert and Tucker 1972; Skoczylas 1972; Read 1980); various cognitive abilities (Darcy 1953; Peal and Lambert 1962; Landry 1974; Segalowitz 1977; Humphrey, 1977; Coronado, 1979; Malherbe 1946; Fishman 1965; Jensen 1962a, 1962b; Johnson 1953, cited in Albert and Obler 1978); place of birth—immigrant or native-born (Carter 1970; Troike 1978; Kimball 1968; Anderson and Johnson 1971; Cardenas and Cardenas 1977; Baral 1979; Ferris 1979); and degree of home-language dominance.

In addition to these background characteristics of the child, numerous factors associated with the teacher, school, and education program can affect the outcome of bilingual instruction (McDonald and Elias 1976; Engle 1975; de Kanter, 1979; Kramer 1980; Izzo 1981).

The procedures used to assign students to bilingual programs can introduce bias into a study along any of these dimensions. For example, bias may occur when parents are permitted to volunteer their children (nonrandom assignment) for a special bilingual program. Parents who volunteer children are usually more involved in their children's schooling than are parents who do not volunteer their children. The former may provide more help and encouragement to the children in their school work than do the parents who remain silent. Moreover, superior students are likely to come from a home environment in which the parents are actively involved with their children's schooling. Volunteered students are likely to be better students than other children are. Thus, the program may show gains due to the inclusion of better students even though the program is really no more effective than regular schooling (see Laumann 1969).

Another possible bias introduced with volunteered students is that parents of children with an unusual gift for languages may want those children to benefit from a special language program. Again, students' progress may have little to do with the specific program; rather, language gifted students would stand out in any language program.[4]

Appropriate Statistical Tests Were Not Applied: Studies that did not apply appropriate statistical tests to demonstrate the presence of program effects were not accepted. Merely presenting differences between two groups is not sufficient proof that the differences did not occur by chance. Statistical tests must be included in the study design to verify that the results were not a chance phenomenon.

English-Speaking Norm-Referenced Design: When the effects of a program are evaluated, the performance of students in the program must be compared with the performance of a similar group of children not in the program. If random assignment is not used, ensuring that the comparison group is similar becomes very difficult. Some studies form what amounts to a control group by comparing growth against test norms to see if students in the special program showed a gain against the norm. In this design, the rate of progress of the bilingual child is compared with the rate of progress of the monolingual norming groups. It is assumed that the expected rate of improvement of students in the program would have been the same as that of the norming group in the absence of the special program. However, there is no reason to believe that the rate of progress of bilingual and monolingual students is the same.

The nature of the learning curve for language-minority children is not known. It is often assumed (see Egan and Goldsmith 1981) that, in the absence of special help, these children will fall further behind the norms over time since they cannot understand instruction as well as the monolingual English-speaking children upon whom the norm is based. We have reason to question this assumption. Using nationally representative data (from the Sustaining Effects Study), we found that although language-minority students began below the monolingual English-speaking group, they did not fall further behind over a three-year period. More research is needed on this point. It calls into question the assumption that the performance of language-minority children worsens as they mature (compared with the performance of monolingual English-speaking students).

A more-important problem with the norm-referenced model is that as the monolingual non-English-speaking limit is approached, a standardized achievement test becomes both a test of communication in English and an achievement test. If students know the answers to the questions but cannot understand the test, their scores will be low. If they then learn enough English to be able to understand the test, their scores may rise dramatically because they can communicate to the test what they already know. Therefore they will register large gains on the test even though their knowledge of what the test purports to be measuring may not have increased. It is possible that small increases in English skills will translate into large gains on the test for the initially lowest-scoring students (evidence of this phenomenon was found in Garcia 1978; Young 1980; A. Cohen 1975; Stern 1975). This violates the assumptions underlying the norm-referenced model, making the growth rate of the monolingual English-speaking normative group an inaccurate estimate of the expected rate of growth for the bilingual student.

We believe this phenomenon accounts for the spectacular gains in percentile scores, especially in math, occasionally reported for bilingual students. It is not so much that they learned better when instructed in the home language as it is that they learned enough English during the school year to be able to communicate to the test what they already knew. If this analysis is correct, then any use of the norm-referenced model based on monolingual English-speaking norms in evaluating bilingual programs is highly suspect. Effects found by using such a norm-referenced design cannot be attributed to the program.

The norm-referenced approach is widely used in education evaluation and is fully suitable in the situation where it is generally used: testing monolingual English-speaking students. In examining the literature, we concluded that norms based on monolingual English-speaking students do not hold up for bilingual populations and that the problem gets worse as the monolingual non-English-speaking extreme is approached. This model makes certain assumptions linking test performance to true achievement that do not fit the nature of achievement growth in language-minority students. Since the most-important consequence of this problem is to register large gains on the test following small increments in improvement in English communication, performance against the norm is meaningless as a program-evaluation measure in the absence of other controls. Therefore we decided to reject studies that relied entirely on comparing the progress of bilingual students to the rate of progress of monolingual English-speaking norms.

School-Year Gains Only, without a Control Group: Most students learn something over the school year, so their scores will increase even if they are rapidly falling behind the norm. Consider the following hypothetical example. Test scores of both the program and the control groups are 100 in the fall. In the spring, the average score for the program group is 125 and that of the control group 150. According to evaluations that consider only program students, the gains would indicate program success. It is clear, however, that since the control group gained more than the program students, the program was far from effective. The point is that a simple examination of gains over the school year for students in a special program yields too little information to permit determining whether the program worked. Researchers must also compare the progress of program students with the normal rate of progress made by students not in the special program. Hence a study design that examines gains over the school year without a control group is unacceptable.

Grade-Equivalent Scores: Grade equivalents do not correspond to the time pattern of learning, and the methods used to produce them are inaccurate. Equal grade-equivalent gains for two students may not represent equal learning. Use of grade equivalents has often been criticized by evaluation experts. Perez and Horst (1982, pp. 11-116) have written, "Grade-equivalent scores provide an illusion of simplicity but, in fact, they are almost impossible to interpret, even for specialists in test construction. Grade-equivalent scores should never be used by anyone for any purpose whatsoever."

Acceptable Studies

Following these methodological criteria, acceptable studies include the following:

1. True experiments in which students were randomly assigned to treatment and control groups.
2. Studies using nonrandom assignment that controlled for possible preexisting differences between the groups either by matching students in the treatment and comparison groups or through using statistical procedures.

Analysis of covariance was by far the most-common statistical method used to control for preexisting differences in nonexperimental studies. Many statisticians have serious reservations about whether this method succeeds in properly adjusting preexisting differences. Similarly, there are doubts that matching is entirely successful.

For this analysis, however, we generally accepted both methods unless there were defects in their application. We assessed the robustness of our conclusions by varying the criteria, including the rejection of all but true experiments.

Generalizability

We carried out an extensive methodological assessment to determine the limits of generalizability of each acceptable study's results and the implications that could be drawn from them. Obviously a study's results apply to the particular group of students studied, but this information alone is not very useful. The ultimate goal is to see if the conclusions apply to all language-minority students or only to some particular group.

Results can acquire generalizability in two ways. First, the students studied can be selected in such a way as to be representative of the entire population of students in whom we are interested—in this case, language-minority children in the United States. Only two of the more than three hundred studies reviewed even attempted national generalizability: Danoff et al. (1977, 1978) and Malherbe (1946). Second, generalizability may come from consistent findings across many different settings. Thus, if every study produced the same results, no matter how limited the generalizability of any individual study, the weight of the collective evidence would be compelling. Since only two of the studies reviewed were nationally representative, we must attach great importance to consistency in the results of the studies when we draw conclusions.

Other Issues

Although the central concern of the study was the question of whether the federal government's heavy emphasis on TBE was justified in terms of the effectiveness of TBE in teaching English and other nonlanguage subjects, we also tried to address some other important issues. It became immediately apparent that program results were mixed and contradictory. Therefore, we attempted to explore the reasons for the contradictory results. First, we coded about thirty studies (without regard for their methodological quality) for a number of variables known to affect the performance of bilingual children. Analysis of these studies led us to conclude that the evaluation reports were so lacking in information that further efforts in trying to assess the effects of any of these variables would be fruitless. Therefore, we decided to discontinue coding every study, wait until we had identified the methodologically sound studies, and then see if we could learn anything about the effects of other variables from the set made up of only the best of the program evaluations. Again, the lack of information about relevant variables provided by the studies doomed the exercise to failure (it even proved impossible to determine the study sample size in three studies).

Results

Of the several-hundred studies covered by the review, thirty-nine were found to apply to our concerns. By comparison, Zappert and Cruz (1977) found eighteen methodologically acceptable studies. We also found studies that had previously been widely cited as evidence for the effectiveness of TBE to be methodologically unacceptable (Skutnabb-Kangas and Toukomaa 1976; St. John Valley 1980; Veilleux 1977; Leyba 1978; Trevino 1968; Modiano 1966; Egan and Goldsmith 1981; Rosier and Holm 1980; and AIR 1975a, 1975c, 1975e).[5]

The studies found acceptable are summarized in appendix 2A, which gives the author, the grades of school encompassed, the number of students in the treatment and control groups combined, the languages used by the program, and the results reported for second-language and math skills. The most-frequent home language was Spanish, but a number of other languages were represented as well. Most of the studies dealing with Spanish speakers included Mexican-American children. And, not surprisingly, most studies took place in the Southwest or West, but the Northeast was also well represented. Most of the study designs were neither longitudinal nor true experiments. Several studies included very large numbers of students.

Although there are few American examples of structured immersion, these programs generally seem to succeed quite well in both L2 and subject-area results. Lambert and Tucker (1972) and Barik and Swain (1975) report outstanding progress in second-language learning through structured immersion, and Pena-Hughes and Solis (1980) showed structured immersion superior to TBE. As for nonlanguage subjects, Lambert and Tucker (1972), Barik et al. (1977), Ramos et al. (1967), and Malherbe (1946) all showed that it is possible to teach math successfully in the second language. These results suggest that if the curriculum is properly structured in L2 so that communication is at a level the child can understand, there will be no negative consequences from teaching math in the second language. We found no data in these studies pertinent to other subject areas, which are often more dependent on verbal skills than is math, although Malherbe (1946) reported an initial deficit in geography scores, which disappeared in a few years when all teaching was in L2. Ramos et al. (1967) reported the least-favorable results for all L2 instruction. They found that all L2 instruction from grade 1 was as effective after five or six years as was a program in which all instruction was in L1 for grades 2 through 4, and in L2 thereafter.

The available data on ESL instruction are limited. Two studies found structured immersion superior to ESL (Lambert and Tucker 1972; Barik et al. 1977). Ames and Bicks (1978), and Balasubramonian et al. (1973) found that TBE programs that included an ESL component were no more effective than ESL alone. Lum (1971) reported that TBE programs that included an ESL component were no more effective than ESL alone on some measures and that ESL alone was superior to TBE on other measures. Legarreta (1979) and Ramirez et al. (n.d.) found that a TBE program with ESL worked better than a TBE program without an ESL component. Ramirez (1973) found ESL superior to submersion.

With respect to TBE, positive outcomes pertaining to language performance were reported by Covey (1973), Carsrud and Curtis (1979), McConnell (1980a, 1980c), Melendez (1980), Morgan (1971), Plante (1976), Legarreta (1979), AIR (1975b), A. Cohen (1975), and Zirkel (1972). However, the case for the effectiveness of TBE is called into question by studies that found no difference in second-language performance between treatment and comparison groups (Ramos et al. 1967; Powers 1978; Morgan 1971; Lampman 1973; Bates 1970; Alvarez 1975; Prewitt Diaz 1979; deWeffer 1972; Ames and Bicks 1978; Plante 1976; Kaufman 1968; Huzar 1973; Legarreta 1979; A. Cohen 1975; Stebbins et al. 1977; Carsrud and Curtis 1979; Matthews 1979; Skoczylas 1972; McSpadden 1979, 1980; Balasubramonian et al. 1973; Cottrell 1971; Olesini 1971; AIR 1975b; Zirkel 1972; Lum 1971). Moreover, some studies found TBE to be less effective than either immersion or ESL (Lum 1971; Pena-Hughes and Solis 1980), and some found TBE to have negative effects by comparison with submersion (Danoff et al. 1977, 1978; Stern 1975; Moore and Parr 1978; A. Cohen 1975; McSpadden 1980; Layden 1972).

A. Cohen (1975) and Ames and Bicks (1978) found that TBE improved acquisition of math skills. However, no effect was found by Danoff et al. (1978), Carsrud and Curtis (1979), Moore and Parr (1978), McSpadden (1979, 1980), A. Cohen (1975), Covey (1973), Stebbins et al. (1977), Powers (1978), Alvarez (1975), Layden (1972), and Ramos et al. (1967). Skoczylas (1972), McSpadden (1980), and Stern (1975) reported a negative effect.

Caution must be exercised in generalizing further from the studies because some methodological issues affecting generalizability remain. For example, Covey (1973) and McConnell (1980a, 1980b, 1980c) report success for programs including TBE. However, the programs also included very low staff-student ratios—one to eight in the program studied by Covey (1981). Therefore strong doubts exist as to whether the reported program effect was due to the use of bilingual instruction or to the small classes. Tucker (1980) argues that differences between the social situation in the United States and Canada limit the generalizability of the Canadian immersion studies. A discussion of the robustness of our results appears in appendix 2B.

A further constraint in drawing conclusions from the data is that the results are open to several alternative explanations. Different interpretation leads to different policy implications. Unfortunately the lack of detail provided by the reports precludes any firm conclusions as to why the results are mixed. Two of the possible alternative explanations, however, merit some discussion.

The most often encountered of the possible explanations for the observed pattern of results are that TBE has been improperly implemented in many settings or that TBE is a poor instructional approach. If program implementation has failed in some places, the mixed pattern of results reflects success where it was correctly implemented and no effect when implementation failed. It follows, therefore, that TBE is highly successful when it is done right and that more attention should be paid in the future to issues of implementation.

Still, several factors argue against full acceptance of the implementation hypothesis, given the present state of knowledge. Without some independent measure of the success of implementation of each project, the implementation hypothesis is a meaningless tautology. The type of documentation needed to make the implementation hypothesis viable is generally lacking in the literature, even in the best of the evaluation studies. About the only support we found for the implementation hypothesis is some tentative evidence that concurrent translation is an ineffective method (see Baker and de Kanter 1981). Yet even if the mixed success of TBE is the result of implementation problems, another serious concern arises. Would it be more cost-effective to switch to alternative instructional methods or to undertake large-scale efforts to redesign and properly implement TBE programs?

The second possible interpretation of the results is that bilingual education is ineffective—that the usual expectation is that the bilingually instructed child will not do any better in English than will the child instructed only in English and often will do worse. Much of the literature suggests that the key to learning English is to practice communicating in English (see Dulay and Burt 1978; Izzo 1981; Carroll 1975; Macmillan 1980; Krashen 1981). The time spent using the home language in the classroom may be harmful because it reduces English practice. (Conversely, the Canadian immersion studies suggest that a considerable part of the school day can be spent in the home language while impressive gains in the second language are made.)

Under this interpretation, those few projects with positive outcomes were successful despite their use of bilingual instruction. They succeeded because other highly favorable instructional settings also were present. Other reports were so lacking in detail about the operation of the program that we cannot be sure what happened, but bilingual programs are usually complex and so offer numerous opportunities for something other than bilingual instruction to have an effect.

The two interpretations for the mixed results found for the effectiveness of TBE lead to different policy implications. If the source of the problem is poor implementation, more effort should be devoted to research on identifying good practices. An extensive program of technical assistance also is essential to ensure that proper implementation occurred in the classroom. But if bilingual education is basically ineffective, the implication for action is straightforward: stop spending money on TBE and do something else.

The research literature offers little guidance in choosing between the alternatives. Obviously the first order of business should be research aimed at identifying which of these hypotheses is correct. Keeping these cautions in mind, we limit the conclusions described later to those that do not require assuming some underlying explanation for the results. Thus, the finding of mixed results for TBE leads us to conclude only that the evidence does not support a government mandate of TBE.

Rejected Studies

We found most of the studies generally cited as evidence for the effectiveness of bilingual education to be unsuited to answering our questions about the effects of bilingual education. Appendix 2C to this chapter summarizes our reasons for rejecting each study. We discuss here the problems we found with four studies widely cited as evidence for the effectiveness of bilingual education.

Rock Point Navajo School: All analyses were conducted in grade-equivalent scores. We have already noted the unsuitability of grade-equivalent scores in program evaluation, and there are other problems with the analyses. The first analysis presented by Rosier and Holm (1980) compared the Rock Point bilingual program students with students from other Navajo schools. The adequacy of the comparison between Rock Point and other schools depends on making a good match between the treatment and comparison groups. Rosier (1977:13) reports that the comparison schools were selected from other Navajo schools using the direct method but notes that very few schools had such programs. Further, more than one-third of the comparison schools received transfer students at grades 3 and up from feeder schools whose instructional programs were not known.

Rosier and Holm (1980) and Willink (1968) note that the Rock Point school has historically outperformed other Navajo schools. Rosier and Holm showed that the control schools scored higher than other Indian schools and interpreted the superiority of Rock Point to the control schools as a positive outcome for the program. Rosier and Holm should have first shown that Rock Point and the control Indian schools were historically equivalent. This demonstration is particularly critical in view of Rock Point's historical superiority. Yet Rosier and Holm failed both to test for equivalence and to apply statistical adjustments for initial differences.

One of the central parts of Rosier and Holm's analysis shows that while grade 2 Rock Point students are behind the comparison schools in English, by grade 6 Rock Point students have moved ahead. This is interpreted as the expected pattern for bilingual education since reading was taught in L1 for the first 2 years. Therefore, the bilingual students should not do as well in English at first, but as the facilitating effect of L1 literacy comes into play, they surpass students taught only in English.

There is a major problem with this interpretation and conclusion. Inspection of Rosier and Holm's data reveals that exactly the same pattern of inferior second-grade and superior sixth-grade performance for Rock Point students occurred in 1970, the year before the bilingual program began (see Rosier and Holm's chart 12). Rather than a program effect, then, all that seems to be happening is the continuation of a historic trend.

In another analysis, Rosier and Holm report that grade 6 students in the Rock Point bilingual program were tested with the 1973 Scholastic Aptitude Test (SAT) and were compared with 1970 Rock Point students who had been tested with the 1964 edition of the SAT. The students in the bilingual program were found to be superior, but again there are difficulties. It is not at all clear that the bilingual sixth graders received initial reading instruction in Navajo. Nor is it clear what effect the different tests had on the scores or how successful published tables equating grade-equivalent scores across different editions of a test really are.

Perhaps the most-serious problem with this analysis was the failure to establish initial similarity between the program and 1970 cohorts. Serious problems can occur with comparing different cohorts of students within the same school by assuming they are equivalent when the number of students is small. Although the law of large numbers says equivalence can be assumed for the entire population, one or two schools are not the entire population. Chance fluctuations can produce considerable differences in ability and performance between any two successive classes. This point is illustrated in the Rock Point data: two successive bilingual fifth grades (1976 and 1977) had average scores of 5.66 and 4.51, about a 25 percent difference in performance from one year to the next.

In their final analysis, Rosier and Holm (1980) describe a comparison between two groups of fourth graders, showing the results of continuous versus interrupted bilingual instruction. The interrupted group began school with Navajo reading-readiness instruction (apparently in kindergarten) but then entered the all-English first-grade program. In the third grade, they returned to the bilingual program. Rosier and Holm argue that these data provide an important evaluation of the program. They attribute the higher scores of the continuous-bilingual-education students to their having learned initial literacy in the home language, but there is another interpretation to these findings. There should be little wonder that children who within a four-year period began schooling in one language, were arbitrarily changed to a second language, and then changed again to a mixture of both languages did not do so well as students with a coordinated exposure to the two languages. Further, Rosier and Holm failed to demonstrate initial equivalency between the two groups.

Rock Point is one of but three American studies to use the sequence of first teaching L1 literacy and then teaching L2 literacy. The facilitating effect on L2 that is hypothesized by first teaching L1 literacy is one of the major justifications for TBE. Consequently Rock Point is an important study, but its adequacy as a test of this hypothesis is doubtful since not all the classes in the bilingual program seem to have been taught literacy first in L1. One of the most-puzzling aspects of the study focuses on how children in grades 4, 5, and 6 were taught initial literacy. Rosier and Holm (1980) state that the fifth and sixth graders were taught initial literacy in Navajo in grade 1. But if the dates reported by Rosier and Farella (1976) are correct, there was no bilingual instruction other than kindergarten reading readiness prior to 1971. By the 1975 testing, students who had been first graders in 1971 would have been in grade 5. Therefore of the three grade 6 classes tested between 1975 and 1977, only one could have been taught initial literacy in Navajo and of the three grade 5 classes, only two would have been taught in Navajo. Since the grade 5 and 6 classes combined over the three years 1975 through 1977 scored the largest gains over the comparison groups, it is not clear how the results should be interpreted.

Finns in Sweden: A recent study of Finnish immigrant children in two Swedish school systems (Skutnabb-Kangas and Toukomaa 1976) is fast becoming one of the most widely cited studies supporting the use of L1 in schools (see Pifer 1979; Troike 1978; McConnell 1980a, 1980c; Baral 1979; Rodriguez-Brown and Junker 1980; Cummins 1980).

It is generally thought that Skutnabb-Kangas and Toukomaa (1976) show that the more schooling in Finnish (L1) children had before beginning instruction in Swedish, the better their Swedish (L2). It is then inferred that this finding supports the use of L1 in the United States for children from non-English-speaking backgrounds.

We rejected this conclusion for several important reasons. The report lacks much of the detail needed to determine exactly what the researchers did. In addition, the authors did not have random assignment, and they did not try to match the comparison and experimental groups or to control statistically for preexisting differences. Further, there is a high attrition rate in the authors' sample.

Missing data pose a particularly severe problem. The authors state that the study covered 687 students (Skutnabb-Kangas and Toukomaa 1976:48), but the key analysis is based on only 150 students. When almost 80 percent of the data are missing, serious distortions can be introduced into the study.

The critical analysis in the Skutnabb-Kangas and Toukomaa study is a table showing the L2 performance level of L1 immigrants with varying amounts of schooling in L1 before immigrating and learning L2. The authors present no statistical analysis of the data, so we carried one out. We made forty-nine tests based on varying assumptions about the data and about exactly what was to be compared to what as derived from the various interpretations of the Skutnabb-Kangas and Toukomaa results found in the literature (see Baker and de Kanter 1981). Of the forty-nine, only six reached the 5 percent level of significance. Since our tests were not independent, this ratio cannot be taken as an overall test of the 5 percent level. Instead the pattern of results must be inspected; the pattern was overwhelmingly one of no relationship between the extent of schooling in L1 and later L2 performance.

We believe the most useful statistic in testing occurrence of the results attributed to Skutnabb-Kangas and Toukomaa is coefficient λ, which gives the percentage improvement in predicting a student's L2 performance that results from knowing that student's L1 performance level. No matter how we looked at the data, λ was always zero, which means there was no relationship between L1 and L2 performance. In short, the Skutnabb-Kangas and Toukomaa data do not support the implications that have been drawn from them.

Indians in Mexico: Modiano (1966), another study widely cited in support of bilingual education, reported that a group of Indian students in Mexico who were taught in their native language for one year before entering an all-Spanish school performed better in Spanish than did students whose first year was in Spanish. We rejected the results of this study for Modiano's failure to control for preexisting differences (even the ages of the two groups were different) in nonrandomly selected groups and for the numerous problems with the study detailed by Engle (1975).

Colorado State Bilingual Education Program: Egan and Goldsmith (1981) and Goldsmith (1981) report a statewide assessment of bilingual programs in Colorado for the 1979-1980 school year. The authors used data from all available school districts in the state where gains in normal curve equivalents (NCEs) could be determined for kindergarten through grade 4. (NCEs are a type of standardized percentile score; the study is fundamentally a norm-referenced study.) The authors argue that since language-minority children would be expected to show a loss against the norm in the absence of treatment, program success is evidenced by classes' showing either no change or an increase. They proceed to count such classes.

Apparently, "no change" was defined as a posttest score within one-third standard deviation of the pretest score, so that some of the classes counted as evidence of success actually may have experienced declining performance. (Since these students were initially low scoring, a decline of one-third standard deviation toward the tail of the distribution would cover a considerable range of scores.)

Goldsmith (1981) concludes that "overall, 87 percent of the program reported gains or maintenance of academic achievement." There are several serious problems with this study. First, the researchers' logic does not overcome the problems found in a norm-referenced design. Second, the statistical analysis does not support the conclusion. The procedure leading to an 87 percent success rate cannot be taken as evidence of program success, given the regression toward the mean artifact in low-achieving populations and the authors' inclusion of a loss of up to one-third standard deviation in very low scoring children as evidence of success. The problem can be illustrated using some test data from a national sample of non-Hispanic students from the Sustaining Effects Study. The percentile score distribution was divided into twenty parts—categories of five percentile points each—and the post-test percentile category was broken out by pretest percentile category. Therefore the movement of students from fall to spring percentile categories can be counted. Since Egan and Goldsmith are dealing with low-achieving students, we limit the example to the four lowest categories in the fall (first through twentieth percentiles). Since Egan and Goldsmith counted losses of up to 7 NCEs (one-third of a standard deviation) as no change, we will count a drop of one category from fall to spring as no change. When we apply Egan and Goldsmith's logic to our data for regular students not in any special program, we find basically the same pattern that Egan and Goldsmith interpreted as a program effect (table 2-1). Clearly, Egan and Goldsmith were observing the effects of measurement error in tests, not program effects.

Conclusions

The literature makes a compelling case that special programs in schools can improve the achievement of language-minority children. There is no evidence, however, that any specific program should be either legislated or preferred by the federal government. Indeed more research and demonstration projects with sound evaluation models are needed to determine which programs are most effective with which types of children in which locations.

Special programs can improve achievement in language-minority students. The literature we reviewed indicates that special programs can improve the achievement of language-minority children. The studies by Pena-Hughes and Solis (1980, 1981), Plante (1976), Huzar (1973), Covey (1973), Kaufman (1968), and Lum (1971) were true experiments, and all showed special programs to have produced positive effects. The ingenious nonex-

Table 2-1
Changes in Students' Reading Ability from Fall to Spring
(*in percentage*)

Fall Percentiles	Spring Percentile				
	Loss	No Change	Gain	No Change	+ Gain
1-5	0	36	64	100	
6-10	0	51	49	100	
11-15	15	33	52	85	
16-20	22	32	46	78	

Note: The students were not enrolled in a special program.

perimental design used by McConnell (1980a, 1980b) also seems to have established firmly the presence of a positive program effect. Positive effects also were reported in the nonexperimental studies of Zirkel (1972), Ames and Bicks (1978), AIR (1975b), Barik and Swain (1975), Olesini (1971), Barik et al. (1977), Ramirez (1973), Morgan (1971), Melendez (1980), Lambert and Tucker (1972), Legarreta (1979), Carsrud and Curtis (1979), A. Cohen (1975), and Malherbe (1946). But although special programs of one sort or another have been shown to be effective, this conclusion says nothing about the effects of any particular instructional approach.

The federal government should not place exclusive reliance on TBE. For more than a decade, the federal government has moved toward institutionalizing TBE as virtually the only approved method of instruction for language-minority children. TBE has been heavily emphasized in Title VII funding decisions; it has been implemented nationwide through the Office for Civil Rights' interpretation of the *Lau* decision; and in 1980 the Carter Administration proposed, with few exceptions, the legal mandate of TBE through federal regulations (that proposal was withdrawn by the Reagan administration).

The literature on the effectiveness of TBE, however, does not justify such heavy reliance on this one method of instruction. In order for the federal government to rely exclusively on one instructional method for meeting the needs of language-minority children, the following two conditions must hold:

1. There must be a strong case that the instructional method is uniformly effective.
2. Effective instructional alternatives should not exist. If the desired outcomes can be reached through more than one approach, the federal government should not constrain the options of local schools.

No consistent evidence supports the effectiveness of TBE. The only American studies designed to be nationally representative found negative effects for TBE in English and no effects for math (Danoff et al. 1978). Another large-scale representative study in South Africa showed that although high levels of achievement in both languages could be attained under a variety of instructional settings, L1 instruction was not essential to the development of nonlanguage subject skills (Malherbe 1946).

Since most of the studies were not representative, much weight must be attached to consistency in their results. These studies are striking in their inconsistency. In general, findings of no significant differences predominate, and negative effects for TBE are almost as frequent as are positive effects. Furthermore, methodological issues in several of the studies reporting positive effects raise strong questions as to the generalizability of the results (Covey 1973; McConnell 1980a, 1980c; Plante 1976).

TBE clearly fails our first test. An occasional, inexplicable success is not reason enough to make TBE the law of the land.

Mandating TBE also fails the second test. There is evidence that alternatives also work sometimes. Instances of success for both ESL and immersion have been found, and several studies show either ESL or immersion to have been superior to TBE. There is hardly justification for the federal government to require a method that regularly comes off second best when it is compared with the alternatives. Since several states have followed the federal lead in developing programs for language-minority children—in some cases, even legislating TBE—our analysis has implications beyond the federal level.

Federal policy should be more flexible. For more than a decade, federal policy has emphasized TBE to the virtual exclusion of alternative methods of instruction. This policy is not justified on the basis of educational effectiveness. Although TBE has been found to work in some settings, it also has been found ineffective and even harmful in other places. Furthermore, both major alternatives to TBE—structured immersion and ESL—have been found to work in some settings.

The commonsense observation that children should be taught in a language they understand does not necessarily lead to the conclusion they should be taught in their home language. They can be taught successfully in a second language if the teaching is done right. The key to successful teaching in the second language seems to be to ensure that the second language and subject matter are taught simultaneously so that subject content never gets ahead of language. Given the American setting, where the language-minority child must ultimately function in an English-speaking society, carefully conducted second-language instruction in all subjects may well be preferable to bilingual methods. Given the lack of consistency of results and the absence of information on how other variables affect program outcome, however, we conclude that it is very hard to say what kind of program will succeed in a particular school. Hence it seems that the only appropriate federal policy is to allow schools to develop instructional programs that suit the unique needs and circumstances of their students.

A widespread structured-immersion demonstration program is especially needed. Until now, the immersion method has been rejected on the basis of untested theoretical arguments.[6] Immersion may not transfer successfully from Canada to the United States, but this is an empirical question that must be answered by direct test.

Given the complexity of the problem, it also seems that the federal government should provide to local schools a source of the most-current information on pedagogical methods for language-minority children so that school districts can make informed choices, adapting methods to their local needs.

Improved bilingual research and program evaluations are needed. More and better research and improved program evaluations in bilingual education are necessary if the needs of language-minority children are to be met adequately. Bilingual education encompasses many complex, difficult issues that have been little (or insufficiently) studied.

The low quality of the methodology found throughout the literature is a serious problem. Studies have evidenced a lack of random assignment between treatment and control groups, the use of study designs that cannot show a treatment effect in the absence of random assignment, and a failure to apply appropriate statistical tests to demonstrate program effects. These problems have particularly characterized Title VII evaluations. The Title VII bilingual program has begun to take steps to improve the quality of local results. Our review, however, has indicated that program evaluations are still of very poor quality.

Some Implications for the Schools

The preceding discussion focused on federal policy implications of the analysis. In this section we suggest some implications from the studies for the local schools.

Having teachers or other adults available in the classroom who speak and understand L1 is probably an essential feature of any successful program. Even immersion programs may require bilingual teachers. All of the examples of immersion programs found in the literature used bilingual teachers. A bilingual teacher may contribute to the educational development of the language-minority child in several ways. First, even though L1 may be used only occasionally, the official recognition of L1 given by the school should have positive effects on student motivation, especially in contrast to the policy of punishing students for speaking their home language, which characterized many schools until recently. Second, immersion programs recognize that in order to learn, students must be allowed to ask questions in L1 when they are unable to formulate the questions in L2. Third, occasional use of L1 may be very effective in keeping the student engaged in learning tasks (Tikunoff, 1981). Time on task is an important factor in learning. Thus, even if we set aside considerations of possible benefits of instruction in L1, we may find that a bilingual teacher or aide in the classroom is an important asset in any special program for the language-minority child.

Concurrent translation methods should be avoided. Many programs use a method often called *concurrent translation* under which a teacher who makes a statement in one language immediately translates the statement into the second language. The idea is that the student will learn L2 as a result of the immediate feedback of the L1 translation. Instead the students tune out the language they understand less well, knowing the teacher will repeat in the home language something they do not grasp in the other language. In other words, the students ignore what is said in L2. So this method, in addition to not teaching students L2, takes time away from teaching students something else. There is some reason to believe that one characteristic of more-successful programs is strict segregation of the situations in which the two languages are used (see Legarreta 1979; de Kanter 1980; Cummins 1979; von Maltitz 1975; Berke 1980).

The level of difficulty of English used by the teacher must be appropriate for the level of development in English of the students. If the teacher talks over the heads of the language-minority students, as in a submersion class, their learning English will be delayed. If the teacher talks below the students' level, again learning will be delayed. Furthermore, the teacher should talk not at the students but with them. It is important that the language-minority children actively engage in communication in English if they are to learn English effectively (see Dulay and Burt 1978; Carroll 1978; Macmillan 1980; Krashen 1981).

The literature offers little guidance as to which instructional approach—TBE, ESL, or immersion—should be used. This is largely because the interaction between instructional method and other factors has not been fully explored. We know that TBE works in some places and fails in others, but we do not know why and therefore cannot specify in what situations TBE should or should not be used. The same is true for immersion and ESL. Although immersion programs seem to have been uniformly successful, all but one immersion study took place outside the United States. Factors differentiating the U.S. situation from the Canadian may or may not make a difference in how well a widespread immersion program would work in the United States. Nevertheless immersion shows enough promise to merit more attention than it has received to date.

Only by trying different approaches while carefully recording what was done and with what results can progress be made toward developing truly effective programs for language-minority students. The federal government should encourage diversity, experimentation, research, and good program evaluation. Change will not occur if the federal government withdraws from the arena. The federal government bears a large share of the responsibility for having institutionalized TBE over the past decade and will have to encourage change and diversity in what it has created.

Appendix 2A:
Summary of Applicable
Studies

Table 2A-1
Summary of Applicable Studies

Author	Date	Grade	Design[a]	Number of Students[b]	Languages[c] L1	Languages[c] L2	Reported Results L2	Reported Results Math
AIR (Corpus Christi)	1975b	K-1	Longitudinal; analysis of covariance	393	Spanish	English	TBE no different from submersion in 1 grade; TBE better than submersion in 1 grade	
Alvarez	1975	2	Longitudinal; analysis of covariance	147	Spanish	English	TBE no different from submersion on 4 tests	TBE no different from submersion on 4 tests
Ames and Bicks	1978	1-9	Analysis of covariance	669	Spanish and French	English	TBE no different from ESL alone	TBE better than ESL alone
Balasubramonian et al.	1973	K-3	Analysis of covariance and other adjustments	317	Spanish	English	TBE no different from ESL alone	
Barik and Swain	1975	K-2	Longitudinal; analysis of covariance	2,253	English	French	Immersion better than ESL	Math taught in L2 no different from math taught in L1
Barik et al.	1977	2-5	Longitudinal; analysis of covariance	*	English	French		Depending on year and grade, math taught in L2 was worse than, no different from, or even better than math taught in L1
Bates	1970	3	Equivalent	56	Spanish	English	Submersion better than TBE	TBE no different from submersion
Carsrud and Curtis	1979	4-5	Longitudinal; analysis of covariance	172	Spanish	English	TBE better than submersion in 1 grade; TBE no different from submersion in 1 grade	TBE no different from submersion
A. Cohen	1975	K-3	Longitudinal; analysis of covariance and other adjustments	90	Spanish	English	TBE no different from submersion on 86 of 100 language skills; submersion better than TBE on 11; TBE better than submersion on 3	TBE no different from submersion in 2 of 3 grades; TBE better than submersion in 1 grade

Author	Year	Grade	Method	N	L1	L2	Result	Result
Cottrell	1971	K-1	Analysis of covariance	470	Navajo	English	TBE no different from submersion	TBE no different from submersion
Covey	1973	9	Random assignment	200	Spanish	English	TBE better than submersion	TBE no different from submersion
Danoff et al.	1977, 1978	2-6	Analysis of covariance and other adjustments; large study	8,900	Several	English	Submersion better than TBE	
deWeffer	1972	1	Analysis of covariance	141	Spanish	English	TBE no better than submersion on an oral test	
Gleason and Rankine	1977	K	Experiment	56	English	French		All L1 better than L2 immersion
Huzar	1973	2-3	Random assignment; one-way analysis of covariance	160	Spanish	English	TBE no different from submersion	
Lambert and Tucker	1972	1-4	Longitudinal; analysis of covariance	213	English	French	L2 performance in an immersion program at or near that of monolingual L2 speakers	Math taught in L2 no different from math taught in L1 (immersion program)
Lampman	1973	2	Matching	40	Spanish	English	TBE no better than submersion	
Layden	1972	3	Experiment	56	Spanish	English	Submersion better than TBE	
Legarreta	1979	K	Analysis of covariance	80	Spanish	English	TBE better than submersion or TBE no different from submersion, depending on test; TBE with ESL better than TBE without ESL component	
Lum	1971	1	Random assignment	55	Chinese	English	ESL alone better than TBE on 3 tests; ESL alone no different from TBE on 2 tests	
McConnell	1980a 1980c	Pre-K-3	Longitudinal; subject as own control	1,020	Spanish	English	TBE better than submersion	
McSpadden	1979	K-1	Analysis of covariance	196	French	English	TBE no different from submersion	TBE no different from submersion

Table 2A-1 (*continued*)

Author	Date	Grade	Design[a]	Number of Students[b]	Languages[c]		Reported Results	
					L1	L2	L2	Math
McSpadden	1980	K-2	Longitudinal; analysis of covariance	263	French	English	Submersion better than TBE in 1 of 3 grades; TBE no different from submersion in 2 grades	Submersion better than TBE in 1 of 3 grade 5s; TBE no different from submersion in 2 grades
Malherbe	1946	4–10	Nationally representative survey (South Africa)	18,773	Afrikaans or English	English or Afrikaans	L2 better the more it is used in school	Initial deficit when instructed in L2 is gone by end of elementary school (also found for geography)
Matthews	1979	2,4, 6,8	Log-linear model	1,011	Many	English	TBE/ESL no different from submersion	
Melendez	1980	7–10	Analysis of covariance	241	Spanish	English	75-100% of reading instruction in L1 better than 50-75% in L1 or 100% in L2	
Moore and Parr	1978	K-2	Analysis of covariance	130	Spanish	English	Submersion better than TBE	TBE no different from submersion
Morgan	1971	1	Matching	193	French	English	TBE better than submersion on 2 tests; no difference on 2 tests	
Pena-Hughes and Solis	1980	K	Random assignment	156	Spanish	English	Immersion better than TBE	
Plante	1976	1-2	Longitudinal; experiment	72	Spanish	English	TBE better than submersion in 1 grade; TBE no different from submersion in 1 grade and for both grades combined	
Powers	1978	2-6	Analysis of covariance	87	Spanish	English	TBE no different from submersion on 2 tests	TBE no different from submersion on 2 tests
Prewitt-Diaz	1979	9	Analysis of covariance	139	Spanish	English	TBE no different from submersion on 3 tests	
Ramirez et al.	n.d.	K-6	Analysis of covariance	NA	Spanish	English	Bilingual plus ESL better than bilingual alone	

Study	Year	Grade	Method	N	L1	L2	Result	Result
Ramirez	1973	K	Analysis of covariance	70	Spanish	English	ESL better than submersion	
Ramos et al.	1967	1-6	Longitudinal; matching	**	Hiligaynon Pilipino	English	TBE no different from immersion[d]	TBE no different from immersion[d]
Skoczylas	1972	1	Analysis of covariance	47	Spanish	English	TBE no different from submersion	Submersion better than TBE
Stebbins et al.	1977	K-3	Longitudinal; analysis of covariance and other adjustments; 5 sites	1,060	Spanish	English	TBE no different from submersion[d]	TBE no different from submersion
Stern	1975	4-6	Analysis of covariance	213	Spanish	English	Submersion better than TBE[d]	Submersion better than TBE[d]
Zirkel	1972	1-3	Matching; analysis of covariance	278	Spanish	English	TBE better than submersion on 1 test; TBE no different from submersion on 4 tests	TBE no different from submersion

* Treatment = 73; control not given.

** Unable to obtain information at present; however, the sample size was large.

[a] For studies not using random assignment, we note the method used to adjust for possible preexisting differences between the treatment and control groups. Analysis of covariance is a statistical method used to adjust for preexisting differences.

[b] In the case of multiyear studies, the number of tested students was counted. Rather than counting the number of unique students, the study counted each year a student was tested as a separate instance.

[c] L1 is the language-minority child's home language; L2 is the child's second language.

[d] This result represents our conclusion from the author's very complex analysis; see Baker and de Kanter (1981) for a detailed discussion.

Appendix 2B: Robustness of the Results

Although there is general agreement in the scientific literature that true experiments provide sound results, there are varying degrees of agreement as to what should be done when true experiments are not used. In this review, we used liberal criteria and accepted nonexperimental studies as long as the researchers had made some reasonable effort to adjust or control for the possible biases that can occur in the absence of random assignment. In general, this meant we accepted studies relying on matching or on the analysis of covariance to adjust test scores statistically for initial differences between the treatment and the comparison groups. Experts disagree somewhat about whether the analysis of covariance adjustment is fully succesful. Further, there may be, in effect, a change in the shape of the learning curve modeled by standardized tests as the monolingual, non-English-speaking limit is approached. This, too, would raise questions about the adequacy of the analysis of covariance adjustment.

To test the robustness of our findings in the face of such methodological disagreements, we can tighten and loosen the criteria for acceptability to see the effects on our conclusions. The most-stringent standard would be to limit consideration to only true experiments. The six true experiments found by our review reported the following. Covey (1973) and Plante (1976) found some positive effects for TBE. No difference between TBE and submersion was reported by Huzar (1973) and by Plante (1976) on some measures. Layden (1972) found TBE inferior to submersion in English and no different on math performance. Lum (1971) found TBE inferior to ESL on some measures but no difference on other measures. Pena-Hughes and Solis (1980) found immersion students superior to TBE students. Thus, the few true experiments produce the same pattern of mixed results found in the larger set of studies.

In addition to the true experiments, several nonexperimental studies, recognizing the problems of the analysis of covariance, used other statistical techniques designed to correct for the shortcomings of the analysis of covariance. Balasubramionian et al. (1973) found no difference between TBE and ESL alone. A. Cohen (1975) found mixed results on a large number of tests, with the majority of cases indicating no difference between TBE and submersion. Danoff (1978) found no effects in math and a negative TBE effect in English. McConnell (1980a, 1980c) reported positive effects. Matthews (1979) found no effects, as did Stebbins et al. (1977). Again, the pattern of mixed results is repeated.

Since essentially the same pattern of results occurs if we limit consideration to true experiments, or to studies using statistical adjustments or both, we conclude that our findings were not affected by the possible methodological problems that may arise in using the analysis of covariance.

Since some researchers would not be so harsh on the use of grade-equivalent scores (GEs) as we were, we also varied our criteria by considering studies using GEs (which would not have been rejected for other reasons). The relaxation of the methodological standards added only three studies. In a true experiment, Kaufman (1968) found TBE superior to submersion on two component scores of a standardized achievement test and no difference on seven component scores in one school. At a second school, there were no differences on any of the nine component tests. Olesini (1971) found TBE superior to submersion on one English and on one math test and no difference on one English and on one math test. Tanguma (1977) found generally positive effects for TBE in both reading and math when compared to submersion. Again, the results are mixed. Even if we consider the few additional positive findings from these studies, we see no reason to modify our conclusion that the evidence for TBE is mixed, and alternative methods of instruction seem to work. Even if the weight of the evidence favored TBE (which is doubtful), there still is no justification for the federal government's placing exclusive reliance on TBE as the sole means for meeting the needs of language-minority students.

A second issue concerning the robustness of the results relates to the generally poor quality of the bilingual evaluation literature. Basically the question is how we know all the studies reporting positive results and rejected for methodological reasons were not right. What if TBE really works, and it is just the poor quality of the studies that keeps us from realizing the success?

Because of this problem, we have carefully constrained our conclusions. We believe the analysis and the studies reviewed are fully sufficient to establish that TBE works in some places and does not work in others. Thus the case for TBE is not strong enough to justify exclusive reliance on this method of instruction. Our conclusion is further supported by our finding that some studies indicating alternative instructional approaches work as well as or better than TBE. We cannot see how further consideration of methodologically doubtful studies could alter these facts. The key point is not that we rejected studies reporting positive results but that we found a number of adequate studies that clearly demonstrate a lack of effectiveness for TBE. If greater effectiveness of TBE is to be demonstrated, better programs are needed as much as or more than better evaluations.

Appendix 2C: Methodological Reasons for Rejecting Studies

Table 2C-1
Methodological Reasons for Rejecting Studies

Study	No Adjustment	Gains Only	Norms	Criterion Tests	Statistics	Local Criteria	GE	No Detail	Other
Ahmann and Lambert 1971	X				X				Posttest only
Ainsworth and Christian 1970	X	X							
AIR 1975e (St. John Valley)	X	X	X		X		X		
AIR 1975a (Alice, Tex.)	X							X	
AIR 1975d (Philadelphia)	X							X	
AIR 1975c (Houston)	X								
Alejandro 1979								X	
Alston et al. 1980a			X				X		
Alston et al. 1980b			X				X		
Arce & Associates 1979	X	X				X			
Arce and Sosa 1975		X				X	X		
Askins et al. 1975		X							
Askins & Associates 1976	X	X				X			
Ayala and Vatsula 1971						X			
Battiste et al. 1975		X						X	
Berget 1980		X				X			
Birmingham 1980		X			X			X	
Boyce 1979	X								
Boyce 1980	X	X							
Cahill and Foley 1973		X	X						
Charlotte-Mecklenburg 1980		X							
Cohen, B., et al. 1971	X								
Cohen, B., and Promisel 1970		X				X			
Collison 1974									Author's interpretation flawed
Condon et al. 1971	X	X							
Corpus Christi 1980a			X		X				
Corpus Christi 1980b			X		X				
Del Buono 1971					X				

Reference	1	2	3	4	5	6	Comments
Demauro 1981				X		X	Correlated test scores and length of time in program with no control for immigration or prior proficiency
Development Associates 1977		X				X	
DiBiasio and Sullivan 1971							
Edwards 1976						X	Literature review
Edwards and Smyth 1976						X	Literature review
Egan and Goldsmith 1981		X		X	X		
Elligett 1980	X						
Ewanyshyn 1978							Not a comparative evaluation; a study of L2 learning
Fairfax County 1980			X				
Ferris 1979	X					X	
Flouris 1978	X					X	
Fort Worth 1975	X					X	
Garcia, A., 1978	X						
Garcia, R., 1977						X	Posttest only
Genesee 1976						X	Literature review
Ghini 1979		X	X			X	
Giles 1971							
Goldsmith 1981			X	X			Literature review
Golub 1977		X				X	
Golub 1981		X					
Goodrick 1977		X				X	
Gudschinsky 1971						X	Literature review

Table 2C-1 *(continued)*

Study	No Adjustment	Gains Only	Norms	Criterion Tests	Statistics	Local Criteria	GE	No Detail	Other
Guerrero 1980		X							
Hall 1970								X	
Harrison 1973	X								
Harrison 1974a			X			X			
Harrison 1974b			X			X			
Harrison 1975a			X			X			
Harrison 1975b			X			X			
Harrison 1976a			X			X			
Harrison 1976b						X			
Harrison 1980		X			X		X	X	
Heuristics 1971						X			No control group
Herbert 1971					X			X	
Horst et al. 1980									Author rejects 19 Bilingual Evaluations (Project Information Package) as unsound
Illinois 1981	X	X	X		X	X	X		
JDRP 1977	X		X				X		
Kalmar 1975					X		X		
Kaufman 1968								X	Included in the analysis
Leyba 1978	X								
Love 1975					X				An evaluation design report, no results
McCarthy 1976		X							

Study			Literature review	Teacher reports of progress	Interpretation of results not clear	Flawed matching	Good design; no findings available	Included in the analysis of robustness
Macnamara 1966			X					
Macnamara 1970								
Merlos 1978		X						
Milwaukee 1972		X						
Milwaukee 1976		X		X				
Miranda 1979				X				
Modiano 1966		X						
Monzon 1981		X				X		
Mortensen 1980		X						
Muller and Leonetti 1970		X				X		
Nearine 1967		X	X					
Offenberg 1970		X	X					
Offenberg 1971		X						
Offenberg 1973		X						
Offenberg et al. 1973, 1974		X	X		X			
Offenberg and Wolowec 1973		X	X		X			
Ojerinde 1978							X	
Olesini 1971		X						X
Orvik 1975		X						X
Payne 1973								X
Payne and Medina 1972								X
Price 1978		X	X					
Pryor 1969		X						X
Pryor 1970								X
Pryor 1971								X
Pryor 1972								

Table 2C-1 (continued)

Study	No Adjustment	Gains Only	Norms	Criterion Tests	Statistics	Local Criteria	GE	No Detail	Other
Richard 1979	X						X	X	No control group
Richardson 1980								X	
Rimm et al. 1975	X					X	X		
Rimm 1978	X		X				X		
Rimm 1980		X							
Rimm 1977	X		X				X		
Rimm 1979	X		X				X		
Rivera 1973	X								
Romero 1977	X						X		
Rosier 1977	X						X		
Rosier and Farella 1976	X						X		
Rosier and Holm 1980	X				X		X		
St. John Valley 1980			X						
Schmid-Schonbein 1980	X		X						
Scott 1979						X			
Scudder 1979									Compared two ESL programs
Skutnabb-Kangas 1979	X				X			X	
Skutnabb-Kangas and Toukomaa 1976	X				X			X	
Smith, M., 1971	X	X							
Smith, F., 1976		X							
Smith and Smith 1978	X	X				X	X	X	
South San Francisco 1979				X		X	X	X	
Sullivan 1973			X		X				
Swain 1978a								X	Mostly a process analysis
Swain 1978b								X	

Study								Comments
SWRL 1975								
Tanguma 1977			X		X	X		Included in the analysis
Trevino 1970		X						
Trevino 1968			X			X		Confounded treatments
Valencia 1970	X							
Valencia 1971		X						
Valencia 1974								
Veilleux 1977	X			X		X		
Vorih and Rosier 1978	X		X	X		X		
Willink 1968	X			X				Compared two types ESL
Winter 1979							X	
Yoloye 1977								Interim report; no relevant results yet
Young 1980	X		X			X		
Zimmer 1976	X		X			X		

Note: Studies that do not address our questions are not listed.

Notes

1. The full report is found in Baker and de Kanter (1981).
2. L1 refers to the child's first or home language. L2 refers to the second language, the language used by society and in the schools (in the case of language-minority students). In the United States, L2 refers to English for the language-minority child; L1 is that child's home language.
3. See Baker and de Kanter (1981) for a full discussion of each study.
4. Equating the treatment and comparison groups for IQ or initial achievement probably does not fully account for this type of language ability. No evidence in the literature review suggests that any of the widely used tests are perfectly correlated with innate language ability. Therefore, to the extent that the tests are unrelated to innate language ability, efforts to control statistically for IQ and pretest will fail.
5. See Baker and de Kanter (1981), chapter 3, for a detailed discussion of the methodological problems found in these studies.
6. Proponents of TBE have raised questions about the generalizability of the immersion studies based on middle-class Canadian children (see Tucker 1980). Genesee (1976) reviewed the status of the Canadian literature and concluded that immersion was applicable to children of lower socioeconomic status and to minorities. Pena-Hughes and Solis (1980) certainly indicate that immersion is workable in the United States, but more research needs to be done because this question ultimately is an empirical one.

References

Ahmann, J. Stanley, and Lambert, B. Geraldine. 1971. "An Evaluation of a Bilingual Education Program 1970-1971." St. Martinville, La.: Saint Martin Parish School Board.

Ainsworth, C.L., and Christian, Chester C. 1970. "Lubbock Bilingual Elementary Education Program, Title VII, Elementary and Secondary Education Act of 1965 Evaluation Report, 1970." Lubbock, Tex.: Lubbock Independent School District.

AIR (American Institutes for Research). 1975a. "Alice Independent School District Bilingual Program, Alice, Texas." *Identification and Description of Exemplary Bilingual Education Programs*. Palo Alto, Calif.: Author.

———. 1975b. "Bilingual Education Program (Aprendemos En Dos Idiomas), Corpus Christi, Texas." *Identification and Description of Exemplary Bilingual Education Programs*. Palo Alto, Calif.: Author.

_____ . 1975c. "Bilingual Education Program (Title VII, P.L. 89-10), Houston, Texas." *Identification and Description of Exemplary Bilingual Education Programs.* Palo Alto, Calif.: Author.

_____ . 1975d. "Let's Be Amigos. Philadelphia, Pennsylvania." *Identification and Description of Exemplary Bilingual Programs.* Palo Alto, Calif.: Author.

_____ . 1975e. "St. John Valley Bilingual Education Project, St. John Valley, Maine." *Identification and Description of Exemplary Bilingual Programs.* Palo Alto, Calif.: Author.

Alejandro, Frank Z. 1979. "The Relationship of Bilingual Bicultural Education and Regular Education in the Verbal and Nonverbal Performance of Chicano Students." Ph.D. dissertation, Catholic University.

Alston, Herbert L.; Gavito, Alfredo A.; and Lopez, Cristobal. 1980a. *Houston Plan for Bilingual Education: 1978-79 School Year Status Report.* Houston: Houston Independent School District.

Alston, Herbert L. and Gavito, Alfredo A. 1980b. *Houston Plan for Bilingual Education 1979-80 School Year Evaluation Report.* Houston: Houston Independent School District Research Evaluation and Accreditation.

Alvarez, Juan M. 1975. "Comparison of Academic Aspirations and Achievement in Bilingual versus Monolingual Classrooms." Ph.D. dissertation, University of Texas.

Ames, J.S., and Bicks, Pat. 1978. "An Evaluation of Title VII Bilingual/Bi-cultural Program, 1977-78 School Year, Final Report, Community School District 22." Mimeographed. Brooklyn, N.Y.: School District of New York.

Anderson, James G., and Johnson, William H. 1971. "Stability and Change among Three Generations of Mexican Americans: Factors Affecting Achievement." *American Educational Research Journal* 8:285-309.

Arce and Associates, Inc. 1979. "Project Rainbow. Pajaro Valley Unified School District. Watsonville, Calif.: 1978-79." Mimeographed. Santa Ana, Calif.: Author.

Arce, Aaron, and Sosa, Xavier. 1975. "ESEA Bilingual/Bicultural Project, 1974-1975 Final Evaluation Report." Austin, Tex.: Austin Independent School District, Office of Research and Evaluation.

Asher, J., and Garcia, R. 1969. "The Optimal Age to Learn a Foreign Language." *Modern Language Journal* 8:334-341.

Askins, Billy E., and Associates. 1976. "A School and Home-Based Bilingual Education Model. End-of-Year Evaluation Report, 1975-76." Mimeographed. Lubbock, Tex.: Clovis Public Schools, New Mexico.

Askins, Billy E. et al. 1975. "Clovis-Portales Bilingual Early Childhood Programs Third Year Evaluation Study (1974-1975)." Lubbock, Tex.: Askins (B.E.) and Associates.

Ayala, Armando, and Vatsula, John. 1971. "Area III Valley Intercultural Report; 1970-71 Final Evaluation Report." Auburn, Calif.: Placer County Office of Education.

Baker, Keith, and de Kanter, Adriana. 1981. "Effectiveness of Bilingual Education: A Review of the Literature. Final Draft Report." Washington, D.C.: Office of Technical and Analytic Systems, U.S. Department of Education.

Balasubramonian, K.; Seelye, H. Ned; and De Weffer, Rafaela Elizondo. 1973. "Do Bilingual Education Programs Inhibit English Language Achievement? A Report on an Illinois Experiment." Paper presented at the Seventh Annual Convention of Teachers of English to Speakers of Other Languages, San Juan, Puerto Rico, May 9–12.

Baral, David. P. 1979. "Academic Achievement of Recent Immigrants from Mexico." *NABE Journal* 111:1-13.

Barik, Henri, and Swain, Merrill. 1975. "Three Year Evaluation of a Large Scale Early Grade French Immersion Program: The Ottawa Study." *Language Learning* 25:1-30.

Barik, Henri C.; Swain, Merrill; and Nwanunobi, Edna A. 1977. "English-French Bilingual Education: The Elgin Study through Grade Five." *Canadian Modern Language Review* 33:459-475.

Bates, Enid May Buswell. 1970. "The Effects of One Experimental Bilingual Program on Verbal Ability and Vocabulary of First Grade Pupils." Ph.D. dissertation, Texas Tech University.

Battiste, Marie, et al. 1975. *Study of Bilingual-Bicultural Projects Involving Native American, Indo-European, Asian and Pacific Language Groups.* Palo Alto, Calif.: American Institutes for Research.

Berget. 1980. "Final Evaluation Report 1979-80." Brentwood, Calif.: Liberty Union High School District.

Berke, I. 1980. Personal communication.

Birmingham Public Schools. 1980. "Bilingual Education Evaluation." Mimeographed. Birmingham, Ala.: Author.

Boyce, Margaret. 1979. "Math Achievement of Participants and Non-Participants in the Bilingual Program." Paper presented at the Rocky Mountain Education Research Association Annual Meeting, Tucson, Ariz., September 26-28.

_____ . 1980. "Math Achievement of Participants and Non-Participants in the Bilingual Program." Paper presented at the Arizona Association for Bilingual Education, March.

Cahill, Robert J., and Foley, Joseph J. 1973. "Evaluation and Evaluative Research in an Urban Bilingual Program." Dedham, Mass.: Heuristics, Inc.

Cardenas, B., and Cardenas, J.A. 1977. "The Theory of Incompatibilities." San Antonio, Texas: Intercultural Development Research Association.

Carroll, J.B. 1975. *The Teaching of French as a Foreign Language in Eight Countries*. New York: John Wiley.

———. 1978. "International Comparisons of Foreign Language Learning in the IEA Project." In Alatis, J.E., ed. *International Dimensions of Bilingual Education*. Washington, D.C.: Georgetown University Press.

Carsrud, Karen, and Curtis, John. 1979. "ESEA Title VII Bilingual Program: Final Report." Mimeographed. Austin, Tex.: Austin Independent School District.

Carter, Thomas P. 1970. "Mexican Americans in School: A History of Educational Neglect." New York: College Entrance Examination Board.

Charlotte-Mecklenburg Schools. 1980. "Title VII Transitional Bilingual Education Summative Report 1979-80." Mimeographed. Charlotte, N.C.: Author.

Christian, Chester, C. 1976. "Social and Psychological Implications of Bilingual Literacy." In Simoes, Antonio ed., *The Bilingual Child*. New York: Academic Press.

Cohen, Andrew D. 1975. *A Sociolinguistic Approach to Bilingual Education*. Rowley, Mass.: Newbury House Publishers.

Cohen, Bernard, and Promisel, David M. 1970. "Final Evaluation Report (1969–1970) New Haven Bilingual Education Program." Darien, Conn.: Dunlap and Associates.

Cohen, Bernard, et al. 1971. "Final Evaluation Report of the 1970-71 New Haven Bilingual Education Program." Darien, Conn.: Dunlap and Associates.

Collison, G.O. 1974. "Concept Formation in a Second Language: A Study of Ghanaian School Children." *Harvard Education Review* 44:441-457.

Condon, Elaine E., et al. 1971. "Project Sell, Title VII: Final Evaluation 1970-71." Union City, Calif.: Union City Board of Education.

Coronado, Leopoldo A. 1979. "The Effects of Differing Degrees of Bilingualism on the Cognitive Performance and Scholastic Achievement of Spanish/English Bilinguals." Ph.D. dissertation, University of Texas.

Corpus Christi Independent School District. 1980a. "Evaluation Report for the Title VII Aprendemos en dos Idiomas Bilingual Program 1979-80." Corpus Christi, Tex.: Author.

———. 1980b. "Follow Through Program Evaluation Report 1979-80." Corpus Christi, Tex.: Author.

Cottrell, Milford C. 1971. "Bilingual Education in San Juan County, Utah: A Cross-Cultural Emphasis." Paper presented at the American Educational Research Convention, New York City, February.

Covey, Donald David. 1973. "An Analytical Study of Secondary Freshmen Bilingual Education and Its Effect on Academic Achievement and Attitude of Mexican American Students." Ph.D. dissertation, Arizona State University.

———. 1981. Personal communication.

Cummins, James. 1978. "Educational Implications of Mother Tongue Maintenance in Minority Language Groups." *Canadian Modern Language Review* 34:395-416.

———. 1980. "The Entry and Exit Fallacy in Bilingual Education." *NABE Journal* 4:25-60.

———. 1979. "Linguistic Interdependence and the Educational Development of Bilingual Children." *Review of Education Research* 2:222-251.

———. 1981. "The Role of Primary Language Development in Promoting Educational Success for Language Minority Students." Paper prepared for the California State Department of Education Compendium on Bilingual-Bicultural Education.

Danoff, Malcolm N.; Coles, Gary J.; McLaughlin, Donald H.; and Reynolds, Dorothy J. 1977. *Evaluation of the Impact of ESEA Title VII Spanish/English Bilingual Education Programs.* Vol. 1; *Study Design and Interim Findings.* Palo Alto, Calif.: American Institutes for Research.

———. 1978. *Evaluation of the Impact of ESEA Title VII Spanish/English Bilingual Education Programs.* Vol. 3: *Year Two Impact Data, Educational Process, and In-Depth Analysis.* Palo Alto, Calif.: American Institutes for Research.

Darcy, N.T. 1953. "A Review of the Literature on the Effects of Bilingualism upon the Measurement of Intelligence." *Journal of Genetic Psychology*, 82:21-57.

De Avila, E.H. 1981. *Relative Language Proficiency Types: A Comparison of Prevalence, Achievement Level, and Socio-Economic Status.* Larkspur, Calif.: Delta Squared.

de Kanter, Ellen Ann Tharp. 1979. "Impact of a Dissonance-Based Intervention Strategy upon Teachers' Attitudes toward Equal Opportunity of Education for Mexican American Students." Ph.D. dissertation, University of Houston.

———. 1980-1981. Personal communication.

Del Buono, Xavier Antonio. 1971. "The Relationship of Bilingual/Bicultural Instruction to the Achievement and Self-Concept of Seventh Grade Mexican-American Students." Ph.D. dissertation, Michigan State University.

Demauro, Gerald. 1981. *The Impact of Bilingual Education on English Acquisition in New Jersey.* Trenton, N.J.: New Jersey State Department of Education.

Development Associates. 1977. "Case Studies of Noteworthy Projects in Bilingual Education." Supporting vol. 3 of A Study of State Programs in Bilingual Education. Washington, D.C.: Author.

de Weffer, Rafaela de Carmen Elizondo. 1972. "Effects of First Language Instruction in Academic and Psychological Development of Bilingual Children." Ph.D. dissertation, Illinois Institute of Technology.

DiBiasio, Guy N. and Sullivan, Richard E. 1971. "Providence Title II Bilingual Education Program. Final Evaluation Report." Kingston, R.I.: Rhode Island University, Curriculum Research and Development Center.

Dulay, Heidi, and Burt, Marina. 1978. "From Research to Method in Bilingual Education." In Alatis, J.E., ed., *International Dimensions of Bilingual Education*. Washington, D.C.: Georgetown University Press.

Edwards, Henry P. 1976. "Evaluation of the French Immersion Program Offered by the Ottawa Roman Catholic Separate School Board." *Canadian Modern Language Review* 33:137-142.

Edwards, H.P., and Smyth, F. 1976. "Alternatives to Early Immersion Programs for the Acquisition of French as a Second Language." *Canadian Modern Language Review* 32:524-533.

Egan, Lawrence, and Goldsmith, Ross. 1981. "Bilingual Bicultural Education: The Colorado Success Story." Mimeographed.

Elligett, Jane K. 1980. "Bilingual Program Achievement Results at Sunset Hills and Tarpon Springs Elementary Schools, Pinellas County, Florida." Clearwater, Fla.: Pinellas County Schools.

Engle, Patricia Lee. 1975. "The Use of Vernacular Languages in Education: Language Medium in Early School Years for Minority Language Groups." *Bilingual Education Series no. 2*. Arlington, Va.: Center for Applied Linguistics.

Ewanyshyn, Eugene. 1978. "Evaluation of a Ukranian-English Bilingual Program 1976-77." Alberta, Canada: Edmonton Catholic School.

Fairfax County Public Schools. 1980. "Evaluation Report: English as a Second Language Program." Mimeographed. Fairfax, Va.: Author, Department of Instructional Services.

Ferris, Melvyn Roger. 1979. "The Effects of the Early and Delayed Second Language Acquisition on the English Composition Skills of Spanish-Speaking Junior High School Students." Ph.D. dissertation, Stanford University.

Fishman, J.A. 1965. "Bilingualism, Intelligence and Language Learning." *Modern Language Journal* 49:227-237.

Flores, Solomon Hernandez. 1969. "The Nature and Effectiveness of Bilingual Education Programs for the Spanish-speaking Child in the United States." Ph.D. dissertation, Ohio State Unviersity.

Flouris, George. 1978. "The Self-Concept and Cross-Cultural Awareness of Greek-American Students Enrolled in the Monolingual and Bilingual Schools." Ph.D. dissertation, Florida State University.

Fort Worth Independent School District. 1975. "Effectiveness of the Bilingual Program in Fort Worth Schools." Mimeographed. Fort Worth, Tex.: Author.

Garcia, A.B. 1978. "Evaluation Report San Jose Area Bilingual Education Consortium, 1977-78." San Jose, Calif.: San Jose Unified School District.

Garcia, Ramiro. 1977. "Bilingual Instruction: Its Relationship to Cognitive and Affective Development—with Implications for Educational Policy Decisions." Ph.D. dissertation, University of California.

Genesee, Fred. 1976. "The Suitability of Immersion Programs for All Children." *Canadian Modern Language Review* 32:494-515.

Ghini, C. 1979. "Terrebone Parish French-English Bilingual Education Project Year End Interim Evaluation Report." Mimeographed. New Orleans: G&A Ltd.

Giles, W.H. 1971. "Cultural Contrasts in English/French Bilingual Instruction in the Early Grades." Paper presented at the Conference on Child Language, Chicago, November.

Gleason, Thomas P., and Rankine, Fred C. 1977. "Reviving a Culture: Kindergarten and French Immersion." Paper presented at the annual meeting of the American Educational Research Association, April.

Goldsmith, R.P. 1981. "Analysis of the Final Evaluation Reports Submitted to the Bilingual Unit of the Colorado Department of Education by Bilingual Education Programs Funded under the Colorado Bilingual/Bicultural Education Act during the 1979-80 School Year." Boulder, Colo.: BUENO.

Golub, Lester S. 1977. "Evaluation Design and Implementation of a Bilingual Education Program Grade 1-12 Spanish/English." Paper presented at the Annual Meeting of the American Educational Research Association, New York, New York, April.

———. 1981. "Literacy Development of Bilingual Children." *Bilingual Journal* 5 (Spring):9-14.

Goodrick, G. Ken. 1977. "Final Evaluation Report Title I ESEA Bilingual Project 1976-77." Houston, Tex.: Houston Independent School District, Program Planning, Research, and Evaluation, August.

Gudschinsky, S.C. 1971. "Literacy in the Mother Tongue and Second Language Learning." Paper presented at the Conference on Child Language, Chicago, November.

Guerrero, F.J. 1980. "Final Evaluation of the 1979-80 State Grant Bilingual Education Program." New Haven, Conn.: New Haven Public Schools.

Hall, R. 1970. "Learning to Read in Two Languages: Statements from the

Research Literature on Reading in Bilingual Programs." Philadelphia: Philadelphia School District.

Harrison, Helene W. 1973. "Evaluation of the San Marcos Independent School District's Bilingual Education Program." San Marcos, Tex.: San Marcos Independent School District.

_____ . 1974a. "Final Evaluation Report of the San Marcos Independent School District's Bilingual Education Program." San Marcos, Tex.: San Marcos Independent School District.

_____ . 1974b. "Final Evaluation Report of the Harlandale Independent School District's Bilingual Education Program." San Antonio, Tex.: Harlandale Independent School District.

_____ . 1975a. "Final Evaluation Report of the San Marcos Consolidated Independent School District's Bilingual Education Program, 1974-75." San Marcos, Tex.: San Marcos Independent School District.

_____ . 1975b. "Final Evaluation Report of the Harlandale Independent School District's Bilingual Education Program, 1974-75." San Antonio, Tex.: Harlandale Independent School District.

_____ . 1976a. "Final Evaluation Report of the San Marcos Consolidated Independent School District's Bilingual Education Program, 1975-76." San Marcos, Tex.: San Marcos Independent School District.

_____ . 1976b. "Final Evaluation for 'The Forgotten Southside,' Harlandale Independent School District's Bilingual Education Program, 1975-76." San Antonio, Tex.: Harlandale Independent School District.

_____ . 1980. "Final Evaluation Report for the State Bilingual Education Program of the Harlandale Independent School District." Mimeographed. Harlandale, Tex.

Herbert, Charles H., Jr. 1971. "Initial Reading in Spanish for Bilinguals." Paper presented at the Conference on Child Language, Chicago.

Heuristics, Inc. 1971. "An Evaluation of the St. John Valley Title VII Bilingual Program, 1970-71." Dedham, Mass.: Author.

Horst, D.P.; Johnson, D.M.; Nava, H.G.; Douglas, D.E.; Friendly, L.D.; and Roberts, A.O.H. 1980. "Technical Discussion and Appendices." *An Evaluation of Project Information Packages (PIPs) As Used for the Diffusion of Bilingual Projects.* Vol. 2. Mountain View, Calif.: RMC Corporation.

Humphrey, Ronald J. 1977. "The Effects of Language Dominance as Determined by the Shutt Primary Language Indicator Test on the Measurement of the Intellectual Abilities and Achievement Ratings of Mexican-American Children in K, 1, 2 Grades." Ph.D. dissertation, Northern Arizona University.

Huzar, Helen. 1973. "The Effects of an English-Spanish Primary Grade Reading Program on Second and Third Grade Students." M.Ed. thesis, Rutgers University.

Illinois State Board of Education. 1981. *The First Annual Program Summary and Evaluation Report of Transitional Bilingual Education Programs in Illinois. 1979-1980.* May.

Izzo, Suzanne. 1981. *Second Language Learning: A Review of Related Studies.* Rosslyn, Va.: National Clearinghouse for Bilingual Education.

Jensen, J. Vernon. 1962a. "Effects of Childhood Bilingualism, I." *Elementary English* 39:132-143.

———. 1962b. "Effects of Childhood Bilingualism, II." *Elementary English* 39:358-366.

JDRP (Joint Dissemination Review Panel). 1977. "Follow Through: The Corpus Christi Independent School District 1976-1977." Mimeographed. Washington, D.C.: U.S. Department of Health, Education and Welfare.

Kalmar, R.R. 1975. "The Culver City Schools' Spanish Immersion Program: Low Cost/High Yield." *CATESOL Occasional Papers no. 2.*

Kaufman, Maurice. 1968. "Will Instruction in Reading Spanish Affect Ability in Reading English?" *Journal of Reading* 17:521-527.

Kimball, William L. 1968. "Parental and Family Influences on Academic Achievement among Mexican-American Students." Ph.D. dissertation, University of California at Los Angeles.

Kramer, V.R. 1980. "The Effect of Auditory Discrimination Training of Spanish Speaking Children on Auditory Discrimination and Sound Letter Associations." In *Outstanding Dissertations in Bilingual Education.* Rosslyn, Va.: National Clearinghouse for Bilingual Education.

Krashen, Stephen D. 1981. "Bilingual Education and Second Language Acquisition Theory." Mimeographed. Paper prepared for the California State Department of Education.

Krashen, Stephen; Long, Michael A.; and Scarcella, Robin C. 1979. "Age, Rate, and Eventual Attainment in Second Language Acquisition." *TESOL Quarterly* 13:573-582.

Lambert, W.E., and Sidoti, N. 1980. "The Selection of Appropriate Languages of Instruction and the Use of Radio for Education in Less Developed Countries." Mimeographed. Washington, D.C.: World Bank.

Lambert, W.E., and Tucker, G.R. 1972. "Bilingual Education of Children: The St. Lambert Experience." Rowley Mass.: Newbury House.

Lampman, Henry P. 1973. "Southeastern New Mexico Bilingual Program. Final Report." Artesia, N.M.: Artesia Public Schools.

Landry, Richard G. 1974. "A Comparison of Second Language Learners and Monolinguals on Divergent Thinking Tasks at the Elementary Level." *Modern Language Journal* 58:10-15.

Laumann, L.F. 1969. *Effect of Project Head Start, Summer 1965: A Second Look at the Equality of Economic Opportunity Study.* Madison: Institute for Research on Poverty, University of Wisconsin.

Layden, Russell Glenn. 1972. "The Relationship between the Language of

Instruction and the Development of Self-Concept, Classroom Climate and Achievement of Spanish Speaking Puerto Rican Children." Ph.D. dissertation, University of Maryland.

Legarreta, Dorothy. 1979. "The Effects of Program Models on Language Acquisition by Spanish Speaking Children." *TESOL Quarterly* 13:521-534.

Leyba, Charles F. 1978. "Longitudinal Study Title VII Bilingual Program Santa Fe Public Schools." Los Angeles, Calif.: California State University.

Love, John M. 1975. "A Process Evaluation of Project Development Continuity. Interim Report II, Part B: Recommendations for Measuring Program Impact." Ypsilanti, Mich.: High/Scope Educational Research Foundation.

Lum, John Bernard. 1971. "An Effectiveness Study of English as a Second Language (ESL) and Chinese Bilingual Methods." Ph.D. dissertation, University of California at Berkeley.

McCarthy, Karen. 1976. "English as a Second Language Program Evaluation." Mimeographed. White Plains, N.Y.: White Plains Public Schools, Office of Research, Testing, and Evaluation.

McConnell, Beverly. 1980a. "Individualized Bilingual Instruction. Final Evaluation, 1978-79 Program." Pullman, Wash.

_____. 1980b. "Individualized Bilingual Instruction for Migrants." Paper presented at the International Congress for Individual Instruction, Windsor, Ontario, October.

_____. 1980c. "Effectiveness of Individualized Bilingual Instruction for Migrant Students." Ph.D. dissertation, Washington State University.

McDonald, Frederick J., and Elias, Patricia. 1976. "Beginning Teacher Evaluation Study, Phase II, 1973-74 Executive Summary Report." Princeton, N.J.: Educational Testing Service.

Macmillan, Deborah L. 1980. "Language Policies for African Primary Education: Summary of the Anglophone Research Literature." Mimeographed. Washington, D.C.: World Bank.

Macnamara, J. 1970. "Comparative Studies of Reading and Problem Solving in Two Languages." Paper presented at the Fourth Annual TESOL Convention, San Francisco, Calif., March.

Macnamara, John. 1966. *Bilingualism and Primary Education*. Edinburgh: Edinburgh University Press.

McSpadden, J.R. 1979. "Acadiana Bilingual Bicultural Education Program. Interim Evaluation Report 1978-79." Lafayette Parish, La: Lafayette Parish School Board.

_____. 1980. "Acadiana Bilingual Bicultural Education Program. Interim Evaluation Report 1979-80." Lafayette Parish, La.: Lafayette Parish School Board.

Malherbe, E.C. 1946. *The Bilingual School*. London: Longmans Green.

Matthews, T. 1979. "An Investigation of the Effects of Background Characteristics and Special Language Services on the Reading Achievement and English Fluency of Bilingual Students.'' Seattle, Wash.: Seattle Public Schools, Department of Planning Research and Evaluation.

Melendez, William Anselmo. 1980. "The Effect of the Language of Instruction on the Reading Achievement of Limited English Speakers in Secondary Schools." Ph.D. dissertation, University of the Pacific.

Merlos, Ramon Luis. 1978. "Effects of Bilingual Education on the Cognitive Characteristics of the Spanish Speaking Children in Chicago Public Schools." Ph.D. dissertation, Loyola University of Chicago.

Milwaukee Public Schools. 1976. "ESEA Title VII Bilingual/Bicultural Education; Programa de Educacion Bilinque/Bicultural 1975-76." Milwaukee, Wis.: Author.

————. 1972. "Milwaukee Bilingual Education Program, 1971-72. Evaluation Report." Milwaukee, Wis.: Author.

L. Miranda and Associates, Inc. 1979. *An Evaluation of the State Funded Illinois Transitional Bilingual Education Program Final Report.* Washington, D.C.: Author.

Modiano, Nancy. 1966. "A Comparative Study of Two Approaches to the Teaching of Reading in the National Language." Ph.D. dissertation, New York University.

————. 1973. *Indian Education in the Chiapas Highlands.* New York: Holt, Rinehart and Winston.

Monzon, Nancy Lee. 1981. "A Comparison of the Monolingual English Immersion and the Bilingual Education Approaches on the English Reading Skills of Limited English Proficient Children, Grades 1, 3, and 5." Ph.D. dissertation, Pennsylvania State University.

Moore, F.B., and Parr, G.D. 1978. "Models of Bilingual Education: Comparisons of Effectiveness." *Elementary School Journal* 79:93-97.

Morgan, Judith Claire. 1971. "The Effects of Bilingual Instruction on the English Language Arts Achievement of First Grade Children." Ph.D. dissertation, Northwestern State University of Louisiana.

Mortensen, Eileen Mary. 1980. "A Comparison of Selected Language, Word-Attack, and Comprehension Skills of Native Spanish-Speaking Elementary Students in a Bilingual Program and Native Spanish-Speaking Elementary Students in a Monolingual Program." Ph.D. dissertation, University of Wisconsin.

Muller, Douglas G., and Leonetti, Robert. 1970. "A Cumulative Summary of the Three Years of the Sustained Primary Program for Bilingual Students, 1967-70." Las Cruces, N. Mex.: Division of Plans and Supplementary Centers. BESE.

Nearine, Robert J. 1967. "Where the Action Is: An Evaluation." Hartford, Conn.: Hartford City Board of Education.

Nixon, Bert Wootton. 1971. "Navajo Parental Attitudes and the Effect of Bilingual Education on Student Self-Concept in San Juan School District 1969-70." Ph.D. dissertation, Brigham Young University.

Offenberg, Robert M. 1970. "Let's Be Amigos: Title VII Bilingual Project Evaluation of the First Year, 1969-70." Philadelphia: Philadephia Public Schools.

_____ . 1972. "Let's Be Amigos: Title VII Bilingual Project Evaluation 1970-71." Philadelphia: Philadephia Public Schools.

_____ . 1973. "Evolution of a Bilingual Evaluation." Paper presented at the Annual Meeting of the American Educational Research Association, February.

Offenberg, Robert M., and Wolowec, Wolodimir. 1973. "Title VII Bilingual Project, Let's Be Amigos: Evaluation of the Third Year, 1971-72." Philadelphia: Philadelphia Public Schools.

Offenberg, Robert M., et al. 1973. "Title VII Bilingual Project, Let's Be Amigos: Evaluation of the Fourth Year, 1972-73." Philadelphia: Philadelphia Public Schools.

Offenberg, Robert M., et al. 1974. "Title VII Bilingual Project, Let's Be Amigos: Evaluation of the Fifth Year, 1973-1974." Philadelphia: Philadelphia Public Schools.

Ojerinde, Adedibu. 1978. "The Use of a Mother Tongue, Yoruba, as a Medium of Instruction in Nigerian Schools." Ph.D. dissertation, Cornell University.

Olesini, J. 1971. "The Effect of Bilingual Instruction on the Achievement of Elementary Pupils." Ph.D. dissertation, East Texas State University.

Orvik, Guy C. 1975. "An Overview of Alaska Native Bilingual Education." *Topics in Culture Learning Vol. 2.* Honolulu: East-West Center, Hawaii University.

Payne, I.V. 1973. "Southeastern New Mexico Bilingual Program. Program Accomplishment Audit, 1972-73." Artesia, N. Mex.: Artesia Public Schools.

Payne, I.V., and Medina, Edward. 1972. "Educational Accomplishment Audit Report, FY 1971-72." Artesia, N. Mex.: Artesia Public Schools.

Peal, E., and Lambert, W. 1962. "The Relation of Bilingualism to Intelligence." *Psychological Monographs* 76:1-23.

Pena-Hughes, Eva, and Solis, Juan. 1980. "abcs." Mimeographed. McAllen, Tex.: McAllen Independent School District.

_____ . 1981. Personal communication.

Perez, Ray S., and Horst, Donald P. 1982. "A Handbook for Evaluating ESEA Title VII Bilingual Education Programs." Rosslyn, Va.: Inter-America Research Associates, March.

Pifer, Alan. 1979. "Bilingual Education and the Hispanic Challenge." New York: Carnegie Corporation.

Plante, Alexander J. 1976. *A Study of the Effectiveness of the Connecticut "Pairing" Model of Bilingual-Bicultural Education.* Hamden, Conn.: Connecticut Staff Development Cooperative.

Powers, Stephen. 1978. "The Influence of Bilingual Instruction on Academic Achievement and Self-Esteem of Selected Mexican-American Junior High School Students." Ph.D. dissertation, University of Arizona.

Prewitt Diaz, Joseph O. 1979. "An Analysis of the Effects of a Bilingual Curriculum on Monolingual Spanish Ninth Graders as Compared with Monolingual English and Bilingual Ninth Graders with Regard to Language Development, Attitude toward School and Self-Concept." Ph.D. dissertation, University of Connecticut.

Price, Aida. 1978. "Evaluation Report 1.S. 184 Demonstration Project in Bilingual/Bicultural Education. Title VII ESEA District 7 Bronx 1977-78." Mimeographed. New York: New York City Board of Education.

Pryor, Guy C. 1969. "Evaluation of the Bilingual Project of Harlandale Independent School District, San Antonio, Texas, in the First, Second, and Third Grades of Four Elementary Schools During 1968-69 School Year." San Antonio, Tex.: Harlandale Independent School District.

_____ . 1970. "Final Educational Accomplishment Audit of the Bilingual Education Program. Harlandale Independent School District, 1969-70." San Marcos: Southwest Texas State University.

_____ . 1971. "Final Educational Accomplishment Audit of the Bilingual Education Program. Harlandale Independent School District, 1970-71." San Marcos: Southwest Texas State University.

_____ . 1972. "Final Educational Accomplishment Audit of the Bilingual Education Program. Harlandale Independent School District, 1971-72." San Marcos: Southwest Texas State University.

Ramirez, A.R.; Salinas, Mary E.; and Liberty, Paul G., n.d. "An Evaluative Study of the ROCK English as a Second Language Program in Spanish-English Bilingual Projects." Edinburgh, Tex.: Bilingual Education Project.

Ramirez, Inez Ruiz. 1973. "The Effect of English as a Second Language Instruction on Oral English Proficiency, Self-Concept, and Scholastic Achievement." Ph.D. dissertation, East Texas State University.

Ramos, M.; Aguilar, J.V.; and Sibayan, B.F. 1967. *The Determination and Implementation of Language Policy*. Philippine Center for Language Study Monograph Series 2. Quezon City, the Philippines: Alemor/Phoenix.

Read, J.S. 1980. "A Sociolinguistic Study of Lau Language Maintenance." *Outstanding Dissertations in Bilingual Education*. Rosslyn, Va.: National Clearinghouse for Bilingual Education.

Richard, L.L. 1979. "Oral Language Gains in a French-English Bilingual Education Program in Iberia Parish (La.) as Measured by a Repetition Instrument." Ph.D. dissertation, University of Texas, Austin.

Richardson, Juanita Casil. 1980. "Length of Time in a Bilingual Program and Academic Achievement among Second Grade Mexican-American

Students." Ph.D. dissertation, University of Houston.

Riegehaupt, Barbara. 1980. "El Marino School: Aqui se habla espanol." *Valley News*, June 3.

Rimm, S. 1977. "Evaluation of the 1976-77 ESEA Title VII Bilingual/ Bicultural Project, St. Paul Public Schools." Watertown, Wis.: Education Assessment Services.

————. 1978. "Evaluation of the 1977-78 ESEA Title VII Bilingual/ Bicultural Project, St. Paul Public Schools." Watertown, Wis.: Education Assessment Service.

————. 1979. "Evaluation of the 1978-79 ESEA Title VII Bilingual/ Bicultural Project, St. Paul Public Schools." Watertown, Wis.: Education Assessment Service.

————. 1980. "Outcome Evaluation of the Title VII Bilingual/Bicultural Program for Laotian/Hmong, St. Paul Public Schools. Final Report." Watertown, Wis.: Education Assessment Service.

Rimm, S., et al. 1975. "Process Evaluation Report of the Bilingual/Bicultural Program of Education ESEA Title VII St. Paul Public Schools." Watertown, Wis.: Education Assessment Services.

Rivera, Carmen Elena. 1973. "Academic Achievement, Bicultural Attitudes and "Self-concepts of Pupils in Bilingual and Non-Bilingual Programs." Ph.D. dissertation, Fordham University.

Rodriguez-Brown, Flora V., and Junker, Linda. 1980. "The Relationship of Student and Home Variables to Language Proficiency and Reading Achievement of Bilingual Children." Paper presented at the Annual Meeting of the American Educational Research Association, Boston, Mass.

Rodriguez-Brown, Flora V., et al. 1976. "Longitudinal Design Consideration for the Evaluation of Bilingual Programs." Paper presented at the Annual Meeting of the American Educational Research Association, San Francisco, California, April.

Romero, Roger Cervantez. 1977. "Student Achievement in a Pilot Cureton Reading, Cuisenaire Mathematics Program, and Bilingual Program of an Elementary School." Ph.D. dissertation, Northern Arizona University.

Rosenthal, A.S.; Milne, A.; Ginsburg, A.; and Baker, K. 1981. "A Comparison of the Effects of Language Background and Socioeconomic Status on Achievement among Elementary School Students." Mimeographed. Washington, D.C.: Applied Urbanetics.

Rosier, Paul Webb. 1977. "A Comparative Study of Two Approaches of Introducing Initial Reading to Navajo Children. The Direct Method and the Native Language." Ph.D. dissertation, Northern Arizona University.

Rosier, Paul, and Farella, M. 1976. "Bilingual Education at Rock Point— Some Early Results." *TESOL Quarterly* 10:379-388.

Rosier, Paul, and Holm, Wayne. 1980. "The Rock Point Experience: A

Longitudinal Study of a Navajo School Program (Saad Naaki Bee Na'nitin).'' *Bilingual Education Series no. 8.* Arlington, Va.: Center for Applied Linguistics.

St. John Valley Bilingual Project. 1980. ''Five Year Evaluation Report 1975-1980, Frenchville, St. Agatha, Van Buren, Madawska.'' Mimeographed. Madawska, Maine: Author.

Schmid-Schonbein, Gisela. 1980. ''Evaluation of the Teaching of English to German Children of Preschool Age.'' *English Language Teaching Journal* 34:173-179.

Scott, Eloise. 1979. ''Buffalo Public Schools Spanish-English Program Evaluation, 1975-77.'' Buffalo, N.Y.: Buffalo Public Schools.

Scudder, B.E.T 1979. ''A Comparative Study of the Effects of the Use of a Diagnostic/Prescriptive Approach versus a Tutorial Approach to the Teaching of English to Non-English Speaking Elementary School Children in a Large Urban School District in Colorado.'' Ph.D. dissertation, University of Colorado.

Segalowitz, N. 1977. ''Psychological Perspectives on Bilingual Education.'' In Spolsky, B., and Cooper, R.L., eds. *Frontier of Bilingual Education.* Rowley, Mass.: Newbury House Publishers.

Skoczylas, Rudolph V. 1972. ''An Evaluation of Some Cognitive and Affective Aspects of a Spanish-English Bilingual Education Program.'' Ph.D. dissertation, University of New Mexico.

Skutnabb-Kangas, Tove. 1979. *Language in the Process of Cultural Assimilation and Structural Incorporation of Linguistic Minorities.* Washington, D.C.: National Clearinghouse for Bilingual Education.

Skutnabb-Kangas, Tove, and Toukomaa, P. 1976. *Teaching Migrant Children's Mother Tongue and Learning the Language of the Host Country in the Context of the Socio-cultural Situation of the Migrant Family.* Helsinki: Finnish National Commission for UNESCO.

Smith, Frederick. 1976. ''Fort Hamilton High School (GRASP).'' Brooklyn, N.Y.: New York City Board of Education.

Smith, Hyrum C., and Smith, Van Nguyen. 1978. ''Evaluating Program Effectiveness: Measuring Input, Process, and Product Variables in New York City Federally Funded High School Bilingual Programs.'' New York City: New York City Board of Education.

Smith, Merle. 1971. ''Pontiac Title VII Bilingual Education Program, 1970-71: Final Evaluation Report.''Pontiac, Mich.: Pontiac City School District.

South San Francisco Unified School District. 1979. ''ESEA Title VII Final Evaluation Report. Spruce School Bilingual Education Program.'' San Francisco, Calif.: Author.

Southwest Educational Development Laboratory (SEDL). 1979. ''Planning Information for Follow Through Experiments (RFP No. 78-101) Task 1B-Final.'' Austin, Tex.: Author, November 19.

Southwest Regional Laboratory for Education Research and Development (SWRL). 1975. *Development of the SWRL English Language and Concepts Program for Spanish-Speaking Children*. Los Alamitos, Calif.: Author.

Stebbins, Linda B.; St. Pierre, Robert G.; Proper, Elizabeth C.; Anderson, Richard B.; and Cerva, Thomas R. 1977. *Education as Experimentation: A Planned Variation Model Vol. 4: An Evaluation of Follow Through*. Cambridge, Mass.: ABT Associates, April.

Stern, Carolyn. 1975. "Final Report of the Compton Unified School District's Title VII Bilingual-Bicultural Project: September 1969 through June 1975." Mimeographed. Compton City, Calif.: Compton City Schools.

Sullivan, Richard E. 1973. "Portuguese-English Title VII Program (Providence, Rhode Island, July 15, 1973). Final Evaluation Report." Kingston, R.I.: Rhode Island University.

Swain, Merrill. 1978a. "Bilingual Education for the English-Speaking Canadian." In Alatis, J.E., ed., *International Dimensions of Bilingual Education*. Washington, D.C.: Georgetown University Press.

———. 1978b. "French Immersion: Early, Late, or Partial?" *Canadian Modern Language Review* 34:577-586.

Tanguma, Ramon Hector. 1977. "Bilingual Education: The Effects of Selected Variables on the Achievement in Selected School Subject Areas of Mexican-American Fifth and Sixth-Grade Students." Ph.D. dissertation, University of Texas at Austin.

Tikunoff, William J. 1981. Personal communication.

Trevino, Bertha. 1968. "An Analysis of the Effectiveness of a Bilingual Program in the Teaching of Mathematics in the Primary Grades." Ph.D. dissertation, University of Texas, Austin.

———. 1970. "Bilingual Instruction in the Primary Grades." *Modern Language Journal* 54:255-256.

Troike, Rudolph C. 1978. *Research Evidence for the Effectiveness of Bilingual Education*. Washington, D.C.: National Clearinghouse for Bilingual Education.

Tucker, G.R. 1980. "Implications for U.S. Bilingual Education: Evidence from Canadian Research." *Focus*, 2.

Valencia, Atilano A., 1970. "The Relative Effects of Early Spanish Language Instruction on Spanish and English Linguistic Development. An Evaluation Report on the Pecos Language Arts Program for Western States Small School Projects." Albuquerque, N.Mex.: Southwestern Cooperative Educational Laboratory, 1970.

———. 1971. "Bilingual/Bicultural Education—An Effective Learning Scheme for First Grade and Second Grade Spanish Speaking, English Speaking, and American Indian Children in New Mexico." Albuquerque, N.Mex.: Southwestern Cooperative Educational Laboratory.

———— . 1974. "The Cognitive and Affective Development of Elementary School Children in a Bilingual-Bicultural Learning Environment. A Study of the Grants Bilingual-Bicultural Education Program, Grants, New Mexico." Grants, N.Mex.: Grants Municipal Schools.

Veilleux, David. 1977. "A Survey of Program Impact of the St. John Valley Bilingual Education Program, 1970-1977." Madawska, Maine.

Veltman, C.J. 1980. "Relative Educational Attainment of Hispanic-American Children, 1976." Paper presented at the Aspira Hispanic Forum for Responsive Educational Policy, Washington, D.C., October.

von Maltitz, Frances Willard. 1975. *Living and Learning in Two Languages: Bilingual/Bicultural Education in the United States.* New York: McGraw-Hill.

Vorih, Lillian, and Rosier, Paul. 1978. "Rock Point Community School: An Example of a Navajo-English Bilingual Elementary School Program." *TESOL Quarterly* 12:263-269.

Willink, E.W. 1968. "A Comparison of Two Methods of Teaching English to Navajo Children." Ph.D. dissertation, University of Arizona, 1968.

Winter, David L. 1979. "A Study Analyzing the Effect a School's Bilingual-Bicultural Program Has on Student Achievement." Ph.D. dissertation, University of Wyoming.

Yoloye, E.A. 1977. "Evaluation of Six-Year Yoruba Primary Project." Paper presented at the Seminar of Government Representatives of Five Yoruba Speaking States of Nigeria, University of Ife, Nigeria.

Young, John. 1980. "Evaluation Report Submitted to the Eastchester Union Free School District." Mimeographed. Eastchester Union Free School District.

Zappert, L.T., and Cruz, B.R. 1977. *Bilingual Education: An Appraisal of Empirical Research.* Berkeley, Calif.: Bay Area Bilingual Education League.

Zimmer, John F. 1976. "An Evaluation of the 1975-76 ESEA Title VII Bilingual-Bicultural Project: St. Paul Public Schools." Minneapolis: Educational Management Services.

Zirkel, Perry Alan. 1972. "An Evaluation of the Effectiveness of Selected Experimental Bilingual Education Programs in Connecticut." Hartford, Conn.: Department of Education.

3

A Comparison of the Effects of Language Background and Socioeconomic Status on Achievement among Elementary-School Students

Alvin S. Rosenthal,
Ann M. Milne,
Fran M. Ellman,
Alan L. Ginsburg,
and *Keith A. Baker*

Considerable controversy surrounds the identification of children who need language-related services and the selection of services to be provided. This chapter is based on the belief that discussion of the delivery of special language services does not go far enough because it remains within the context of language. The educational problems of children from non-English-speaking backgrounds have multiple causes, not least among them socioeconomic disadvantage. To the extent that these complex causes are not recognized and that language is assumed to be the only cause, children may be misassigned to language-based services—not merely in the choice between bilingual and English-as-a-second-language (ESL) instruction, but in the choice between language-based and other compensatory services. As a result, these children may be deprived of adequate and appropriate help.

The federal government has actively sought to help language-minority students to obtain an adequate education through Title VII of the Elementary and Secondary Education Act (ESEA), the *Lau* Remedies, and the recent proposed rules. There is little controversy about the need to provide special services to language-minority students who may need them, but the design and instructional approaches that should be used have often been hotly debated. Most of the disagreement has concerned the use of ESL services and bilingual education. Both Title VII and the *Lau* Remedies favor bilingual-bicultural education.

For both Title VII and *Lau,* the implicit assumption in the definition of students eligible for language-related services is that students have difficulty learning subject matter presented in English because their primary language is not English. As Dulay and Burt (1980) point out, however, many language-

The authors wish to thank Michael R. Olneek and David Myers for helpful suggestions.

minority students speak English better than their home language and can communicate in English; they simply have not scored at norm levels in English-language skills. Language-minority students are not the only people who score below the norm; half the native English-speaking students score below the norm in English.

To the extent that poor school performance of language-minority students reflects the same factors that produce below-average performance for half the native English-speaking students, neither bilingual instruction nor ESL services will improve the opportunity of these students to participate effectively in school. Consequently these students may become (or remain) low achievers.

The major focus of this chapter is the extent to which socioeconomic status variables explain the low achievement of the language-minority population. If socioeconomic variables are found to be important and if they are ignored in federal policies for identifying and serving language-minority students, many students may be assigned to language-related services instead of to other types of compensatory education, which are more appropriate for them.

Few studies have assessed the relative effects of language and socioeconomic status on achievement. Coleman et al. (1966), Jencks et al. (1972), and Baral (1979) noted the relationship between socioeconomic status and educational achievement. AIR (1977), Danoff (1978), Brown et al. (1980), and Carsrud (1980) investigated the correlation between language background and achievement. And Paulston (1974), Epstein (1977), Bowen (1977), and Cummins (1979) suggested that language and socioeconomic status might be interrelated in their effect on educational achievement.

This question was pursued in several empirical studies—notably Mayeske et al. (1973) and Veltman (1980)—that attempted to assess the relative effects of language and socioeconomic status on educational achievement. In a reanalysis of Coleman's *Equality of Educational Opportunity* data, Mayeske reported that for Hispanics, the small relationship that was found between home language and achievement was completely accounted for by the low socioeconomic status of the Hispanic population. Veltman (1980) reported similar findings using parental education as a measure of social class. De Avila (1980) also found that among blacks, Anglos, and Hispanics, socioeconomic status accounts for a significant part of the variance in school achievement. De Avila argues further that more of the variance could be explained by the extent to which the Hispanic population has limited proficiency in English.

De Avila's study illustrates the difficulties with the empirical research in this area: the data are based on an inadequate sample, the variables under investigation and the analyses used are not defined, and the methodological approach is inadequate. Moreover, our review of the literature found no studies that examined both achievement level and achievement *change* (school-year learning) while controlling for socioeconomic status and language background.

Our analysis addresses the appropriateness of the service mandates provided by federal policies for language-minority students. The data available for the analysis allowed us to classify students according to the presence of a home language other than English and to the students' reliance on this home language. This classification allowed us to parallel federal policies for identifying students for language-related services. Both the *Lau* Remedies and Title VII of ESEA rely on home-language indicators as a first step in the identification process; beyond that, they use various approaches to determine which students need language services.

Analytic Approach

In the analysis, two types of achievement are used: achievement level and achievement change. Achievement level represents the effect of the previous home background and schooling processes up to the time of measurement. Achievement level is the student's score on an achievement test administered in the fall. Differences in achievement level among groups may suggest differences in home enrichment or in previous discrimination.

Learning, or achievement change, is the difference in achievement at two points in time: the beginning and the end of the school year. School-year learning includes influences of both the home environment and schooling. The influence of home-background variables, however, is limited by controlling for achievement level in measuring achievement change.

The independent variables used in the analysis are language and socioeconomic status. Existing research has shown that socioeconomic status and achievement are positively related, so this topic is not pursued here. Rather we concentrate on the relative importance of language and socioeconomic status in explaining achievement differences between language groups.

We compare differences in achievement between Spanish-predominant and English-only students.[1] To maximize the possible differences between the two comparison groups, we excluded from comparisons those Spanish-background students who have a non-English home language but rely on English. However, the estimation procedure uses data for both comparison and noncomparison groups. Three comparisons are made:

1. We compare the difference in achievement between the two language groups. This is the uncontrolled-language effect.

2. We compare the difference in achievement between the two groups, controlling for socioeconomic status. This is the residual language effect remaining after socioeconomic status is taken into account.
3. We estimate the socioeconomic status effect with language controlled. This is the effect of socioeconomic status after language has been taken into account.

The relative effects on achievement of language with socioeconomic status controlled and of socioeconomic status with language controlled can be directly compared.

Statistical Models

The description in this section of our statistical approach is limited to the structural relationships and does not discuss the actual estimation procedures, which are presented in appendix 3A.

Equations 3-1 and 3-2 model the effect of language on achievement where socioeconomic status is not controlled. Equation 3-1 is for achievement level, and equation 3-2 is for learning. (Learning is estimated in an analysis-of-covariance framework, with posttest as the dependent variable and pretest as one of the independent variables.) Equations 3-3 and 3-4 are similar to equations 3-1 and 3-2, respectively, with the addition of a socioeconomic-status-control variable.

In each equation, we estimate a predicted value for achievement (level or learning). We then use these values to estimate the achievement of the Spanish-predominant students if they had the language ability, or the socioeconomic status of the English-only group, or both. Thus the English-only group becomes a normative reference point.

The structural equations for the regressions of achievement on language background are these:

$$\text{Achievement level: } A_F = b_0 + b_1 SP + b_2 OL + b_3 LP \qquad (3\text{-}1)$$

$$\text{Learning: } A_S = a_0 + a_1 A_F + a_2 SP + a_3 OL + a_4 LP \qquad (3\text{-}2)$$

where A_F = fall achievement in reading or math; A_S = spring achievement in reading or math; SP = Spanish language usually used in the home coded as 1, otherwise coded as 0; OL = other non-English language, not Spanish, usually used in the home coded as 1, otherwise coded as 0; LP = Spanish or other language predominant coded as 1, English predominant coded as 0; and a_i and b_i are coefficients. For equations 3-1 and 3-2, the predicted achievement for the Spanish-predominant group if they had the language ability of the English-only group is given as $-(b_1 + b_3)$ for achievement level and $-(a_2 + a_4)$ for learning.

The structural equations for the regressions of achievement on language background and socioeconomic status are these:

Achievement level: $A_F = b_0 + b_1 SP + b_2 OL + b_3 LP + b_4 SES$ (3-3)

Learning: $A_S = a_0 + a_1 AF + a_2 SP + a_3 OL + a_4 LP + a_5 SES$ (3-4)

where SES = a socioeconomic status factor and the other symbols are defined as in equations 3-1 and 3-2. For equations 3-3 and 3-4, the language effect, controlling for socioeconomic status, is again $-(b_1 + b_3)$ for achievement level and $-(a_2 + a_4)$ for learning. The socioeconomic-status effect, the estimate of equating the socioeconomic status of the Spanish-predominant group to that of the English-only group, is b_4 (SES_K) for achievement level and $a_5(SES_K)$ for learning, where K = (mean SES of the English-only group) — (mean SES of the Spanish-dominant group).

The four equations include no interaction terms. In other analyses, not presented here, we have examined the interactions of home language with predominance and the interactions of these variables with socioeconomic status. Using ordinary-least-squares techniques, we found that inclusion of the interaction terms did not add significantly to the variance explained ($p > 0.01$, assuming a simple stratified random sample), so we limited our analytical models to those without interactions. Analyses were undertaken for each grade separately and all six grades together. In the analyses, the means of the achievement variables were removed for each grade.

To estimate the parameters in the regression models, we have specified our equations in the LISREL framework (see Jöreskog 1973; Jöreskog and Sörbom 1979). This estimation procedure allows for errors in measurement for both the dependent variables and the independent variables, as well as correlated measurement errors and specification errors across equations. By taking this information into account, we can obtain more-precise estimates than we can obtain with more commonly used estimation techniques, such as ordinary least squares. We have estimated the equations by using the computer program MILS.[2] (A detailed specification of the statistical model is provided in appendix 3A.)

Variables and Data

To assess the relationship of achievement to socioeconomic status and language, we used data from a household survey conducted as part of the

Sustaining Effects Study of Title I (Hoepfner et al. 1977). The Sustaining Effects Study, conducted during school year 1976-1977, was a nationally stratified cluster sample of 81,000 students in grades 1 through 6 from more than 240 schools. The household survey obtained additional data through interviews with the parents of 15,579 randomly selected students. Table 3-1 presents the means of variables used in the analysis for all students in the sample and for students by language classification.

The dependent variable, achievement, was measured by student scores on the Comprehensive Test of Basic Skills (CTBS). Achievement level was measured as the student's score for reading and for math on the CTBS, given at the beginning of the school year (fall). School-year learning was measured by the student's score for reading and for math at the end of the school year (spring), with the fall score used as a control.[3] Reading and math tests were assumed to tap different underlying dimensions of achievement.

The independent variables used in the analysis were two home-language-background variables and four socioeconomic indicators. The two home-language-background variables were language usually spoken in the home and reliance on a language other than English. Home language was identified through parental responses to this question: "Which of these languages are spoken regularly in your home: English, Spanish, Portuguese, Chinese, Japanese, Italian, or other?" Home language was classified as only English used regularly, Spanish used regularly, or a language other than English, but not Spanish, used regularly.

Students were classified as English-language predominant or other-language predominant on the basis of the extent to which a language other than English was relied upon in the home. Students for whom the only usual home language was English were classified as English predominant. All students for whom English was not mentioned as being usually spoken in the home were classified as other-language predominant. To classify the remainder of the students, an additional survey question was used. Parents had been asked whether English or another language was used when helping the student with school work. If only English had been mentioned, students were classified as English predominant. The rest of the students were classified as other-language predominant.

A socioeconomic status factor was formed by combining four indicators: parental education, family income, a measure of parents' occupation, and race (white or nonwhite).[4] The computation of the socioeconomic factor is part of the analysis, as described in appendix 3A.

Results

Table 3-2 presents the results of the comparisons between Spanish-predominant and English-only students. The mean differences in the table

Table 3-1
Means and Standard Deviations for All Students and for Students by Language Classification

Characteristic	All Students	English Only	Spanish		Other Language	
			English Predominant	Spanish Predominant	English Predominant	Other Language Predominant
Sample size	12,996	11,475	600	369	446	106
Socioeconomic status factor	0 (1)	.056 (1.132)	−.685 (1.183)	−1.215 (.994)	.339 (1.215)	−.014 (1.350)
Parent education (years)	12.6 (2.8)	12.7 (2.6)	10.8 (3.2)	9.2 (2.9)	13.5 (3.0)	12.6 (3.5)
Family income ($)	15,922 (10,577)	16,216 (10,545)	11,790 (8,967)	10,150 (5,802)	17,783 (12,950)	16,201 (13,244)
Percentage white	83.7 (36.9)	83.7 (36.9)	88.7 (31.6)	95.1 (21.5)	71.5 (45.1)	64.5 (47.8)
Percentage professional-managerial occupation	25.9 (43.8)	26.6 (44.2)	15.6 (36.3)	7.1 (25.8)	35.8 (47.9)	30.5 (46.0)
Deviation from grade means						
Fall reading	0 (55.8)	2.2 (55.3)	−23.4 (52.7)	−49.3 (49.6)	10.6 (53.2)	−7.2 (44.6)
Spring reading	0 (60.0)	2.5 (59.2)	−26.1 (57.1)	−52.4 (56.0)	9.6 (59.9)	−9.7 (53.1)
Fall math	0 (54.0)	1.4 (53.9)	−17.1 (51.3)	−31.7 (47.7)	7.2 (54.3)	4.2 (53.1)
Spring math	0 (61.8)	1.9 (61.8)	−24.7 (59.7)	−33.4 (49.5)	6.8 (60.9)	3.8 (60.0)

Note: Means and standard deviations are weighted, with standard deviations in parentheses.

Table 3-2
Mean Differences for Total Language, Language Controlling for Socioeconomic Status and Socioeconomic Status Controlling for Language between Spanish-Predominant and English-Only Students
(in vertical-scale score units)

	Achievement	All Grades	Grade					
			1	2	3	4	5	6
Uncontrolled language effect	Level							
	Reading	50.3	25.4	42.6	58.2	53.0	60.8	73.3
	Math	31.4	24.8	28.4	30.3	33.3	43.6	34.1
	Learning							
	Reading	8.8	13.2	17.2	9.1	9.7	6.2	−4.2
	Math	8.9	9.3	1.3	21.0	9.6	7.4	−4.7
Language, controlling for socioeconomic status	Level							
	Reading	10.7	3.3	13.6	15.7	5.1	11.6	18.4
	Math	−1.5	2.8	3.3	1.1	−8.5	1.3	−9.9
	Learning							
	Reading	2.8	6.9	10.3	1.8	3.9	1.9	−8.6
	Math	−2.2	3.3	−8.2	5.5	.3	−3.4	−16.4
Socioeconomic status, controlling for language	Level							
	Reading	36.2	22.2	31.4	37.0	40.2	42.8	45.9
	Math	29.7	22.4	24.6	25.1	35.3	35.7	36.9
	Learning							
	Reading	9.8	17.2	11.8	9.5	9.5	7.1	7.1
	Math	12.5	11.6	12.7	17.6	11.2	12.3	13.5

refer to the expected (or average) difference in achievement due to language or socioeconomic status differences between the two groups.[5] For example, the "all-grades" total language effect for reading-achievement level, 50.3 vertical-scale score points,[6] indicates that a Spanish-predominant student scores an average of 50.3 points lower on the reading-achievement vertical-scale score than an English-only student, regardless of socioeconomic status. Conversely, the "all-grades" language effect controlling for socioeconomic status is 10.7; this means that a Spanish-predominant student scores an average of 10.7 points lower than an English-only student with an equivalent socioeconomic status.[7]

In the case of the all-grades reading-achievement level, the value for the socioeconomic status effect in table 3-2 is 36.2. This example indicates that in a comparison of two students with the same language background, one of whom had the average socioeconomic status of the Spanish-predominant group while the other had the average socioeconomic status of the English-only group, the student with the average Spanish-predominant socioeconomic status would score 36.2 points lower than the other student.

The total language effects differ from grade to grade and are larger for achievement level than for learning (see table 3-2). For achievement level, the effects tend to increase over the grades, and they tend to increase more for reading than for math. In grade 1 the difference is 25.4 for reading and 24.8 for math, while in grade 6 the difference has increased to 73.3, and 34.1 for reading and math achievement, respectively. For learning, differences between the groups are smaller and are not consistent across grades. The difference between groups for reading and math when all grades are analyzed is 8.8 and 8.9, respectively.

When socioeconomic status is controlled in the models, the language effect decreases (and in some cases becomes negative) and is often insignificant. For achievement level, the language effects, controlling for socioeconomic status, are only 10.7 for reading when all grades are analyzed together and negative (-1.5) for math. For the individual grades, the achievement-level effects vary and are not consistent across grades.

For learning, the language effects, controlling for socioeconomic status, are small— $+2.8$ for reading and -2.8 for math—when all grades are analyzed together. As with acheivement, there is no consistent increase or decrease across grades.

The main difference in achievement between the language groups is attributable to socioeconomic status rather than to language. When socioeconomic status is controlled, the differences between the groups attributable to the language variables diminish greatly (or even reverse, in which case Spanish-predominant students would achieve at a higher level than would be predicted for English-only students of the same socioeconomic status).

The socioeconomic status effects for achievement level, when control-ling for language, are 36.2 for reading and 29.7 for math when all grades are analyzed together. In addition, the effects of socioeconomic status on reading and math achievement increase monotonically from grades 1 to 6. The socioeconomic status effects on learning tend to decrease from grades 1 to 6 for reading but not for math. With all grades analyzed together, the mean effects of socioeconomic status on learning are 9.8 for reading and 12.5 for math.

In these analyses, socioeconomic status had a larger effect on reading and math achievement than language had when socioeconomic status was controlled. In fact, the socioeconomic status effects, controlling for language, are nearly the size of the uncontrolled total language effects. For achievement level, the socioeconomic status effects are almost as large as the language effects uncontrolled for socioeconomic status; for math in grades 4 and 6, the socioeconomic status effects are actually larger. For learning, the socioeconomic status effects are greater than the uncontrolled language effects in all but three comparisons (reading, grade 2; math, grade 3; and reading, grade 4).

Discussion

The major conclusion from this analysis is that most of the difference in achievement level and in learning between the Spanish-predominant group and the English-only group is actually attributable to differences in socioeconomic status. Once socioeconomic status has been controlled, the effects of language become negligible, especially for learning. In fact, with comparable socioeconomic status, the Spanish-predominant group occa-sionally shows an advantage over the English-only students, particularly for learning.

Low-achieving students from non-English-speaking home-language background may have problems in school as a result of language and socioeconomic status factors. To the extent that bilingual programs select low-achieving students from non-English-speaking home backgrounds without taking socioeconomic status into consideration, students may receive inappropriate services. There are two types of problems. First, many children who may appear to need language-related services to improve their achievement may in fact be better served by compensatory services of other types. Well-designed services intended to compensate for economic and educational disadvantage are more subject-matter intensive, are delivered by subject-matter specialists rather than language specialists, and are often given in smaller group settings.

Second, for some children the causes of low achievement may include lack of English proficiency as well as socioeconomic disadvantage. These children would no doubt benefit from a variety of services. However, the rights of students with limited-English proficiency are now assured by Title VI of the Civil Rights Act and the *Lau* Remedies, but the rights of the socioeconomically disadvantaged are not, so there are understandable pressures on school districts to place children about whom there is any doubt in language-related services. As other studies have shown, districts with limited funds tend not to deliver multiple services to individual children (Birman 1979; Comptroller General 1980; Kimbrough and Hill 1981). To the extent that this situation results in misplacement, many children may be deprived of services from which they could benefit. In addition, placement of children who do not have language-based needs in language-service classes hampers the already limited capacity of the nation's school districts to provide language-related services to children who truly need them.

The finding that much of the difference attributed to language is a result of socioeconomic status differences means that care must be taken in selecting students for special language services. The choice among regular classes, special compensatory education classes, and special language classes must be made carefully to ensure that students derive the greatest benefit from school attendance.

Appendix 3A:
Statistical Models
and Estimation

Two separate models were estimated, corresponding to one model for equations 3-1 and 3-2 and another model for equations 3-3 and 3-4. The models were estimated for each grade and for all grades together. The models estimated for all grades together used achievement data with the means for each grade removed. All correlation matrices were formed deleting an observation when any variable had a missing value; the correlations were weighted by the original sampling design weights.

We used the computer program MILS (written by Ronald Schoenberg), a program similar to the LISREL program (Jöreskog and Sörbom 1978). Where LISREL allows estimation through the methods of maximum likelihood only, MILS also allows the use of generalized least squares. Generalized least squares has the advantage (for purposes of estimation) of having no stringent distributional assumptions, as opposed to the requirements of multivariate normality for the maximum-likelihood procedure used in LISREL.

Figure 3A-1 presents the model estimated for the total effects of language on achievement (equations 3-1 and 3-2); figure 3A-2 presents the model estimated for the effects of socioeconomic status and language on achievement (equations 3-3 and 3-4). The two models are similar, with the one in figure 3A-2 having an additional socioeconomic-status factor and its indicators. In the figures, the circles refer to the factors, and the squares refer to the indicators of the factors.

Model Specification

Symbols Used

The model specifications used several symbols, which appear in the appendix figures and tables. The following abbreviations for variables are used:

FR	= Fall reading achievement.
SR	= Spring reading achievement.
FM	= Fall math achievement.
SM	= Spring math achievement.
SP	= Spanish language usually used in the home coded as 1, otherwise coded as 0.

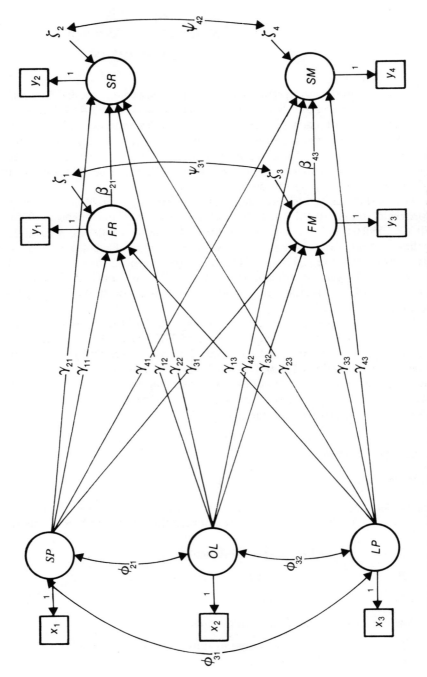

Figure 3A-1. Model Estimated for Equations 3.1 and 3.2 Using MILS Program

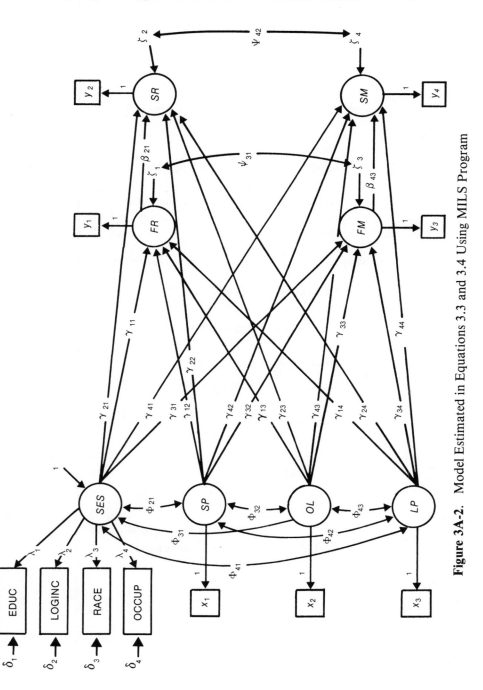

Figure 3A-2. Model Estimated in Equations 3.3 and 3.4 Using MILS Program

OL   = Other non-English-language, not Spanish, usually used in the home coded as 1, otherwise coded as 0.

LP   = Spanish or other language predominant coded as 1, English predominant coded as 0.

SES   = Socioeconomic factor.

EDUC = Parent education (socioeconomic status indicator).

LOGINC = Logarithm of family income (socioeconomic status indicator).

RACE = White coded as 1, nonwhite coded as 0 (socioeconomic status indicator).

OCCUP = At least one parent professional, managerial, or technical worker coded as 1, otherwise coded as 0 (socioeconomic indicator).

The following meanings are associated with the other symbols:

γ_{ij} = Regression coefficient of achievement (i) on the exogenous factor (j).

β_{ij} = Regression of spring achievement (i) on fall achievement (j).

ζ_i = Error of structural equations.

ϕ_{ij} = Variances ($i=j$) and covariances ($i \neq j$) of exogenous factors.

ψ_{ij} = Variances ($i=j$) and covariances ($i \neq j$) of structural equation errors.

λ_i = Regression of indicators of exogenous factors on the exogenous factors.

s_i = Errors in the regression of exogenous factor indicators on the factors.

y_i = Perfect indicators of the achievement factors.

x_i = Perfect indicators of the language factors.

Model 1

This model corresponds to equations 3-1 and 3-2.

Structural Model

$$FR = \gamma_{11} SP + \gamma_{12} OL + \gamma_{13} LP + \zeta_{11}$$

$$SR = \gamma_{21}SP + \gamma_{22}OL + \gamma_{23}LP + \beta_{21}FR + \zeta_{22}$$

$$FM = \gamma_{31}SP + \gamma_{32}OL + \gamma_{33}LP + \zeta_{33}$$

$$SM = \gamma_{41}SP + \gamma_{42}OL + \gamma_{43}LP + \beta_{43}FM + \zeta_{44}$$

Measurement Model: The observed indicators of the endogenous and exogenous factors are assumed to be perfect measures in the model.

Variances and Covariances: Variances of independent factors (ϕ_{11}, ϕ_{22}, ϕ_{33}) are free. Covariances among the exogenous factors (ϕ_{ij}, $i \neq j$) are also free.
Covariances among errors in the structural model are assumed to be nonzero for the fall tests (ψ_{21}) and the spring tests (ψ_{43}).

Model 2

This model corresponds to equations 3-3 and 3-4.

Structural Model

$$FR = \gamma_{11}SES + \gamma_{12}SP + \gamma_{13}OL + \gamma_{14}LP + \zeta_{11}$$

$$SR = \gamma_{21}SES + \gamma_{22}SP + \gamma_{23}OL + \gamma_{24}LP + \beta_{21}FR + \zeta_{22}$$

$$FM = \gamma_{31}SES + \gamma_{32}SP + \gamma_{33}OL + \gamma_{34}LP + \zeta_{33}$$

$$SM = \gamma_{41}SES + \gamma_{42}SP + \gamma_{43}OL + \gamma_{44}LP + \beta_{43}FM + \zeta_{44}$$

Measurement Model

$$EDUC = \lambda_1 SES + s_1$$

$$LOGINC = \lambda_2 SES + s_2$$

$$RACE = \lambda_3 SES + s_2$$

$$OCCUP = \lambda_4 SES + s_4$$

The following observed indicators of the endogenous and exogenous factors are assumed to be measured without error:

y_1 = SP

y_2 = OL

y_3 = OP

x_1 = FR

x_2 = SR

x_3 = FM

x_4 = SM

Variances and Covariances: The variance of SES (ϕ_{11}) is set to 1 (standardized), and the variances of other independent factors (ϕ_{22}, ϕ_{33}, ϕ_{44}) are free to vary. Covariances among the independent factors (ϕ_{ij}, $i \neq j$) are also free.

In addition, the covariances among the errors in the structural model are free for the fall tests (ψ_{21}) and the spring tests (ψ_{43}).

Problems in Model Estimation

In estimating the two models, we observed that the data were weak in terms of supporting the estimates of the ψ matrix; this means that these estimates are imprecise. However, the imprecision of these coefficients does not seem to have produced any problems elsewhere in the model.

The general consistency of coefficients across grades is evidence that the estimation results are reasonable. The patterns of differences in the coefficients, such as the increases in each of the elements in the β matrix from grades 1 to 6, are consistent with theoretical expectations.

Discussion of Model Estimation

The parameter estimates from the analysis of the two models are presented in tables 3A-1 and 3A-2. The following discussion focuses on the statistical fit of the models to the data. The fit of each of the models for each grade is about the same. The χ^2 values range from 237 to 371 for model 1 and 436 to 531 for model 2. The χ^2 for the all-grades analyses are much higher because the sample size includes all students in the six grades.

The fit of model 2 is fair; the ratio of χ^2 to degrees of freedom is about 24 for each grade. Given the sample size of 2,000, the overall fit is acceptable. The fit of model 1 is much poorer. While the χ^2 values are lower, there are only 2 degrees of freedom, yielding a ratio of χ^2 to degrees of freedom

Table 3A-1
Coefficient Estimates from MILS Model Equations 3.1 and 3.2

Coefficient		All Grades	1	2	3	4	5	6
β	2, 1	0.90	0.84	0.87	0.86	0.89	0.93	0.93
	4, 3	.85	.81	.78	.83	.82	.88	.90
γ	1, 1	−26.48 N	−6.57 N	−21.04	−28.27	−39.28	−26.33	−44.20
	1, 2	9.51 N	1.68 N	7.72 N	24.17	5.35 N	12.89 N	6.44 N
	1, 3	−23.80 N	−18.81	−21.54	−29.94	−13.68 N	−34.48	−29.07
	2, 1	−5.69 N	−7.77 N	−7.23 N	−8.15 N	−9.02 N	−2.42 N	.16 N
	2, 2	−.51 N	−.99 N	−2.09 N	2.41 N	−2.21 N	2.69 N	−1.21 N
	2, 3	−3.11 N	−6.40 N	−9.96 N	−.97 N	−.65 N	−3.82 N	4.00 N
	3, 1	−19.77 N	−10.62	−13.52	−20.38	−33.65	−18.25	−26.81
	3, 2	7.37 N	4.51 N	5.92 N	17.18	4.22 N	10.83	2.41 N
	3, 3	−11.59 N	−14.16 N	−14.86 N	−9.94 N	.32 N	−25.34	−7.31 N
	4, 1	−10.35 N	−5.62 N	−16.21 N	−10.31 N	−11.09 N	−8.47 N	−12.11 N
	4, 2	−.55 N	1.82 N	−8.07 N	−.05 N	−1.35 N	2.85 N	3.49 N
	4, 3	2.65 N	−3.72 N	14.93	−10.71 N	1.49 N	1.03 N	16.79 N
φ	1, 1	.06	.07	.07	.07	.06	.06	.05
	2, 1	−.00 N	−.00 N	−.00	−.00 N	−.00	−.00 N	−.00 N
	2, 2	.04	.03	.04	.04	.05	.03	.03
	3, 1	−.03	−.03	−.02	−.03	−.03	−.02	−.02
	3, 2	−.01	−.01	−.01	−.01	−.01	−.00	−.00
	3, 3	.03	.04	.03	.04	.04	.03	.03
ψ	1, 1	3,160	1,123	2,433	3,102	3,598	4,046	4,707
	2, 2	1,025	1,373	1,003	843	1,001	976	960
	3, 1	2,024	751	1,350	1,714	2,566	2,788	3,127
	3, 3	2,955	1,279	2,049	2,258	3,505	4,125	4,575
	4, 2	307	380	271	319	313	298	288
	4, 4	1,730	1,210	1,402	1,689	1,741	2,080	2,243
$\chi^2(2)$		1,728	371	311	309	237	255	323
Sample size		12,996	2,279	2,077	2,080	1,977	2,054	2,529

Note: Estimation of model in figure 3A-1 by generalized least squares. All coefficients are significant beyond the 0.01 level, assuming a simple (weighted) random sample, except those annotated "N."

Table 3A-2
Coefficient Estimates from MILS Model Equations 3.3 and 3.4

Coefficient	All Grades	Grade					
		1	2	3	4	5	6
λ 1	2.23	2.18	2.20	2.29	2.27	2.10	2.27
2	.43	.46	.42	.48	.44	.42	.40
3	.10	.11	.10	.10	.10	.12	.08
4	.26	.26	.27	.26	.24	.26	.26
β 2,1	.83	.61	.77	.80	.82	.88	.88
4,3	.77	.67	.69	.72	.74	.81	.83
γ 1,1	28.52	17.46	24.75	29.15	31.62	33.68	36.15
1,2	-2.35 N	5.38 N	-5.62 N	-3.52 N	-11.33 N	4.14 N	-.10 N
1,3	-3.37 N	-5.68 N	-1.34 N	-1.52 N	-3.96 N	-1.67 N	-6.48 N
1,4	-8.34 N	-8.68 N	-7.99 N	-12.13 N	6.23 N	-15.75 N	-18.33 N
2,1	7.69	13.53	9.27	7.48	7.46	5.57	5.61
2,2	-1.65 N	-2.34 N	-3.33 N	-3.50 N	-6.00 N	1.03 N	4.43 N
2,3	-2.53 N	-3.07 N	-5.05 N	-3.05 N	-3.00 N	1.45 N	-2.08 N
2,4	-1.19 N	-4.60 N	-6.96 N	1.74 N	2.07 N	-2.97 N	4.13 N
3,1	23.38	17.60	19.36	19.79	27.82	28.14	29.03
3,2	.04 N	1.20 N	-.11 N	-3.67 N	-9.67 N	6.87 N	8.32 N
3,3	-3.33 N	-2.72 N	-2.78 N	-.52 N	-3.80 N	-1.47 N	-7.25 N
3,4	1.46 N	-4.01 N	-3.15 N	2.58 N	18.17 N	-8.15 N	1.53 N
4,1	9.83	9.14	9.98	13.82	8.82	9.66	10.59
4,2	-4.32 N	-2.06 N	-11.12 N	-1.50 N	-6.39 N	-1.18 N	-2.68 N
4,3	-3.38 N	-.10 N	-11.50 N	-9.43 N	-2.55 N	.18 N	2.69 N
4,4	6.51 N	-1.20 N	19.33 N	-3.98 N	6.12 N	4.62 N	19.09 N
φ 2,1	-.06	-.06	-.05	-.07	-.06	-.06	-.07
2,2	.06	.07	.07	.07	.06	.06	.06
3,1	.01 N	.01 N	.01 N	.02	.01 N	.01 N	.01 N
3,2	-.00	-.00	-.00	-.00	-.00	-.00	-.00
3,3	.04	.03	.04	.04	.05	.03	.03
4,1	.03	.04	.03	.04	.04	.03	.03
4,2	-.03	-.03	-.02	-.03	-.03	-.02	-.02
4,3	-.01	-.01	-.01	-.01	-.01	-.00	-.00

4, 4	.03	.04	.03	.04	.04	.03	.03
ψ 1, 1	2,431	858	1,805	2,337	2,749	3,052	3,560
2, 2	986	1,241	956	819	966	957	941
3, 1	1,499	503	933	1,269	1,856	2,018	2,269
3, 3	2,496	992	1,731	1,951	2,863	3,478	3,861
4, 2	326	421	293	316	336	328	318
4, 4	1,631	1,158	1,298	1,493	1,668	1,989	2,122
s 1	2.79	2.77	3.01	2.83	2.73	3.38	2.37
2	.39	.39	.34	.40	.40	.37	.42
3	.14	.15	.13	.14	.14	.15	.12
4	.13	.12	.13	.13	.13	.12	.14
$\chi^2(24)$	2,836	612	512	531	436	506	459
Sample size	12,996	2,279	2,077	2,080	1,977	2,054	2,529

Note: Estimation of model in figure 3A-2 by generalized least squares. All coefficients are significant beyond the 0.01 level, assuming a simple (weighted) random sample, except those annotated "N."

of over 100. This indicates that the language variables alone do very poorly in predicting achievement.

The coefficient values in most cases are significantly different from 0, except for a few values of γ_{ij} and most of the γ_{ij} language-variable coefficients. In fact, even when socioeconomic status is excluded from the model (model 1), many of the γ_{ij} language coefficients are not significantly different from 0.

Notes

1. The small number of students who rely on non-English, non-Spanish languages in the sample made their use in comparison groups questionable. We do not believe this limits the policy implications of our analysis because previous research has shown that children from Spanish backgrounds are the dominant group among language-minority school-age children (Waggoner 1978; Milne and Gombert, chap. 4 of this book; Veltman 1980).

2. MILS is an advanced version of LISREL (Jöreskog and Sörbom, 1978) and is available from Ron Schoenberg, National Institutes of Health, Building 31, Room 4C11, Bethesda, Maryland 20205.

3. This analysis used vertical-scale scores that were created independently for reading and math tests (Hemenway et al. 1978). These scores are a standardized common metric across the entire sample of grades (grades 1 to 6), designed to control differences in levels of the test used across different grades and test dates. Analyses were undertaken using all grades together (adjusting for mean differences among grades) and for each grade separately. Approximately 2,000 students in each grade took the fall and spring reading and math tests.

4. For the parental-education variable, the maximum value of either the mother's or the father's education was coded from categorical variables, with fewer than eight years of schooling coded as 7; nine to eleven years of schooling coded as 10; high school coded as 12; some college coded as 14; college coded as 16; and more than college coded as 18. The occupation measure was coded as 1 if at least one parent was a professional, managerial, or technical worker; otherwise, it was coded as 0. Race was determined from parental response to a survey question. When there was no response to the question or when the parents responded "Hispanic," teacher identification of the child as white or nonwhite was used.

5. To obtain the values in table 3-2, coefficients were used from the analysis as presented in appendix 3A. The language effects are the negative of the sum of the Spanish-language coefficient and the language-predominant coefficient, while the socioeconomic status effect is 1.27

times the socioeconomic status coefficient. The value of 1.27 is the difference between the mean English-only socioeconomic status factor score ($+0.0559$) and the mean Spanish-predominant factor score (-1.2145). The γ_{ij} coefficients referenced can be found in tables 3A-1 and 3A-2. Reference is also made to the coefficients in equations 3-1 through 3-4 as an aid to the reader.

6. The value 50.3 is computed by taking $-(\gamma_{11} + \gamma_{13})$ from table 3A-1, which is $-(-26.48 + -23.80)$. γ_{11} is the same as b_1 and γ_{13} the same as b_3 in equation 3-1.

7. This is found by taking $-(\gamma_{12} + \gamma_{14})$ from table 3A-2, which is $-(-2.35 + -8.34)$. (γ_{12} is the same as b_1 and γ_{14} the same as b_3 in equation 3-3.) The SES effect, controlling for language, is found by taking the γ_{11} coefficient (28.52) in table 3A-2 and multiplying it by 1.27. (γ_{11} is the same as b_4 in equation 3-3.)

References

American Institutes for Research (AIR). 1977. *Evaluation of the Impact of ESEA Title VII Spanish/English Bilingual Education Program. Vol. 1: Study Design and Interim Findings.* Palo Alto, Calif.

Baral, D.P. 1979. "Academic Achievement of Recent Immigrants from Mexico." *NABE Journal* 3:1-13.

Birman, B.F. 1979. *Case Studies of Overlap between Title I and Public Law 94-142: Services for Handicapped Students.* Menlo Park, Calif.: SRI International.

Bowen, J.D. 1977, "Linguistic Perspectives on Bilingual Education." In Bernard Spolsky and Robert Cooper, eds., *Frontiers of Bilingual Education.* Rowley, Mass.: Newbury House Publishers.

Brown, G.H.; Rosen, N.; and Hill, S. 1980. *The Condition of Education for Hispanic Americans.* Washington, D.C.: National Center for Education Statistics.

Carsrud, K.E. "Evaluation of Achievement Outcomes: Austin's Experience." Paper presented at the National Conference on Longitudinal Evaluation of Bilingual Programs, Austin, Tex., August.

Coleman, J.S.; Campbell, E.; Hobson, C.; McPartland, J.; Mood, A.; Weinfeld, F.; and York, R. 1966. *Equality of Educational Opportunity.* Washington, D.C.: U.S. Government Printing Office.

Comptroller General. 1980. *Report to Congress: An Analysis of Concerns in Federal Education Programs: Duplication of Services and Administrative Costs.* Washington, D.C.: General Accounting Office.

Cummins, J. "Linguistic Interdependence and the Educational Development of Bilingual Children." *Review of Educational Research* 49:222-251.

Danoff, M.N. 1978. *Evaluation of the Impact of ESEA Title VII Spanish/ English Bilingual Education Program: Overview of Study and Findings.* Palo Alto, Calif.: American Institutes for Research.

De Avila, E.A. 1980. "Relative Language Proficiency Types: A Comparison of Prevalence, Achievement Level and Socio-Economic Status." Report submitted to the Rand Corporation.

Dulay, H., and Burt, M. 1980. "The Relative Proficiency of Limited English Proficient Students." In James E. Alatis, ed., *Georgetown University Round Table on Languages and Linguistics 1980, Current Issues in Bilingual Education.* Washington, D.C.: Georgetown University Press.

Eptstein, N. 1977. *Language, Ethnicity, and the Schools: Policy Alternatives for Bilingual-Bicultural Education.* Washington, D.C.: George Washington University Institute for Educational Leadership.

Hemenway, J.A.; Wang, M.; Kenoyer, C.; Hoepfner, R.; Bear, M.; and Smith, G. 1978. *The Measures and Variables in the Sustaining Effects Study.* Santa Monica, Calif.: System Development Corporation.

Hoepfner, R.; Wellisch, J.; and Zagorski, H. 1977. *The Sample for the Sustaining Effects Study and Projections of Its Characteristics to the National Population.* Santa Monica, Calif.: System Development Corporation.

Jencks, C.; Smith, M.S.; Acland, H.; Bane, M.; Cohen, D.; Gintis, H.; Heynes, B.; and Michelson, S. 1972. *Inequality: A Reassessment of the Effect of Family and Schooling in America.* New York: Basic Books.

Jöreskog, K. "A General Method for Estimating a Linear Structural Equation System." In Arthur Goldberger and Otis Dudley Duncan, eds., *Structural Equation Models in the Social Sciences.* New York: Seminar Press.

Jöreskog, K., and Sörbom, D. 1978. *LISREL IV: Analysis of Linear Structural Relationships by the Method of Maximum Likelihood.* Chicago: International Educational Services.

———. 1979. *Advances in Factor Analysis and Structural Equation Models.* Cambridge, Mass.: ABT Books, 1979.

Kimbrough, J., and Hill, P. 1981. *The Cumulative Effects of Federal Education Programs.* Santa Monica, Calif.: Rand Corporation.

Mayeske, G.W.; Okada, T.; Cohen, W.; Beaton, A., Jr.; and Wisler, C. 1973. *A Study of the Achievement of Our Nation's Students.* Washington, D.C.: U.S. Government Printing Office.

Paulston, C.B. 1974. "Implications of Language Learning Theory for Language Planning: Concerns in Bilingual Education." Bilingual Education Series, Vol. 1. Washington, D.C.: Center for Applied Linguistics.

Veltman, C.J. 1980. "Relative Educational Attainments of Hispanic-American Children, 1976." Report Prepared for the Aspira Center for Educational Equity.

Waggoner, D. 1978. "Non-English Language Background Persons: Three U.S. Surveys." *TESOL Quarterly,* Vol. 12, pp. 247-262.

4

Students with a Primary Language other than English: Distribution and Service Rates

Ann M. Milne and
Jan M. Gombert

A number of attempts have been made to estimate the size of the population with limited English-language proficiency in the United States. Such estimates are important for federal policies related to the education of children who require special language services. The federal government has obligations to these children under Title VI of the Civil Rights Act, as interpreted by the Supreme Court in *Lau* v. *Nichols* (1974) and enforced by the Education Department's Office for Civil Rights (OCR) through compliance agreements known as the *Lau* Remedies. In addition, the federal government provides funds for bilingual education programs under Title VII of the Elementary and Secondary Education Act, and estimates of children in need of language services are important for establishing annual appropriations for this program.

It is equally necessary to estimate the distribution of children with limited English proficiency across geographic units such as states and also across administrative units such as school districts and schools. The relative concentration of language-minority children is clearly related to the ability of schools or districts to provide services to these children. This fact was duly noted in regulations written by the Department of Education in 1980 in an attempt to codify the *Lau* Remedies. Although the proposed rules were subsequently withdrawn, they required that full, unmodified classes in bilingual education be provided only in schools where there were more than twenty-five eligible students who were enrolled in two consecutive grades below grade 9 and who had a common primary language other than English. This requirement recognized the difficulty of providing appropriate services to children more sparsely distributed and perhaps also the related scarcity of teachers knowledgeable in the relevant languages.

Thus the relative concentration of children with limited English proficiency, more than their sheer numbers, is the critical factor in the ability of educational units to provide high-quality, appropriate, language-related services. Such concentrations, and their relationship to current provision of services, can be estimated from only one set of data bases: the annual or

113

biennial surveys conducted by OCR. Not only are these surveys representative at the level of the nation, the states, and selected school districts, but they also represent all schools within sampled districts. Thus, they allow estimates of the relative concentration of users of languages other than English within schools—information critical to a determination of the number of schools that have sufficient concentrations of similar-language students to provide appropriate services.

This chapter presents estimates of school-level concentrations, along with distributions across larger demographic and geographic units, and estimates of the service rates associated with these concentrations and classifications. The estimates are linked to the definitions used in the proposed regulations, for this study was initially undertaken as an attempt to evaluate the probable impact of those regulations.

Methodology

The Data Base

This study is based on data obtained by the OCR, Department of Education, in its fall 1978 survey of elementary and secondary schools and school districts.[1] The survey was the latest in a series of annual or biennial surveys conducted to determine the extent to which districts and schools are providing services to various groups covered by civil-rights guarantees.[2]

Although the size of the surveys has varied from year to year, the 1978 survey was conducted on a stratified sample of approximately half of all school districts having enrollments of more than three hundred students in the fifty states and the District of Columbia. Within these 6,000 or so districts, all schools (approximately 54,000) were surveyed.

Some 2,100 districts were included in the sample with a probability of one (required inclusion) because of high interest to OCR. The remaining districts were selected on the basis of several needs: to project data to state, regional, and national levels; to include a certain percentage of each minority or language group; and to survey districts in which data from the 1976 survey suggested potential discrimination.

The sample can be weighted to support projections to state, regional, and national levels. Addition of metro codes (central city, SMSA, non-SMSA) allows representation of these demographic characteristics; the census of schools within districts permits analysis of school types; and finally, because of the emphasis on larger districts, approximately 72 percent of the students in public schools in the United States were covered by the survey.

The survey was conducted using two forms: form 101, which required summary data at the district level, and form 102, completed by individual schools. All analyses reported here were based on form 102, and data for the districts and higher levels were aggregated up from the school level.

The 1978 OCR survey question that identified our population of interest asked for a count of "pupils in membership who speak or use a language other than English more often than English." The specific question or definition used in any survey of the language-minority population will determine the estimates of the size of that population. We were particularly interested in the extent to which the OCR definition corresponds to any step in the screening process required by the proposed rules. Those rules required a series of steps to identify and assess the needs of language-minority children. The first step would identify all children with a "primary language other than English," where the primary language is defined as the first language the student acquired or a language the student normally uses. In the second step, appropriate tests would determine the degree of English proficiency of all students so identified. Finally, those deemed limited in English would take further tests to determine their relative proficiency in English as compared with the primary language. Each step would identify a successively smaller subset of students, finally ending up with a group of those in need of various services.

It is difficult to overlay the population counted by OCR with any subset identified by the proposed rules. Although the OCR question should identify children whose dominant language is not English, it is not clear that all such children will have limited proficiency in English. As a result the eligible population may be overestimated if those served under the proposed rules included only children limited in English proficiency who are dominant in the home language. However, if children comparably limited in both languages were to be eligible for the unmodified services required by the rules, the OCR estimates could be an undercount because degree of English proficiency is not identified. Also, the OCR survey may undercount eligible children because of the compliance orientation of the survey.

Regardless of the size of the total population, however, there is no reason to believe that the relative concentrations of these children across various classifications—our major concern here—is skewed in any particular direction. Because of the difficulty of labeling the children identified by OCR using a term denoting a degree of English proficiency, we have chosen to refer to them as PLOTE students, an acronym standing for "primary language other than English." This label fairly closely reflects the criterion used in the OCR identification question.

The OCR survey asked for the number of identified PLOTE students "who are enrolled in a Bilingual program, High Intensity Language Training, An English-As-A-Second-Language program or any non-language class taught in a language other than English." This number was not to include "pupils enrolled in a class to learn a language other than English."

Without knowing the degree of English proficiency of enrolled students, we cannot estimate the probable appropriateness of such services; we can only report on the incidence of the services.

The data base is limited by missing data. By far the most serious gap is the total lack of data for the city of Chicago. This omission will affect all counts that include Illinois. There are also lesser instances of missing data, including, for New York, enrollment data by ethnic category for fifteen schools and PLOTE student enrollement or services data for twenty-seven schools.

Analyses Conducted

Our major goal was to identify the relative concentration of PLOTE students across a number of demographic and geographic classifications. Although our primary focus was on distributions within schools, we were also interested in classifications such as district size, urban status, and state. Within each classification, we counted total PLOTE students, as well as PLOTE students within racial-ethnic categories. The racial-ethnic categories used by OCR were American Indian or Alaskan native, Asian or Pacific Islander, Hispanic, black (not of Hispanic origin), and white (not of Hispanic origin). The black and white categories were grouped as "other." One cannot necessarily identify the primary language of a student within a particular racial-ethnic category who is identified as having a primary language other than English. For example, it is unclear what primary language is used by black PLOTE students, and PLOTE students in other categories in some cases may speak a primary language different from that implied by their racial-ethnic category. However, for explanatory simplicity, we will refer to the groups as language groups.

We made a number of demographic and geographic classifications.

State: Counts of the total number of PLOTE children and of PLOTE students served were developed for each individual state. The counts for Illinois are low as a result of the absence of data from Chicago.

Region: We selected the ten Department of Education regions rather than the Census regions because we believe the former geographic areas are better related to language questions. Also, OCR compliance procedures are primarily conducted through regional offices.

Urban Status: Each district in the OCR sample was assigned a metro code from census mapping designating its status as a central city, suburban area, or "non-SMSA" (an area not included in a Standard Metropolitan Statistical Area, SMSA. Non-SMSAs are not truly rural but include small cities and towns.) These analyses were conducted by region to control possible anomalies created by weighting.

District Size: Districts were divided into the following enrollment classifications: under 300; 300 to 2,499; 2,500 to 4,999; 5,000 to 9,999; 10,000 to 24,999; and 25,000 and over. These categories are based on size breaks commonly used by the National Center for Education Statistics. They are an attempt to compromise between equalizing the number of students and equalizing the number of districts across size categories. Although the 1978 survey did not intend to sample districts with enrollments under 300 students, 180 such districts were included. Some presumably lost enrollment between the 1976 survey (the data used to stratify the sample) and 1978, and some may have been "forced" because of OCR interest. The sample districts in this category may not be representative.

School Level: The OCR data base does not identify enrollment or PLOTE students by grade; rather, it indicates the grades served by each school. Therefore a simple algorithm was devised to identify elementary and secondary schools: if the majority of grades in a school were grade 8 or below, that school was termed elementary; all other schools, eliminating the special-education and unclassifiable schools, were classified as secondary. This approach corresponds to distinctions in the proposed rules.

Schools and Districts with Small PLOTE Populations: The proposed rules would require bilingual education (instruction in required subjects given through both English and the primary language) for all students with limited English proficiency who are superior in the primary language. The rules might also require bilingual education for students comparably limited in both languages. This basic provision would be modified for small student populations and for students in grades 9 and above.[3] To qualify as small, a population would consist of twenty-five or fewer eligible students who are enrolled in two consecutive grades in a school and who have a common primary language other than English.

We were particularly interested in determining the number of schools (and the number of districts in which these schools are located) that would be required to meet the full, unmodified provisions of the proposed rules. An exact count was not possible because we do not know the grade and the bilingual entitlement (degree of need) of individual students in the OCR file. We derived a pair of simple algorithms to estimate whether a given school would be subject to the unmodified rules:

1. PLOTE students per school divided by half the number of grades per school, where a school with more than twenty-five PLOTE students

with a common language per nonoverlapping grade pair would qualify as subject to the proposed rules.
2. PLOTE students per school, where more than twenty-five total PLOTE students with a common language would define a school as subject to the proposed rules.

Neither estimate takes into account the fact that children with language problems tend to be disproportionately clustered in the lower elementary grades. However, the actual applicability of the unmodified rules would probably fall somewhere between definitions 1 and 2.

Analyses were conducted separately for all schools (excluding "other" or unclassifiable schools). Schools were then classified as subject to the proposed rules (required to provide unmodified bilingual education) if they satisfied either of the definitions and contained a majority of grades below grade 9. Schools with small populations and all secondary schools were deemed not subject. These analyses were done for each racial-ethnic group and for the total group of PLOTE students. Any elementary school above the count for any racial-ethnic group was included in the total column as subject to the unmodified rules. We then counted the number of districts that contained any subject schools in any racial-ethnic group to determine the number of school districts that would be affected by the unmodified bilingual-education requirements.

Lau **Compliance Districts:** Under current federal policies (those which the proposed rules attempted to codify), OCR has compliance agreements relating to bilingual education with approximately 500 school districts. The exact substance of these agreements is not clear, nor is it clear that all agreements were in effect before the 1978 OCR survey. Generally a district is required to enter a compliance agreement when it is found—as in a court case—to be discriminating against students with limited English proficiency or when it applies for funds under the Emergency School Aid Act (ESAA). We obtained a list of districts with *Lau* compliance agreements and found that 394 of these (80 percent) were represented in the 1978 OCR sample. We then determined the total number of PLOTE students and the number of such students served in these districts.

All analyses in each classification were weighted to the appropriate level, with the exception of the *Lau* district analyses. While some 80 percent of *Lau* districts were represented in the sample, it is not clear that they are representative of *Lau* districts nationally.

Results

National Distribution of PLOTE Students and Service Rates

Table 4-1 shows the number of PLOTE students in each language (racial-ethnic) category and also expresses that number as a percentage of total

Table 4-1

National Estimates of PLOTE Students in Public Elementary and Secondary Schools

	Number of PLOTEs	PLOTEs as Percentage of Language Group	Percentage of Total PLOTE Population	Percentage of PLOTEs Served
American Indian or Alaskan native	27,816	8.3	3	39.3
Asian	87,064	14.7	9	54.8
Hispanic	736,940	26.1	79	63.0
Other[a]	82,008	0.2	9	47.4
Total	933,828	2.2	100	60.2

[a]Those whose racial-ethnic background is white or black (not of Hispanic origin).

enrollment in that category and as a percentage of the total PLOTE population. The table also presents the service rate (percentage of PLOTE students who receive language-related services) in each language category. Of the 41,863,103 students enrolled in the nation's public schools, 933,828 (2.2 percent) are classified as having a primary language other than English. Estimates are for districts with enrollments over 300.

Comparison of the various language categories, however, shows a wide range in the percentage of PLOTE students. While only 8.3 percent of American Indian and Alaskan natives speak a language other than English more often than English, more than 26 percent of Hispanic students apparently rely on the primary language. This fact, combined with the relative numbers of each racial-ethnic group enrolled in public schools, means that nearly 80 percent of the public-school PLOTE population is made up of Hispanics. This heavier incidence of Hispanic PLOTE students appears to be reflected in their service rate, which, at 63 percent, is the highest for any other PLOTE group and raises the national PLOTE service rate to just over 60 percent. The lower service rates for other groups, especially for American Indian and Alaskan natives, may reflect their relatively greater dispersion or sparsity in the population.

Distribution and Service Rates by State

Of all PLOTE students, 67.5 percent are enrolled within three states: California (27.5 percent), Texas (27.5 percent), and New York (12.5 percent).[4] (These same three states together enroll 24 percent of all U.S. students.) Each of eight other states has between 1 and 5 percent of all

PLOTE students enrolled in their schools; each of the remaining thirty-nine states and the District of Columbia enrolls less than 1 percent. In terms of the percentage of each state's total enrollment represented by PLOTE students, the states rank somewhat differently. New Mexico leads the list, with 10.2 percent of its total enrollment made up of PLOTE students; Texas is second with 9.1 percent and Arizona third with 7.7 percent. Twelve other states have PLOTE enrollments equalling 1 percent or more of state public-school enrollment. (The state-by-state totals and each state's share of national PLOTE students are shown in table 4A-1 in the appendix.)

By language group, PLOTE students are distributed as follows:

Hispanic PLOTE students: Texas enrolls 34 percent of all Hispanic PLOTE, California 28 percent, and New York 12 percent.

American Indian PLOTE students: Arizona and New Mexico have 40 percent and 33 percent, respectively, of the national total of American Indian PLOTE; Alaska is third with 6 percent.

Asian PLOTE students: 40 percent of Asian PLOTE are enrolled in California; New York is second with 9 percent.

Service rates for PLOTE students vary widely from state to state, with a national mean service rate of 60.2 percent. The lowest service rate, 8.3 percent, is found in West Virginia; Hawaii has the highest service rate: 99.6 percent. No simple relationship exists between the size of PLOTE student enrollment within a state and the state's service rate. High service rates are found in states with relatively low PLOTE enrollments, as well as in states with large numbers of PLOTE students.

Distribution and Service Rates by District Size

The enrollment patterns and service rates by district size are shown in table 4-2. Within each category, between 1.3 and 3.8 percent of total enrollment is made up of PLOTE students, with the largest districts having the highest concentrations. Although only 27 percent of all public-school students are enrolled in the largest districts (enrollments of 25,000 or more), 46 percent of PLOTE students are enrolled in such districts. This pattern holds for each language group, with one exception: 66 percent of American Indian PLOTE students are in districts with enrollments between 300 and 5,000.

The largest districts also have the highest service rate, 64 percent; the lowest service rate, 45.9 percent, is in districts with enrollments of 300 to 2,499. The higher service rates in larger districts may reflect the greater ease of providing appropriate services where needy students are sufficiently con-

Table 4-2
PLOTE Student Distribution and Service Rates, by District Size

District Enrollment	Number of PLOTEs	PLOTEs as Percentage of Enrollment	Percentage of PLOTEs Served
0-299	1,127	1.7	53.2
300-2,499	108,317	1.3	45.9
2,500-4,999	97,611	1.3	61.2
5,000-9,999	116,671	1.5	57.3
10,000-24,999	184,997	2.5	61.1
25,000 or more	425,105	3.8	64.0
Total	933,828	2.2	60.2

centrated. These higher rates may also reflect the greater availability of bilingual teachers in such areas.

Distribution and Service Rates by Urban Status

Table 4-3 presents PLOTE student distribution and service rates for central cities, other areas of SMSAs excluding the central city, and non-SMSA areas. Perhaps reflecting only another aspect of the district-size analyses just presented, higher concentrations of PLOTE students occur in central cities than in other areas.

Central cities, which enroll only 26 percent of all public-school students, enroll 55 percent of all PLOTE students. This pattern holds for each language group except American Indian PLOTE students, 93 percent of whom are enrolled in non-SMSA areas.

Service rates are essentially equal in central cities and suburban areas, at 62.6 percent and 63 percent, respectively; they are lowest in non-SMSA areas, at 49.8 percent, again perhaps reflecting the difficulty of providing services in sparsely settled areas.

Table 4-3
PLOTE Student Distribution and Service Rates, by Urban Status

Urban Status	Number of PLOTEs	PLOTEs as Percentage of Enrollment	Percentage of PLOTEs Served
Central City	513,656	4.8	62.6
Other SMSA	238,939	1.5	63.0
Non-SMSA	181,233	1.2	49.8
Total	933,828	2.2	60.2

Distribution and Service Rates by School Level

The unmodified bilingual-education requirement in the proposed rules would be applicable only to elementary schools (below grade 9), which currently enroll 81 percent of all PLOTE students in the United States. (In comparison, 69 percent of total school-age children are enrolled in elementary schools.) A high proportion (82 percent) of Hispanic PLOTE students are in elementary grades; 73 to 76 percent of other PLOTE children are in elementary schools. The relatively high percentage of PLOTE children in elementary grades is consistent with expectations and lends credence to our further analyses of distributions across elementary schools.

Elementary schools also have higher service rates than do secondary schools—64.5 percent versus 41.8 percent, respectively; however, service rates differ by language group, as table 4-4 shows. The relatively lower service rates for all but Asian PLOTE students in secondary schools may reflect the higher dropout rates for other PLOTE groups, particularly Hispanics.

Distribution across Schools

Our major concern was with the distribution of PLOTE students within individual schools and with the number of schools that would have been required to comply with the unmodified bilingual-education provisions of the proposed rules. Although the OCR data base was lacking a number of the qualifiers that would have allowed us to pinpoint this population precisely, we were able to develop two algorithms to estimate the schools most likely to be subject to the rules. Table 4-5 presents the number of schools that would be subject (and the number not subject) to the unmodified rules under each definition, along with the number and percentage of total PLOTE students enrolled in each group of schools and the parallel service rates.

Table 4-4
PLOTE Service Rates, by School Level

	Elementary-School Service Rate	*Secondary-School Service Rate*
American Indian or Alaskan native	45.5	22.2
Asian	55.7	52.1
Hispanic	67.7	40.9
Other	48.5	44.0
Total	64.5	41.8

Table 4-5

Distribution of PLOTE Students and Service Rates in Schools Subject to and Not Subject to Unmodified Service Provisions of Proposed Rules

Definition	Subject Status	Number of Schools	Percentage of Schools	Number of PLOTEs	Percentage of PLOTEs	Number of PLOTEs Served	Percentage of PLOTEs Served
More than 25 PLOTE students with common language enrolled per two grades	Subject	2,251	3	500,266	54	329,515	66
	Not subject	76,226	97	431,249	46	231,215	54
More than 25 PLOTE students with common language enrolled per school	Subject	4,822	6	634,124	69	429,670	67
	Not subject	73,655	94	288,391	31	131,061	45

Only 3 to 6 percent of all public schools in the country have high enough concentrations of PLOTE students to require compliance with the full rules. Or, to phrase it differently, only 3 to 6 percent of schools have sufficient concentrations to be reasonably expected to mount full-scale, appropriate, cost-efficient bilingual programs. The service rates in these subject schools may reflect this reality; within schools with high concentrations, the service rates are 66 to 67 percent, while in schools with lower concentrations, the service rates are 45 to 54 percent.

These subject schools enroll 54 to 69 percent of all PLOTE students. Thus some 54 to 69 percent of such students are sufficiently concentrated within given schools to make full-scale bilingual education feasible. The rest are so sparse or widely distributed as to raise the possibility of providing some form of modified service—itinerant teachers, busing to a central location, or other approaches based on district-level rather than school-level provision of service. If each district that has at least one school subject to unmodified rules were to implement a district-wide service program, 82 to 91 percent of all PLOTE students in the nation could receive bilingual services. That is, the 4 to 9 percent of school districts that include all subject schools by our definitions enroll 82 to 91 percent of all PLOTE students. The proportions are comparably high for each language-ethnic group, with the exception of Asian PLOTE students. For example, districts covered under our second definition would enroll 90 percent of all American Indian PLOTE students and 94 percent of all Hispanic PLOTE students but only 60 percent of all Asian PLOTE students.

It would thus appear that a very small proportion of schools and school districts, enrolling very high percentages of PLOTE students, were the effective target of the proposed rules. As the final analyses demonstrate, these districts are already the target of OCR activity, and although the exact behavior of districts under the proposed rules might have changed, their identity would have remained essentially the same.

Description of Lau Districts

Distribution: The *Lau* compliance districts may enroll as many as three-fourths of all PLOTE students. (This may even be an underestimate, given the absence of PLOTE counts for Chicago.) These districts significantly overlap with the districts identified as being subject to the basic unmodified bilingual-education provision of the proposed rules. Apparently no districts with large concentrations of PLOTE students have gone unidentified by OCR. Each of the two largest *Lau* districts in the OCR sample (New York City and Los Angeles) enrolls in excess of 90,000 PLOTE students; the largest non-*Lau* district in the sample enrolls just over 3,000. Of the 394 *Lau* districts in the sample, 108 have 1,000 or more PLOTE students; in contrast, only 21 of the 5,260 non-*Lau* districts in the sample have that many.

Generally the *Lau* districts reflect the overall demographic distribution of PLOTE children, in exaggerated form. Texas, California, and New York contain 75 percent of the *Lau*-district PLOTE students. Most *Lau*-district PLOTE students (61 percent) are in districts of 25,000 or more. However, *Lau* districts with enrollments of between 300 and 2,499 average the highest percentage of PLOTE students in relation to total enrollment: 25 percent PLOTE children as opposed to 5 percent for the largest districts. No *Lau* districts with enrollments below 300 students were found. Central cities enroll 72 percent of the *Lau*-district PLOTE students. (Again, American Indians do not follow the pattern; these PLOTE students are concentrated in non-SMSA areas and in districts with enrollments between 2,500 and 25,000.)

Service Rates: On the whole, service rates for PLOTE students are slightly higher in *Lau* districts than in districts in general—64.8 percent versus 60.2 percent. The *Lau* district service rate is in the range of service rates for schools with high concentrations of PLOTE students (see table 4-5) and may in fact represent those same schools.

By state, service rates in *Lau* districts vary from a low of 28.6 percent to a high of 100 percent. Each of these extremes, however, is found in a state with relatively few PLOTE students, relatively few *Lau* districts, or both.

By district size, service rates vary from 58.1 percent (districts of 5,000 to 9,999) to 72.7 percent (districts of 2,500 to 4,999). These rates are fairly consistent across language groups.

Service rates show little difference across urban-status categories, ranging from 58.4 percent in non-SMSAs to 68 percent in suburbs.

Summary and Conclusions

While the population of children with a primary language other than English may not overlap completely with the population of eligible children, there may be fewer children who need language-related services than has been estimated previously (O'Malley 1981). Moreover, these children appear to be concentrated in a limited number of areas. Specifically the analyses showed that:

1. A total of 933,828 students, or 2.2 percent of U.S. enrollment, are classified as PLOTE students; 79 percent of these students are of Hispanic background.
2. Three states—California, Texas, and New York—enroll 67.5 of all PLOTE students.

3. The percentage of PLOTE students enrolled in the largest school districts (46 percent) overrepresents those districts' share of total national enrollment (27 percent).
4. The majority (55 percent) of PLOTE students are enrolled in central cities.
5. Most PLOTE students (81 percent) attend elementary schools.
6. Most PLOTE students covered by the compliance agreements or by the proposed rules are concentrated within 3 to 6 percent of schools and 4 to 9 percent of school districts.
7. Districts currently under compliance agreements with OCR may enroll as many as three-fourths of the total PLOTE population, or even more if Chicago were counted.

More specifically, large proportions of PLOTE students are enrolled in districts already under compliance agreements with OCR, and these districts are essentially the same as those that would have been targeted under the basic bilingual-education requirement of the proposed rules. The extent to which the proposed rules would have replaced the current procedures in these districts—with more- or less-restrictive procedures—is a policy question not addressed by these analyses.

The rates of language-related services to PLOTE children vary according to demographic classification around a national rate of 60.2 percent. This analysis did not address the adequacy of these services. Adequacy of content cannot be addressed by the OCR data; adequacy of coverage is also difficult to determine because the data do not enable any assessment of English-language proficiency or of relative proficiency in English and the primary language. An accurate evaluation would require a second, separate assessment procedure.

**Appendix 4A:
State Shares of
PLOTE Enrollment**

Table 4A-1
Enrollment by State, All Districts

State			Total			
	Enrollment	Number of PLOTEs	Percentage PLOTEs	Number Served	Percentage Served	Percentage Share of Total PLOTEs
California	4,096,379	257,061	6.3	174,059	67.7	27.5
Texas	2,808,974	256,807	9.1	142,503	55.5	27.5
New York	3,035,936	116,746	3.8	77,852	66.7	12.5
New Jersey	1,300,068	44,332	3.4	26,484	59.7	4.7
Arizona	508,086	39,299	7.7	19,340	49.2	4.2
Florida	1,513,285	28,492	1.9	15,550	54.6	3.1
New Mexico	273,568	27,973	10.2	13,590	48.6	3.0
Massachusetts	1,032,889	27,806	2.7	15,503	55.8	3.0
Connecticut	568,959	18,465	3.2	9,501	51.5	2.0
Michigan	1,911,387	12,508	0.7	7,978	63.8	1.3
Illinois	2,075,363	11,368	0.5	7,023	61.8	1.2
Pennsylvania	2,019,508	8,803	0.4	6,334	72.0	0.9
Washington	766,927	7,200	0.9	4,259	59.2	0.8
Louisiana	817,228	6,387	0.8	2,359	36.9	0.7
Virginia	1,054,341	6,247	0.6	4,213	67.4	0.7
Colorado	549,011	5,968	1.1	4,557	76.4	0.6
Ohio	2,063,953	5,139	0.2	2,407	46.8	0.6
Rhode Island	166,033	5,081	3.1	2,387	47.0	0.5
Maryland	819,331	4,332	0.5	3,533	81.6	0.5
Utah	320,779	4,144	1.3	2,179	52.6	0.4
Oregon	451,340	3,791	0.8	1,921	50.7	0.4
Indiana	1,108,977	3,289	0.3	1,055	32.1	0.4
Wisconsin	872,155	3,175	0.4	2,071	65.2	0.3
Oklahoma	587,366	2,889	0.5	1,041	36.0	0.3
Minnesota	776,790	2,507	0.3	1,153	46.0	0.3
Alaska	86,307	2,190	2.5	1,329	60.7	0.2
Idaho	194,546	2,188	1.1	1,200	54.9	0.2
Kansas	423,272	2,027	0.5	915	45.1	0.2

Montana	141,443	1,651	1.2	769	46.6	0.2
Maine	220,655	1,626	0.7	987	60.7	0.2
Hawaii	169,602	1,479	0.9	1,473	99.6	0.2
District of Columbia	108,903	1,476	1.4	1,180	79.9	0.2
Iowa	554,335	1,451	0.3	952	65.6	0.2
Georgia	1,067,671	1,429	0.1	817	57.2	0.2
Nevada	145,813	1,253	0.9	946	75.5	0.1
Missouri	883,666	1,081	0.1	274	25.4	0.1
North Carolina	1,170,307	963	0.1	445	46.2	0.1
Nebraska	255,438	713	0.3	259	36.3	0.1
Tennessee	863,528	706	0.1	294	41.7	0.1
South Dakota	125,385	541	0.4	136	25.2	0.1
Delaware	113,565	405	0.4	318	78.5	0.0
New Hampshire	158,819	395	0.2	135	34.2	0.0
Alabama	761,928	388	0.1	211	54.4	0.0
South Carolina	638,574	360	0.1	104	28.9	0.0
Kentucky	686,360	319	0.0	104	32.6	0.0
Arkansas	442,296	301	0.1	46	15.3	0.0
Mississippi	487,473	296	0.1	114	38.4	0.0
Wyoming	89,673	270	0.3	76	28.1	0.0
North Dakota	97,114	269	0.3	29	10.6	0.0
West Virginia	397,620	181	0.0	15	8.3	0.0
Vermont	80,177	60	0.1	22	37.5	0.0
Total	41,863,103	933,828	2.2	562,004	60.2	100.0

Source: AUI Policy Research, December 15, 1980.
Note: No data on the number of PLOTE students or the number served are available for the city of Chicago.

Table 4A-2
Hispanic Enrollment by State, All Districts

State	Enrollment	Number of PLOTEs	Percentage PLOTEs	Number Served	Percentage Served	Percentage Share of Total PLOTEs
Texas	721,374	250,212	34.7	140,318	56.1	34.0
California	840,127	209,376	24.9	149,395	71.4	28.4
New York	333,355	90,439	27.1	63,968	70.7	12.3
New Jersey	99,026	35,673	36.0	21,702	60.8	4.8
Arizona	111,251	26,825	24.1	14,540	54.2	3.6
Florida	100,426	23,062	23.0	13,960	60.5	3.1
New Mexico	114,173	18,320	16.0	9,562	52.2	2.5
Massachusetts	27,795	14,664	52.8	9,013	61.5	2.0
Connecticut	28,657	12,433	43.4	7,965	64.1	1.7
Illinois	113,468	7,455	6.6	4,986	66.9	1.0
Michigan	31,686	6,937	21.9	4,529	65.3	0.9
Pennsylvania	27,547	6,355	23.1	4,743	74.6	0.9
Colorado	80,233	4,202	5.2	3,329	79.2	0.6
Washington	21,680	3,769	17.4	1,911	50.7	0.5
Ohio	20,878	3,265	15.6	1,752	53.7	0.4
Wisconsin	10,176	2,375	23.3	1,707	71.9	0.3
Oregon	9,749	2,332	23.9	1,121	48.1	0.3
Indiana	14,052	2,089	14.9	859	41.1	0.3
Idaho	7,223	2,035	28.2	1,149	56.5	0.3
Louisiana	6,159	1,763	28.6	680	38.6	0.2
Virginia	5,575	1,543	27.7	975	63.2	0.2
Oklahoma	8,596	1,439	16.7	437	30.4	0.2
Utah	12,217	1,161	9.5	556	47.9	0.2
Kansas	10,393	1,152	11.1	499	43.3	0.2
Rhode Island	2,752	1,111	40.4	636	57.3	0.2
Maryland	6,419	1,009	15.7	89	88.2	0.1
Minnesota	5,668	912	16.1	376	41.2	0.1
Nevada	6,631	869	13.1	668	76.9	0.1
District of Columbia	1,244	822	66.1	690	83.9	0.1

Georgia	2,324	522	22.5	287	55.0	0.1
Iowa	3,701	490	13.3	338	68.9	0.1
Delaware	1,562	369	23.6	307	83.3	0.1
Nebraska	5,166	316	6.1	99	31.3	0.0
Missouri	4,549	313	6.9	111	35.5	0.0
North Carolina	1,890	259	13.7	108	41.8	0.0
Wyoming	5,316	234	4.4	62	26.3	0.0
Alaska	1,098	129	11.8	104	80.4	0.0
North Dakota	534	109	20.4	1	0.9	0.0
Tennessee	874	101	11.6	36	35.3	0.0
New Hampshire	449	91	20.2	46	50.6	0.0
Alabama	502	64	12.7	9	14.1	0.0
Arkansas	947	62	6.6	5	8.1	0.0
South Carolina	816	57	7.0	27	47.4	0.0
West Virginia	467	51	10.9	6	11.8	0.0
Montana	1,440	50	3.5	22	43.2	0.0
Mississippi	501	36	7.2	2	5.6	0.0
South Dakota	419	29	7.0	12	42.3	0.0
Kentucky	525	27	5.1	4	13.4	0.0
Maine	277	19	6.8	0	0.0	0.0
Hawaii	11,600	7	0.1	7	100.0	0.0
Vermont	56	6	9.9	0	0.0	0.0
Total	2,823,547	736,940	26.1	464,511	63.0	100.0

Source: AUI Policy Research, December 15, 1980.

Note: No data on PLOTE students or PLOTE students served are available for the city of Chicago.

Table 4A-3
Asian Enrollment by State, All Districts

State	Enrollment	Number of PLOTEs	Percentage PLOTEs	Number Served	Percentage Served	Percentage Share of Total PLOTEs
California	196,890	34,832	17.7	18,461	53.0	40.0
New York	45,910	8,223	17.9	5,268	64.1	9.4
Texas	16,924	4,196	24.8	1,603	38.2	4.8
Virginia	12,448	3,576	28.7	2,568	71.8	4.1
New Jersey	16,554	3,322	20.1	1,707	51.4	3.8
Washington	19,207	2,893	15.1	1,911	66.0	3.3
Louisiana	3,844	2,459	64.0	979	39.8	2.8
Massachusetts	8,303	2,359	28.4	998	42.3	2.7
Illinois	22,228	2,260	10.2	1,296	57.3	2.6
Maryland	11,389	2,117	18.6	1,780	84.1	2.4
Florida	8,811	1,964	22.3	634	32.3	2.3
Michigan	10,745	1,570	14.6	674	42.9	1.8
Hawaii	117,585	1,472	1.3	1,466	99.6	1.7
Pennsylvania	10,143	1,434	14.1	845	58.9	1.6
Minnesota	6,205	1,225	19.7	606	49.5	1.4
Colorado	6,265	1,205	19.2	945	78.4	1.4
Utah	3,112	839	27.0	522	62.2	1.0
Arizona	4,790	709	14.8	327	46.2	0.8
Connecticut	3,813	691	18.1	230	33.3	0.8
Oregon	7,135	690	9.7	358	51.8	0.8
Oklahoma	3,597	683	19.0	478	69.9	0.8
Georgia	3,323	679	20.4	404	59.5	0.8
Iowa	2,728	678	24.8	382	56.3	0.8
Kansas	3,633	619	17.0	288	46.6	0.7
Ohio	8,450	567	6.7	105	18.6	0.7
Missouri	4,707	566	12.0	132	23.3	0.7
Wisconsin	3,924	516	13.2	238	46.1	0.6
Tennessee	2,134	487	22.8	226	46.3	0.6
North Carolina	2,971	437	14.7	190	43.5	0.5

District of Columbia	775	406	52.4	282	69.5	0.5
Indiana	3,961	325	8.2	106	32.7	0.4
Rhode Island	1,187	323	27.2	251	77.6	0.4
Nebraska	1,451	310	21.4	143	45.9	0.4
Alaska	1,612	276	17.1	227	82.4	0.3
Nevada	2,367	270	11.4	239	88.6	0.3
New Mexico	1,444	240	16.6	199	82.8	0.3
Alabama	1,116	239	21.4	155	64.9	0.3
Kentucky	1,347	229	17.0	95	41.5	0.3
South Carolina	1,975	209	10.6	47	22.5	0.2
Arkansas	1,194	204	17.1	38	18.7	0.2
Mississippi	920	191	20.8	111	57.9	0.2
West Virginia	1,063	108	10.1	7	6.2	0.1
South Dakota	515	101	19.6	54	53.8	0.1
Maine	563	78	13.8	29	37.4	0.1
Montana	784	76	9.6	19	25.1	0.1
Idaho	1,262	70	5.5	25	35.6	0.1
North Dakota	495	50	10.1	24	47.8	0.1
Delaware	756	32	4.3	11	34.0	0.0
New Hampshire	404	25	6.2	14	54.9	0.0
Wyoming	434	23	5.4	11	46.6	0.0
Vermont	224	10	4.3	2	25.9	0.0
Total	593,614	87,064	14.7	47,709	54.8	100.0

Source: AUI Policy Research, December 15, 1980.

Note: No data on PLOTE students or PLOTE students served is available for the city of Chicago.

Table 4A-4
American Indian Enrollment by State, All Districts

State	Enrollment	Number of PLOTEs	Percentage PLOTEs	Number Served	Percentage Served	Percentage Share of Total PLOTEs
Arizona	33,556	11,212	33.4	4,218	37.6	40.3
New Mexico	22,436	9,220	41.1	3,739	40.6	33.1
Alaska	19,277	1,726	9.0	972	56.3	6.2
Utah	5,307	1,654	31.2	909	55.0	5.9
Montana	10,954	1,488	13.6	710	47.7	5.4
Oklahoma	64,525	599	0.9	66	11.1	2.2
Louisiana	3,777	475	12.6	57	12.0	1.7
South Dakota	8,501	304	3.6	0	0.0	1.1
Texas	4,219	302	7.2	56	18.7	1.1
California	40,421	239	0.6	95	39.6	0.9
Florida	1,500	140	9.3	8	5.7	0.5
Ohio	2,070	58	2.8	14	23.7	0.2
Minnesota	10,063	57	0.6	2	4.3	0.2
Mississippi	346	52	15.1	0	0.0	0.2
Michigan	16,132	48	0.3	9	17.7	0.2
Nebraska	2,096	34	1.6	2	6.0	0.1
Washington	16,180	32	0.2	28	86.7	0.1
New York	5,922	30	0.5	3	10.0	0.1
Idaho	2,944	26	0.9	0	0.0	0.1
Arkansas	1,101	21	1.9	0	0.0	0.1
Colorado	2,537	9	0.4	4	40.0	0.0
Illinois	2,178	8	0.4	0	0.0	0.0
Nevada	2,548	8	0.3	4	50.0	0.0
Maryland	1,524	7	0.5	7	100.0	0.0
Oregon	7,254	7	0.1	9	133.3	0.0
Connecticut	1,378	6	0.5	0	0.0	0.0
Virginia	857	6	0.7	2	33.3	0.0
Massachusetts	816	6	0.8	0	0.0	0.0
Georgia	547	6	1.1	2	33.3	0.0

Tennessee	337	6	1.8	0	0.0	0.0
New Jersey	863	5	0.6	2	40.0	0.0
Pennsylvania	1,034	5	0.4	3	66.7	0.0
Wyoming	1,125	4	0.4	0	0.0	0.0
Kansas	2,989	4	0.1	0	0.0	0.0
Missouri	1,101	3	0.3	0	0.0	0.0
District of Columbia	26	2	7.7	0	0.0	0.0
Iowa	1,515	1	0.1	0	0.0	0.0
New Hampshire	83	1	1.3	0	0.0	0.0
Alabama	839	1	0.1	0	0.0	0.0
South Carolina	828	1	0.1	4	400.0	0.0
North Carolina	16,568	1	0.0	0	0.0	0.0
Kentucky	191	1	0.5	0	0.0	0.0
Hawaii	387	0	0.0	0	—	0.0
Wisconsin	8,635	0	0.0	0	—	0.0
Indiana	706	0	0.0	0	—	0.0
Rhode Island	329	0	0.0	0	—	0.0
West Virginia	159	0	0.0	0	—	0.0
Maine	595	0	0.0	0	—	0.0
North Dakota	5,055	0	0.0	0	—	0.0
Delaware	169	0	0.0	0	—	0.0
Vermont	146	0	0.0	0	—	0.0
Total	334,643	27,816	8.3	10,924	39.3	100.0

Source: AUI Policy Research, December 15, 1980.

Note: No data on PLOTE students or PLOTE students served are available for the city of Chicago.

Table 4A-5
Other Enrollment by State, All Districts

State	Enrollment	Number of PLOTEs	Percentage PLOTEs	Number Served	Percentage Served	Percentage Share of Total PLOTEs
New York	2,650,748	18,054	0.7	8,613	47.7	22.0
California	3,018,942	12,614	0.4	6,108	48.4	15.4
Massachusetts	995,974	10,778	1.1	5,492	51.0	13.1
Connecticut	535,112	5,335	1.0	1,306	24.5	6.5
New Jersey	1,183,625	5,331	0.5	3,073	57.6	6.5
Michigan	1,852,824	3,953	0.2	2,766	70.0	4.8
Rhode Island	161,765	3,646	2.3	1,500	41.1	4.4
Florida	1,402,548	3,326	0.2	948	28.5	4.1
Texas	2,066,457	2,097	0.1	526	25.1	2.6
Louisiana	803,448	1,690	0.2	643	38.0	2.1
Illinois	1,937,489	1,645	0.1	741	45.0	2.0
Maine	219,219	1,530	0.7	958	62.6	1.9
Ohio	2,032,554	1,249	0.1	536	42.9	1.5
Maryland	799,998	1,199	0.1	856	71.4	1.5
Virginia	1,035,461	1,121	0.1	667	59.5	1.4
Pennsylvania	1,980,783	1,009	0.1	743	73.7	1.2
Indiana	1,090,258	874	0.1	90	10.3	1.1
Oregon	427,203	763	0.2	434	56.8	0.9
Arizona	358,489	554	0.2	254	45.9	0.7
Colorado	459,977	551	0.1	280	50.9	0.7
Washington	709,861	506	0.1	409	80.9	0.6
Utah	300,143	489	0.2	192	39.2	0.6
Minnesota	754,854	313	0.0	168	53.8	0.4
Wisconsin	849,421	284	0.0	126	44.3	0.3
Iowa	546,391	282	0.1	232	82.5	0.3
New Hampshire	157,883	278	0.2	75	27.1	0.3
North Carolina	1,148,879	267	0.0	147	55.0	0.3
Kansas	406,257	252	0.1	127	50.5	0.3
District of Columbia	106,858	246	0.2	208	84.6	0.3

State						
Georgia	1,061,477	222	0.0	125	56.1	0.3
Missouri	873,309	199	0.0	31	15.6	0.2
New Mexico	135,515	193	0.1	90	46.6	0.2
Oklahoma	510,648	168	0.0	59	35.0	0.2
Tennessee	860,184	112	0.0	33	29.2	0.1
North Dakota	91,030	110	0.1	4	3.5	0.1
Nevada	134,267	107	0.1	35	33.1	0.1
South Dakota	115,951	106	0.1	70	65.4	0.1
South Carolina	634,955	93	0.0	26	28.0	0.1
Alabama	759,471	84	0.0	47	56.0	0.1
Kentucky	684,297	63	0.0	6	8.9	0.1
Alaska	64,320	59	0.1	26	44.3	0.1
Idaho	183,116	56	0.0	26	46.1	0.1
Nebraska	246,725	53	0.0	16	29.4	0.1
Vermont	79,750	45	0.1	20	44.7	0.1
Montana	128,265	37	0.0	18	50.0	0.0
West Virginia	395,931	22	0.0	2	10.7	0.0
Mississippi	485,706	16	0.0	1	6.3	0.0
Arkansas	439,054	14	0.0	3	21.1	0.0
Wyoming	82,799	8	0.0	3	38.4	0.0
Delaware	111,077	4	0.0	0	0.0	0.0
Hawaii	40,030	0	0.0	0	—	0.0
Total	38,111,299	82,008	0.2	38,860	47.4	100.0

Source: AUI Policy Research, December 15, 1980.

Note: No data on PLOTE students or PLOTE students served are available for the city of Chicago.

Notes

1. That survey was conducted for OCR by Killalea Associates, Inc. The analysis files for the current study were built by Decision Resources from the Killalea data base.

2. While preliminary data tapes are available for the 1980 OCR survey, they do not yet contain the district sampling weights that would allow data aggregation across districts.

3. The allowed modifications include magnet schools and itinerant bilingual teachers serving several schools, both alternatives presumably being less expensive than providing bilingual teachers for entire classes.

4. Analyses were also done for the ten Department of Education regions. Not surprisingly the regions that include California, Texas, and New York (regions 9, 6, and 2) have the largest numbers of PLOTE students. The largest concentrations of American Indian PLOTE students are also in these regions—in Arizona (region 9) and New Mexico (region 6).

References

Milne, Ann M., and Gombert, Jan M. 1981. "Students with a Primary Language Other than English: Distribution and Service Rates." Report prepared for the Office of Planning, Budget, and Evaluation, U.S. Department of Education, under contract no. 300-80-0778, September 4.

O'Malley, J. Michael. 1981. *Children's English and Services Study: Language Minority Children with Limited English Proficiency in the United States.* Rosslyn, Va.: InterAmerica Associates.

**Part II
Local-Policy Issues**

5

Case Studies of Delivery and Cost of Bilingual Education

Margaret Carpenter-Huffman
and *Marta K. Samulon*

This chapter describes the current delivery and cost of bilingual programs in six school districts. We undertook the study to help the Department of Education estimate the cost of regulations proposed in August 1980 for bilingual programs.

Several researchers have estimated that bilingual programs add to the cost of education between $150 and $300 per student with limited English proficiency (Alston 1977; Cardenas, Bernas, and Kean 1976a, 1976b; Garcia 1977; Guss Zamora et al. 1979; Robledo et al. 1978). School districts, in contrast, report added costs per student ranging up to $1,000.[1] Our study provided an opportunity to discover the basis for the discrepancy; resolution of this issue would clearly be useful to the Department of Education in its deliberations concerning its future bilingual-education policies.

Scope and Objectives of this Study

Our immediate objective was to obtain better information for the Department of Education to use in estimating the cost of the proposed rules. This information would be better in two senses: it would be empirical, rather than hypothetical, and it would capture some of the variety in provision of services that we suspect exists in the nation's school districts.[2]

During visits to local school districts, we examined the possibility of estimating the effects of the rules on the cost of education in these districts. If district staff could identify the number of students who fall into each of the categories defined by the rules and if we could establish the added cost of bilingual programs now provided in the given districts, we could roughly estimate the effects of the rules on cost by extrapolating the added cost to the newly identified student populations.

To a large extent, the resources available for the study constrained its objectives. Only three months elapsed between initiation of the study and oral presentation of preliminary findings; two consultants helped us structure and administer the on-site interviews. Despite these time constraints, we explored fundamental questions about the delivery and cost of bilingual education and examined a broad range of issues posed by the Education Department.

Primarily, we wanted to answer several questions fundamental to federal policy in bilingual education:

1. How does provision of bilingual education vary among school districts?
2. Why do these variations arise?
3. How do these variations affect cost?

Our findings in these areas may not represent the situation in the nation's school districts as a whole, but they illustrate the linkages between the school-district environment, procedures for delivering services, and cost. Our findings provide a firmer basis for further work by the Department of Education than would the usual procedure that estimates a cost per student by merely dividing the funds earmarked for bilingual programs by the number of students these funds are purported to serve. Such an approach not only is based on erroneous assumptions but also provides no insight into what services the funds are providing and why. Without such insights, there is no way to know whether the costs incurred by one school district are appropriate to another.

Much of the work reported here was aimed at gaining an understanding of the linkages just described, which is valuable in itself. This understanding also is necessary for establishing economic cost, which measures the value to the nation of the resources required to provide bilingual programs. By *resources* we mean the teachers, materials, administrators, and other factors that together provide the required service. Thus, we built costs from resources, as did the cost analysis of the Department of Education (Department of Education 1980b).

This study focused on determining the processes and costs of language-assistance instruction because instruction is the main purpose of education, instruction usually consumes the bulk of educational resources, and uncertainties about the added cost of instruction were displayed in an earlier cost analysis of the Department of Education. We also collected information on related functions, such as staff development, purchase of materials, and program administration, and on a variety of other issues surrounding the proposed rules. The most important of these is the availability of qualified teachers.

Selection of Sample Sites

We selected six school districts of various sizes, locations, program types, and enrollments of students with limited English proficiency. Because of the short time available for the study, we could not visit a nationally representative sample of school districts and included no districts located in the Midwest or East. Further, since we wanted to learn as much as possible about the delivery and cost of bilingual programs, we visited no districts lacking any special services for students with limited English proficiency.

To ensure the availability of relevant data, we chose districts from those nominated by Rand Corporation colleagues who were familiar with the districts' programs and characteristics. Before selecting a district for inclusion in the sample, we interviewed the bilingual-education director over the telephone to get descriptions of the district's enrollment and special services for students with limited English proficiency.

We visited districts in California, Texas, and Washington. They included two small rural districts, one medium-size suburban district, and three large urban districts (table 5-1). The bilingual programs in the sample sites serve speakers of Spanish as well as Chinese, Vietnamese, Japanese, Korean, Laotian, Samoan, Russian, Arabic, and Filipino dialects. Enrollment ranges from fewer than 3,000 students to more than 150,000.

Table 5-2 shows the percentage of students in various ethnic categories at the sample sites. Four districts (A, C, E, and F) have significant black populations, ranging from 21 percent to 75 percent of the total enrollment. In these same districts, Anglo enrollments are declining, so minority enrollments are increasing proportionately. The Asian populations in districts A, C, and E include large influxes of Indochinese refugees.

Although two small rural districts, B and D, have significant American Indian populations (25 percent and 15 percent of enrollment), the Indian students are not served by the bilingual program. The Indians in these districts object to having their language taught in school, since it is closely tied to the tribal religion. The bilingual programs in districts B and D serve Hispanics, most of whom are children of migrant workers.

Table 5-1
Enrollment, Type, and Language Groups Served for Sample School Districts

Enrollment	Type	Language Groups	Number of Districts
Under 5,000	Rural	Spanish	2
10,000-50,000	Suburban	Spanish, Vietnamese	1
Over 50,000	Urban	Spanish, Vietnamese	1
Over 50,000	Urban	Spanish, Chinese, Filipino, Vietnamese, Korean, Samoan, Laotian, Japanese	1
Over 50,000	Urban	Spanish, Chinese, Filipino, Vietnamese, Japanese, Korean, Russian, Arabic	1

Table 5-2
Ethnic Composition of Students at Sample Sites
(percentage)

District	White	Black	Hispanic	Asian and Pacific Islanders	American Indian and Other
A	19	26	16	30	9
B	40	0	30	5	25
C	60	21	4	12	3
D	40	1	43	1	15
E	27	45	26	2	0
F	4	75	20	1	0

Data-Collection Method

District superintendents or bilingual-program directors approved our visits. Once in the district, we first interviewed central office staff, including district superintendents, persons in the budget office, and administrators of bilingual programs. We also interviewed counselors instructional consultants, and other support staff who work with language-assistance programs. We collected budgets, school plans, and program descriptions to supplement interview data.

Rand staff drew a random sample of schools offering special services to language minorities. Then we randomly selected at least one type of teacher to interview from among the types of teachers providing services at each of the schools selected. The types of teachers identified were ESL, bilingual, resource, and classroom teachers. Rand staff also interviewed the principal and aides at each school. During the interview with the principal, we obtained general information about the school. With teachers, we reviewed daily schedules and recorded their estimates of the number of minutes of instruction provided to students proficient in English and students with limited English proficiency. We also recorded the teachers' education and experience.[3]

Programs for Language-Minority Students
at Sample Sites

The short time available for the study prohibited much classroom observation. Instead we conducted extensive interviews with school staff members to obtain descriptions of both the organization and content of instruction for students with limited English proficiency. We reviewed daily class schedules and recorded the number of minutes per day during which these students receive instruction in various subjects. We also noted whether instruction is delivered in English, bilingually, or with bilingual support. As a result, we could calculate the percentage of the instructional day during which these students received instruction in various subjects, according to the language modes used. We recognize that teacher self-reports may not be completely reliable; however, our findings are consistent among the sample sites and are intuitively reasonable, as the discussion will demonstrate.

Instruction for Students with Limited English Proficiency

Curriculum: In the sample districts, subjects available to students with limited English proficiency include ESL, formal instruction about the primary, non-English language, and instruction in the district's typical curriculum (academic and other subjects). Instruction is given in English, bilingually, or in English with bilingual support.

ESL is instruction about English for people who speak little or no English. It focuses on oral language development, introduction to reading, writing and reading improvement, and English vocabulary. Courses are usually taught by monolingual English speakers.

Instruction about a non-English language is formal instruction about Chinese, Spanish, or other primary languages dealt with in the districts' bilingual programs. Bilingual teachers usually teach these courses.

Academic subjects include mathematics, science, language arts, social studies, and health. These subjects may be taught bilingually, in English with bilingual support, or in English only.

Other subjects include music, art, physical education, class opening and closing periods, typing, and the like. Although these subjects may be taught bilingually or in English with bilingual support, they are usually taught in English only.

Bilingual instruction is delivered in a number of ways in the sample districts. The classroom teacher may teach a concept in English and repeat the instruction in the primary language (or vice-versa). Or instruction may be conducted entirely in English for one class period and in the primary language for another class period. Or a teacher may conduct a class entirely in English for half the week and in the primary language for the rest of the week. Bilingual instruction may be provided in either a self-contained classroom or a pull-out program.

Bilingual support is provided by bilingual aides or teachers under the direction of a classroom teacher. These instructors use the students' primary language to help them with concepts presented in English; they confer with the classroom teacher to determine the students' greatest need.

In some settings, bilingual support is provided on a pull-out basis, that is, students are removed from the regular classroom for their bilingual instruction. In others, a bilingual aide or the classroom teacher provides bilingual support within the classroom by grouping students according to English ability. After aides are presented in English, the teacher or the aide explains the ideas to groups of students who speak little or no English in the students' primary language.

Monolingual English instruction is delivered using only the English language.

Organization of Instruction: Districts use several arrangements to deliver instruction to language-minority students: self-contained classes, part-time, pull-out programs, and newcomer centers. Among the factors affecting instructional approach are staff availability and the size and concentration of students in a particular language group. Faced with shortages of staff able to teach in a certain language or with small concentrations of students with a certain language, districts are likely to use part-time, pull-out instruction. In some districts, students whose English is severely limited are more likely to be placed in self-contained classes that provide bilingual instruction; students with some English proficiency are more likely to receive part-time language assistance. Districts with declining enrollments and changing ethnic compositions are more likely to use part-time, pull-out programs to provide services to students with limited English proficiency as a way of responding to the demand for bilingual teachers without reducing existing staff, which is largely monolingual English speaking.

Bilingual, self-contained classes are usually found in kindergarten through grade 6 in our sample. Each class is conducted by a bilingual, biliterate teacher, who is a member of the teaching staff. Both ESL and formal instruction about the non-English language are provided in the classroom.

Instruction is given bilingually or with bilingual support. That is, the teacher either delivers instruction in two languages, or the teacher or a bilingual instructional aide clarifies concepts in the students' primary language after instruction is delivered in English.

Students who are proficient in English are usually included in self-contained, bilingual classes. The district's ability to integrate students in these classes depends on district enrollment trends and the non-English language of the bilingual class. The shortage of Anglo students forced some districts to integrate students with limited English proficiency with other minority students who are expected to provide the English role model for their less-proficient peers.

Bilingual, self-contained classes at the elementary level are available in five of the districts we visited. The policy of the sixth district, district C, is to serve language minorities with other approaches.

As table 5-3 illustrates, self-contained classroom programs in the districts studied share a number of similarities. Students in self-contained classes receive approximately one period per day of formal instruction about their primary language. They also receive one period of formal ESL instruction in addition to other English language-arts instruction (spelling, reading, handwriting) during the day.

The bulk of bilingual instruction deals with academic subjects. Total instruction delivered bilingually varies from 23 percent of the day in district F (instruction in academics only) to 71 percent of the day in district E (48 percent for academics, 23 percent for other subjects). Subjects taught with bilingual support may supplement the bilingual instruction students receive in self-contained classes. Bilingual support is also usually provided for instruction in academic subjects; this support ranges from 8 percent of the instructional day in district B to 20 percent in district D.

In the sample districts, more self-contained classes are provided for Spanish-speaking students than for those from other primary-language groups because there is a shortage of bilingual personnel who speak the other languages.

Bilingual team teaching is used in districts A, B, and D to compensate for a shortage of fully trained bilingual teachers, usually for elementary students. Students are grouped in the classroom according to English and primary-language ability. During ESL or primary-language instruction, the teacher may exchange groups of children with another member of the teaching staff. The schedules of children who are in team-teaching programs appear similar to those of children in bilingual, self-contained classes.

Table 5-3
Instructional Time in Self-Contained Classrooms for Elementary-Level Students with Limited English Proficiency, by Subject Area
(percentage)

			Academic Subjects			Other Subjects		
District	ESL	Primary Language	Bilingual	Monolingual English	English with Bilingual Support	Bilingual	Monolingual English	English with Bilingual Support
A	14	15	28	6	18	0	19	0
B	8	16	51	0	8	17	0	0
C[a]								
D	8	9	20	14	20	18	4	7
E	19	10	48	0	0	23	0	0
F	19	23	23	13	10	0	12	0

[a]Mode not available in this district.

Pull-out programs place students with limited English proficiency in classes conducted by English-speaking classroom teachers who are not necessarily bilingual or biliterate in the students' language. Usually students proficient in English are also enrolled in the class. Children needing ESL or bilingual support in academics are removed from class ("pulled out") for part of the day and taught by special staff. Students in this type of program receive little or no instruction about their primary language either in class or during pull-out, as shown in table 5-4. In most of the districts the bulk of these students' time is spent in a monolingual English class. In the five districts for which there is information about this option, students with limited English proficiency received between 18 percent and 85 percent of their instruction entirely in English.

In general, students receiving language-assistance instruction on a pull-out basis receive much less instruction of this type than do students served in self-contained classes. Instruction delivered bilingually to students in part-time programs ranges from none of the day in districts A and F to 38 percent in district D (20 percent in academic subjects and 18 percent in other subjects). Bilingual support in pull-out programs ranges from none of the students' day in districts C, E, and F to 27 percent in district D.

In the five districts for which we obtained information on pull-out services, ESL instruction is provided during 7 to 15 percent of the students' day. In three of these districts, formal ESL instruction amounts to 10 percent or less of the students' day. In district E, students receive instruction about their primary language during 17 percent of the day. This is not typical of the other districts in the sample.[4] Pull-out instruction is used for formal instruction about a primary language or for bilingual instruction in academic subjects, but most often it is used in these districts to teach ESL.

Table 5-4
Instruction Time per Subject Area in Elementary-Level Part-Time or Pull-Out Programs
(percentage)

| District | ESL | Primary Language | Academic Subjects | | | Other Subjects | | |
			Bilingual	Monolingual English	English with Bilingual Support	Bilingual	Monolingual English	English with Bilingual Support
A	7	0	0	51	22	0	20	0
B[a]								
C	10	0	5	67	0	0	18	0
D	8	9	20	14	20	18	4	7
E	15	17	0	54	0	0	14	0
F	15	0	0	59	0	0	26	0

[a]Information on this delivery mode was not available for this district.

Students who speak relatively rare languages for which there is a shortage of bilingual teachers tend to be served by pull-out programs, as are students who are not represented in sufficiently large numbers in a particular school or district to warrant conducting a self-contained class. Students may also be served by pull-out programs because their parents have chosen not to place them in self-contained, bilingual classes.

Pull-out programs enable the districts to use their bilingual staffs more extensively. These programs permit teachers to serve larger numbers of students by providing each student with less instructional time than he or she would receive in a self-contained classroom.

Newcomer centers are provided in districts A and C to cope with an influx of students with limited English proficiency who are recent immigrants to the United States and who are judged to be two or more years below grade level. Classes are composed entirely of newcomers. For this reason, as well as because of fiscal limitations, students must leave these programs after one or two semesters; then they may remain in the bilingual program or move into a regular classroom.

We randomly chose to visit the elementary Spanish newcomer center in district A. The program there provides instruction in ESL and basic skills but no formal instruction about Spanish (table 5-5). Formal ESL is taught during approximately 23 percent of the students' day. Classroom instruction is supplemented by visits to a language lab. The rest of the students' day is spent in instruction in basic skills and social studies in programs especially designed for newcomers.

Table 5-5
Instructional Time per Subject Area at Newcomer Centers
(percentage)

District	ESL	Primary Language	Academic Subjects			Other Subjects		
			Bilingual	Monolingual English	English with Bilingual Support	Bilingual	Monolingual English	English with Bilingual Support
Elementary level								
A	23	0	0	0	60	0	17	0
C	12	0	0	51	24	0	13	0
Secondary level								
A	46	0	17	5	13	0	19	0
C	17	0	17	33	0	0	33	0

Teachers in this newcomer center said that they try to teach in English and use Spanish as needed to convey ideas the students may have missed. Approximately 60 percent of the students' basic-skills instruction is delivered in English with bilingual support. About 17 percent of the students' day is spent receiving English-language instruction in other subjects.

Students at Newcomer High School in district A usually receive intense ESL instruction—an average of 46 percent of daily instructional time. Approximately 30 percent of daily instruction is delivered bilingually or with bilingual support.

The newcomer centers in district C are part-time programs for both elementary and secondary students, who spend one-third to one-half of their school day in special classes designated for newcomers (table 5-5). About 32 percent of the district's students with limited English proficiency are served in these centers. Elementary newcomer center classes include one period of ESL and two of basic-skills instruction, delivered with bilingual support. At the secondary level, approximately 66 percent of the students' instruction is delivered in English because the students are mainstreamed into a regular secondary-school program. Half of that time is spent in classes not requiring a high degree of English comprehension—arts, crafts, physical education, or shop, for instance.

Because of its part-time nature, district C's program is less intensive than district A's. Program staff indicated that because of a shortage of spaces to accommodate all newcomers, some of these students are placed in regular high-school programs, at best receiving some ESL and tutorial assistance.

The shortage of trained personnel also affects services to newcomers. In district C, one part-time newcomer center for Laotian students was headed by a bilingual teacher whose languages are English, Spanish, and Filipino. He communicated with his students in English. The other person staffing the center was also bilingual, but in Tagalog and English. A third teacher was a monolingual English speaker. A Laotian tutor was available for some translating.

Services to Secondary-School Students with Limited English Proficiency: We found secondary students with limited English proficiency to be less evenly and less well served than those enrolled in primary schools in our sample. We observed large variations in the amount of bilingual instruction available to these students, ranging from none to 38 percent of instructional time (table 5-6). Special academic courses for these students are essentially unavailable in three districts.

ESL instruction is available at the secondary level in all six districts. ESL courses usually substitute for typical English or language-arts classes and account for 17 percent to 25 percent of the students' daily instructional time.

Table 5-6
Instructional Time per Subject Area in Secondary-Level Language-Assistance Services
(percentage)

			Academic Subjects			Other Subjects		
District	ESL	Primary Language	Bilingual	Monolingual English	English with Bilingual Support	Bilingual	Monolingual English	English with Bilingual Support
A	25	0	38	17	0	0	20	0
B	17	0	5	78	0	0	0	0
C	17	0	33	17	0	0	33	0
D[a]								
E	17	0	3	40	0	0	40	0
F	17	3	0	63	0	0	17	0

[a]Time was not adequate to obtain data on this program.

As table 5-6 indicates, we found little formal instruction about the students' primary language. In district F, formal instruction about Spanish is provided for one class period per week on the average; in four districts, students receive no instruction about their primary language.

Teachers in secondary schools described special problems in serving their students with limited English proficiency. They frequently indicated that it is difficult to assemble a full class of students speaking a common language. The need to disperse students for racial and ethnic integration intensifies this problem. Staff teaching a diverse group of students gear their courses to an ESL, instead of a bilingual, approach.

The need to serve a variety of students produces some innovative approaches. We observed a science class taught by a monolingual English teacher to students from a variety of language groups, including Vietnamese, Chinese, and Filipino. Each group of students gathered around an instructional aide who spoke their language. The classroom teacher presented the core ideas of the lesson in English, and each aide translated the ideas into the group's native language.

A bilingual math class in district A was taught by a teacher fluent in Cantonese and English. His students were Chinese, Vietnamese, and other Southeast Asians. The teacher indicated he taught most of the lesson in English and occasionally used Cantonese to explain certain concepts. Students in the class who were fluent in both Cantonese and Vietnamese translated as necessary for their peers who understood only Vietnamese.

Teacher Assignments and Characteristics

In our analysis of staff characteristics, we categorized the teachers interviewed as regular classroom teachers (who teach monolingual English-speaking classes), bilingual and newcomer-center teachers, and ESL teachers. We found that teachers who work with students with limited English proficiency are generally less experienced than regular classroom teachers (table 5-7). In the sample districts, regular classroom teachers had taught for an average of 15 years, compared with 8.5 years for bilingual classroom teachers and those in newcomer centers. Teachers of ESL are somewhat more experienced, having taught for 12 years on an average. We hypothesize that ESL teachers are drawn from the pool of excess teachers in the sample districts.

The less-experienced teachers in bilingual classrooms and newcomer centers have a higher percentage of master's degrees than do the other teachers in the sample, probably primarily reflecting the recency of requirements for master's degrees for teaching positions.

As one would expect, more teachers in bilingual classrooms and newcomer centers hold bilingual teaching certificates and are fluent in the target language. On the other hand, nearly a fifth of the regular classroom teachers interviewed said that they have bilingual teaching certificates. Thus there is an appreciable population of teachers qualified to provide bilingual services who are not doing so as part of their district's formal program.

A surprisingly high percentage of ESL teachers report that they are fluent in the target language. These teachers often have dual responsibilities as bilingual and ESL teachers in pull-out programs.

Added Cost of Programs at Sample Sites

Past research on the added cost of bilingual programs has defined such cost as the cost of resources that would be purchased with categorical funds to provide services to LEP students with limited English proficiency. The added cost per student has been taken to be the total cost of added resources divided by the number of limited-English-proficient students served. This procedure

Table 5-7
Teacher Assignments, by Teacher Characteristics

Teacher Assignment	Number	Percentage with Master's Degree	Average Years Experience	Percentage Fluent in Target Languages	Percentage with Bilingual Teaching Certificate
Bilingual classroom or newcomer center	62	42	8.5	79	54
ESL instruction	34	27	12	50	5
Regular classroom	39	20	15	14	19

may not estimate economic cost because it may not adequately measure added resources delivered to students with limited English proficiency.

The actual added cost of resources required may be different from the cost of resources added under a categorical program. In most of the school districts visited, for example, teachers in self-contained classrooms are paid less than are teachers in monolingual English classrooms because they are less experienced. Therefore the cost of additional resources, such as instructional aides, is somewhat offset by the lower teacher salaries, and the economic cost is less than the cost of the aides.

The approach used in previous research does not accurately measure resources delivered to students with limited English proficiency because the cost per student has been computed only on the basis of the number of such students. If other students benefit directly or indirectly from the resources added for the students with limited English proficiency, this procedure inflates the added cost per target student.

Procedures for Computing Added Cost

Previous studies of the cost of bilingual programs have been designed to determine the amount of additional funding that would be required to support the establishment or expansion of such programs. This objective is different from ours. Categorical funding usually purchases designated resources, whereas we want to measure the total added cost of resources provided to students with limited English proficiency, regardless of the nature of resources used or of the sources of funds required to purchase them.

Procedures for computing added cost have been developed by several authors (see Fisher 1970:193). In their terminology, bilingual education is an example of joint production because the same set of resources is often used jointly to produce education for both students with limited English proficiency and monolingual English students. Generally all students benefit from added resources, unless special provisions are made to avoid this. For example, the addition of an instructional aide to a classroom changes the mix of resources delivered to all students in that classroom. In some classrooms, the aide may work mainly with the students with limited English proficiency, thereby giving the teacher more time for the monolingual English students. Alternatively the aide may work with only a subset of the students with limited English proficiency for most of the day, or both teacher and aide may work with the whole class simultaneously. We saw wide variations in the use of aides during our site visits. Even time-and-motion studies would not tell precisely how to apportion teachers and aides among both types of students because the interactions between teachers and aides often affect both categories of students simultaneously.

Therefore, the only defensible approach to take in measuring the cost of added resources for students with limited English proficiency is to spread the added cost of the aide over all of the students in the classroom.

Beyond the classroom, most educational services, such as central administration, support instructional services for all of the students in the district, regardless of their membership in special populations. Therefore the added cost per student of bilingual education should be estimated in this way:

1. Estimate the total cost of education, including the bilingual program, for all students.
2. Divide the total cost by the total number of students to obtain the cost per student.
3. Estimate what the total cost of education would be for the same number of students without the bilingual program (the baseline cost).
4. Divide the baseline cost by the number of students.
5. Subtract the cost per student obtained in step 4 from the cost per student obtained in step 2.

The problem with this formulation is that we cannot perform step 3 from empirical information; that is, we cannot establish what the total cost of education at the sample site would be without the bilingual program because we cannot match any of our sites with a site that is the same except that it has no bilingual program. Even a comparison of the situation at a given site before and after the bilingual program would run the risk of being confounded by other changes such as declining enrollment or implementation of other new programs. The absence of a bona-fide baseline cost poses an especially important problem for determining the average teacher salary and the average class size for instruction without the bilingual program.

Establishing Total Cost of Bilingual Programs

To establish the total cost of bilingual programs, we conducted the cost analysis in five steps:

1. Define the functions to be costed.
2. Determine how these functions are performed by the sample school districts.
3. Identify resource requirements by function in the sample school districts.
4. Estimate resource costs by function in the sample school districts.
5. Estimate added costs of bilingual education in the sample school districts.

The functions important to the delivery of bilingual education are these:

1. Instruction: Bilingual instruction or bilingual support in academic sub-
    jects, instruction about the student's primary language, ESL instruc-
    tion, development and purchase of instructional materials and equip-
    ment, other instructional activities (such as field trips).
2. Student identification and assessment for program placement.
3. Staff development.
4. Program administration.
5. Other support activities, such as parental involvement and student
    counseling.

We carried out the full analysis for the cost of instruction. We also examined identification and assessment, staff development, and program administration in as much detail as time allowed. Although development of instructional materials and other activities such as parental involvement also
are important, in the sample school districts they were minor compared with
the functions on which we concentrated. Therefore we relied largely on
budgetary figures to obtain estimates of the costs of these functions.

Added Cost of Instruction

The cost of instruction is largely the cost of instructional personnel. Therefore we concentrated on establishing this cost.

Estimating Total Cost of Instructional Personnel: To obtain sufficient data
on instructional personnel for cost analysis, we visited as many schools as
possible in each school district. This was necessary because local specifications for use of instructional and personnel are too general for cost analysis
and because the details of personnel use may vary widely among the schools
in each district.
    At each school we obtained the following information:

1. The total enrollment and the enrollment of students with limited English
    proficiency.
2. The total number of classrooms and the number of bilingual-program
    classrooms.
3. The total number of students and the number of students with limited
    English proficiency enrolled in bilingual-program classrooms.
4. The number of instructional aides provided for students with limited
    English proficiency whether or not they are in bilingual-program class-
    rooms.

5. The number of pull-out teachers providing part-time instruction for the bilingual program.
6. The total number of students with limited English proficiency each pull-out teacher teaches, the number of students in each pull-out group, and the length of time each group is taught.
7. Typical schedules for students with limited English proficiency and monolingual English students at the secondary level.
8. The number of periods that bilingual-program teachers teach at the secondary level and the number of students in each class period.

These data permitted a determination of how many of what types of instructional personnel in the bilingual program are provided to how many students with limited English proficiency and to how many students proficient in English, in cases in which the latter are instructed by the same personnel as the former. The data also permitted us to compute average class size at the schools visited.

We did not include instructional personnel who provide remedial reading or math to underachieving students, even though many students with limited English proficiency participate in such programs, because these programs arise for reasons other than the students' language background. Because of the tendency of school administrators to assign personnel across the boundaries of categorical programs, we based our judgments about whether a teacher or aide should be excluded or included in the calculation on the basis of what that person was doing rather than on the source of funds to support that person.

Table 5-8 summarizes the use of instructional personnel in the sample school districts. Recall that district C provides no self-contained classrooms

Table 5-8
Use of Instructional Personnel

	Self-Contained Classrooms				Pull-Out Classes			Total
			Students			Students		Students with
District	Teachers	Average Aides per Classroom	Limited English Proficiency	Total	Teachers	Limited English Proficiency	Total	Limited English Proficiency
A	266	0.9	6,400	8,300	115	4,300	4,300	9,900[a]
B	3	1.0	77	100	7	240	270	310[a]
C					77	2,500	2,500	2,500
D	16[b]	0.5	220	420	4	150	280	280[a]
E	280	0.2	8,500	8,500	69	3,000	3,000	11,500
F	63	1.0	1,300	1,900	6	140	140	1,300[a]

[a]Some students in pull-out classes are also in bilingual classrooms.
[b]Team teaching.

for the bilingual program, whereas the majority of students with limited English proficiency in all other districts but B are in such classrooms. Note also that districts A, B, and F have essentially one aide per self-contained classroom, whereas district E has a much lower average.

To compute the total cost of instructional personnel for all students, we needed unit costs—that is, the average salaries (plus fringe benefits) for various types of teachers and aides. We obtained district-wide averages for teacher and aide salaries, plus fringe benefits, from district budget or personnel offices. In most school districts, we estimated average salaries for bilingual, ESL, and resource teachers from data gathered during teacher interviews. In the interviews, we obtained information on teacher education and experience, which, together with salary information, permitted us to compute average teacher salaries by type.

One school district provided a listing of all bilingual and ESL teacher salaries from which we computed the required averages. We compared the average salaries of the teachers we interviewed with the districtwide averages. The average salaries of interviewees were within 5 percent of the districtwide averages for three of the six categories of teachers interviewed. In each of the remaining three categories, we interviewed fewer than five teachers; their salaries were higher than average. To minimize bias in teacher-salary estimates, we used only two teacher groupings in the other school districts so that we would have as many teachers as possible in each group.

Using this information, we first computed the total cost of instructional personnel per student with limited English proficiency by multiplying the unit cost of instructional personnel of each type by the number of personnel of each type and then dividing by the total number of students to whom the instructional personnel are provided.

To determine the added cost of instructional personnel per student with limited English proficiency, we needed to subtract what would be the cost per student of instructional personnel without the bilingual program from the total cost per limited-English-proficient student. Since the baseline figure was not available, we devised special strategies to estimate it.

Estimating Cost of Instructional Personnel with No Bilingual Program: To estimate what the per-student cost of instructional personnel would have been without a bilingual program, we needed to estimate the average teacher salary and the average class size without the program. We assumed that the average teacher salary is the district-wide average. This figure includes the salaries of teachers in the bilingual program, who are generally paid less because they have been hired more recently and have fewer years of teaching experience than other teachers. Although the number of bilingual classroom teachers at several sites is small relative to the total number of teachers, removing their salaries from the computation of the average would have raised the average somewhat. To use this higher average would require an assumption that younger teachers would not have been hired in the same numbers without the bilingual program. Although there is no reason to make such an assumption, we display the results of adopting it in one of the examples to follow.

We also had to make several assumptions to estimate what the average class size would be without the program. The first difficulty arose in trying to determine the average class size for the district as a whole from district data. District figures on the total number of teachers at various levels include music teachers, physical education teachers, and special-education teachers, with the result that apparent class sizes are low. Therefore we estimated average class sizes from data gathered at each school. Class sizes varied significantly among the visited schools, so we had to decide when to use the class size in a given school and when to use the average of all schools visited.

In the examples we consider the computations appropriate to determining the added cost of teachers for students with limited English proficiency in a self-contained classroom and, at the secondary level, in a period of language-assistance instruction. The class size of such bilingual-program classrooms in a given school was usually closer to the overall class size in that school than it was to the average class size in all of the schools visited in the school district. Thus the bilingual-program classroom teacher appeared simply to replace a monolingual English-classroom teacher in that school. Therefore, we used the average class size in that school as the class size without the bilingual program.

To have used the average class size in the school district to compute the per-student cost without the bilingual program would have attributed the cost of school-specific variations in class size to the bilingual program. Although there was no reason to believe that these variations are caused by the presence of students with limited English proficiency in the schools, possibly classroom teachers have been added to the staffs of some schools because of the presence of such students. If this is true, the appropriate class size would be computed by dividing total enrollment by some reduced number of classrooms. To make such a computation, we would have to decide how many bilingual-program classrooms are additional to, and how many are replacements for, monolingual English classrooms. Because we had no evidence that schools have been staffed in this way, not to mention the difficulty in knowing what procedure would be appropriate in each case, we did not attempt this computation. We illustrate the effects of making this assumption in one of the following examples.

In the case of part-time programs—that is, the provision of language-assistance instruction by teachers who remove students with limited English proficiency from self-contained classrooms—we took the class size for instruction without the bilingual program to be simply our estimate of the average class size in the school district. This is because school-level variations in class size probably do not affect the size of pull-out groups.

The relevant cost per student at a given school without the bilingual program depended on the situation being considered. This is proper because it allows us to compensate for variations in the delivery of instruction that do not arise from the bilingual program.

Examples of Computing the Added Cost of Instructional Personnel: The first two of the following three examples are for self-contained classrooms and a pull-out teacher at the elementary level. The third is for a bilingual-program teacher at the secondary level. District A is used for all examples because this district uses a wide variety of approaches for furnishing bilingual education and because the use of a single district avoids confusion arising from variations among districts in teacher salaries.

Self-Contained Classrooms: District A provides bilingual instruction in self-contained classrooms whenever enough students require services and a qualified bilingual teacher is available. This teacher is usually assisted by a bilingual aide.

School 4 in district A instructs 433 students in fourteen classrooms, for an average class size of 30.9. There are 126 students enrolled in four bilingual classrooms. Of these students, 79 are Hispanic students with limited English proficiency. What is added to the cost of instructing these students because they have deficiencies in English? The added cost for delivering bilingual instruction to a student may be determined by:

$$\text{added cost per student} = \frac{(4\,BT + 4A)}{126} - \frac{T}{30.9},$$

where BT = average bilingual-teacher salary, plus fringe benefits, in district A, A = average aide salary, plus fringe benefits, in district A, and T = average teacher salary, plus fringe benefits, in district A.

The first term in the equation measures the cost of instruction for each student in the bilingual classrooms, regardless of whether the student is limited in English proficiency. This procedure is dictated by the joint-production nature of bilingual education. Aides are not included in the computation of the cost of instruction without the bilingual program (the second term) because district A does not provide aides to every classroom.[5] The average teacher salary for the district and the average class size in school 4 were used to estimate the cost of instruction without the bilingual program.

Completing the computation, if BT = \$22,884, A = \$7,535, and T = \$27,377, the added cost per student is \$80 and the total added cost for students with limited English proficiency is $6,320, for a total added cost of $10,080. The total added cost is less than the cost of the salaries for the four aides because the cost of their salaries is largely offset by lower salaries paid to bilingual teachers than to regular classroom teachers.

Now let us consider the effects of varying assumptions about average teacher salary and average class size without the program. Assuming that district A would not have hired an equal number of younger teachers without a bilingual program, we may remove the salaries of the younger teachers from the computation of average salary. The resulting figure is only slightly higher ($28,023) than the value of T because bilingual teachers represent a little more than 10 percent of the total teaching staff. Using this revised value, the added cost per student would have been $59 rather than $80.

The average class size has a much stronger effect on the computation. Assuming that one teacher would not have been added to the staff without the bilingual program, the average class size in school 4 would have been 33.3,[6] and the added cost per student would be $144. If both revised assumptions were used, the added cost per student would be $124.

Pull-Out Instruction: In addition to the 79 Hispanic students with limited English proficiency served in the bilingual classrooms, school 4 also has 55 students with limited English proficiency who speak languages other than English or Spanish and for whom language-assistance instruction has not been provided in a self-contained classroom. Instead district A has provided an ESL teacher and a bilingual aide who teach these students in six groups, averaging 9.2 students each. Each group is away from the classroom for one-sixth of each instructional day. From our school visits, we estimate that the average class size at the elementary level in district A is 31. What is added to the cost of instruction for these students because they have deficiencies in English?

$$\text{Added cost per student} = \frac{1}{6} \frac{(ESLT + A)}{9.2} - \frac{1}{6} \frac{T}{31},$$

where $ESLT$ = average ESL teacher salary in district A, and T and A are defined as before. If $ESLT$ is $27,827, the added cost per student is $494 and the total added cost for students with limited English proficiency is $27,170. The total added cost is a large proportion of the total cost of the ESL teacher and aide because only a small part of the regular classroom teacher's salary may be deducted.

The difference shown in the two examples between the added cost for self-contained classrooms and for pull-out programs is not unusual. It arises primarily because of the generally lower class size in pull-out programs.[7]

Instruction at the Secondary Level: District A provides language-assistance instruction to secondary students with limited English proficiency during one or more of their regular classroom periods. School 13 has three bilingual teachers, assisted by two aides, for 115 such students. Although the average class size in school 13 is 23.7, the average class size in the bilingual classrooms is 28. All students in the bilingual classrooms are limited in English proficiency. What is the added cost of instruction for these students?

The added cost per student is the product of the added cost per student for one period of bilingual instruction and the number of periods that each student receives bilingual instruction. Since each teacher teaches five periods, the added cost per student of each period of bilingual instruction is:

$$\frac{(3\ BT + 2A)}{(15 \times 28)} - \frac{T}{(5 \times 23.7)} = \$32,$$

where BT = average bilingual teacher salary, plus fringe benefits in district A, A = average aide salary, plus fringe benefits, in district A, and T = average teacher salary, plus fringe benefits, in district A.

In this example, the added cost is negative primarily because of the larger bilingual class size. Although this example is not typical (we found negative added cost at only four of the sixty schools for which we obtained data), it is included to illustrate the overriding influence of class size on cost.

The 115 students with limited English proficiency require a total of 690 student-periods of instruction, since 115 students × 6 (periods per day) = 690 student/periods; the three bilingual teachers furnish 420 student-periods of instruction, since 15 × 28 = 420. Therefore, each bilingual student receives (420/690) × 6 = 3.65 periods of bilingual instruction, and the total added cost of bilingual instruction per student is 3.65 X − $32 = − $117. This example is typical in that secondary students with limited English proficiency almost never receive language-assistance instruction for the entire school day, thus decreasing the added cost per secondary student.

Added cost has been shown to the nearest dollar only for the purposes of illustrating the computational method. The cost estimates derived here are not this accurate; later the findings are summarized to one significant figure, the limit of possible accuracy in this case.

Total Added Cost of Instructional Personnel: In the three smaller school districts in the sample (districts B, D, and F), the data gathered on cost per student essentially covered the district. In the larger districts, however, the average added cost per student derived from the data was adjusted to represent the district as a whole. This was necessary because of the large variations in added cost by delivery mode and level.[8]

District A again illustrates the computation of average added cost per student for the district. The central offices provided a list of teachers in self-contained bilingual-program classrooms and in pull-out programs. Comparison of this list with the numbers of teachers of each kind in the sample showed that we had sampled larger numbers of teachers in self-contained classrooms relative to pull-out teachers than are provided in the district as a whole. Therefore we adjusted our figures accordingly. The computations were made separately for the elementary and secondary levels because of the differences in cost per student at the two levels.

The adjustment was accomplished in the following steps. First, the average added cost per student at each level was computed for each type of program (table 5-9).

Next was computed the total number of students at each level who receive services from each type of program. For this operation, we assumed that the number of students with limited English proficiency per teacher of each type is the same for the sample as for the district as a whole. Table 5-10 displays the results.

Next the total added cost was computed by multiplying the number of students at each level for each type of program by the appropriate average added cost per student and summing the results. Finally, the average added cost per student of $159 for district A was obtained by dividing the total added cost by the total number of students.

This computation slightly overstates the added cost for pull-out students in district A who are also in self-contained, bilingual classrooms. To compute added cost for these students, we should have included a fraction of the pull-out teacher and aide with the self-contained bilingual-program classrooms. Instead, to compute the added cost for students receiving both types of services, we added the separate per-student cost of each service. Of the three large districts for which we had to adjust our district-wide averages, only district A provided overlapping services.

Using similar procedures, we computed the average added cost per student in each of the six school districts. The results (table 5-11) show that the average added cost per student varies widely among the districts visited. Because average teacher salary might account for part of this variation, it is displayed in the table. District E, which has the lowest average teacher salary,

Table 5-9
Added Personnel Cost for District A, by Level and Type of Program

	Added Cost per Student	
Program Organization	Elementary	Secondary
Self-contained	$200	− $ 24
Pull-out	446	636[a]

[a]Some middle schools had bilingual programs similar to those in elementary schools, including pull-out programs.

Table 5-10
Number of Students with Limited English Proficiency in District A,
by Level and Type of Program

	Number of Students with Limited English Proficiency	
Program Organization	Elementary	Secondary
Self-contained	3,528	5,056
Pull-out	2,018	146
	—683[a]	—146[a]
Total	4,863	5,056

[a]Pull-out students are also served in self-contained classrooms.

also has the lowest added cost. Yet the added cost for district A, with the highest average teacher salary, is the second lowest in the table. Thus, average teacher salary cannot account for all the variation shown in the table.

Another contributing factor undoubtedly is the percentage of students in pull-out programs, also shown in table 5-11, because districts with lower percentages of students in pull-out programs have lower added cost per student. Once again, the relationship is not linear. Probably several factors would need to be considered simultaneously to account for most of the variation in added cost per student displayed in the table. Table 5-8 shows that district F, for example, has one aide for every bilingual classroom, whereas district E has fewer aides; this helps to account for the difference between these two districts.

Apparent Source of District Reports of Large Added Cost per Student for Bilingual Education: At this point we may speculate about the source of district reports of the large additional funding required for bilingual educa-

Table 5-11
Added Cost of Instructional Personnel

District	Added Cost per Student	Average Teacher Salary (000s)	Percentage of Students in Pull-out Programs[a]
A	$159	$27.4	46
B	426	21.5	75
C	504	26.8	100
D	332	22.6	54
E	85	20.9	26
F	220	22.0	17

[a]Includes students in both self-contained classrooms and pull-out programs.

tion. In particular, our estimates of added cost per student for pull-out instruction can be compared with additional funds reported by two of the sample districts. (The other districts in the sample did not report cost for pull-out instruction.) One reported that an additional $600 per student would be needed for pull-out instruction; the other, $1,100.

Our estimates of the added cost of pull-out instruction for these districts are only 40 to 50 percent of these figures. Both districts presented these figures as estimates of additional funding needed rather than as estimates of bona-fide added cost. This is the source of most of the discrepancy, since we computed the added cost of instruction by subtracting from the total cost our estimate of the cost of instruction without the bilingual program. The districts in question simply used the total budget for the additional teacher salaries to estimate added cost.

District administrators point out that since the pull-out teachers must be added to the teaching staff, their salaries represent an additional expense. The question is, then, what does the discrepancy between this expense and our estimate of added cost represent? The response is that most of the difference measures resources indirectly added to the classrooms from which students are pulled out through a reduction in the average class size.

An additional 15 to 20 percent of the discrepancy arises from the districts' use of average teacher salary to compute the cost of additional teachers. In each district, teachers actually assigned to the bilingual program earned 75 to 85 percent of the average teacher salary.

Instructional Materials and Equipment: Because the use of instructional equipment was of particular interest in some previous research (Cardenas et al. 1976b), we initially attempted to determine through teacher interviews whether students with limited English proficiency and those proficient in English differed significantly in their use of such equipment. In general, teachers reported that use of equipment, though it might vary in detail, was about the same for each type of student. Also classroom teachers, regardless of which type of students they taught, tailor-made a variety of instructional materials for their classrooms. Thus we also failed to identify significant differences in materials development at the classroom level.

Chiefly for these reasons, we relied on budgetary figures to identify the cost of instructional materials and equipment and assumed that these figures represent added cost. This overstates added cost, since we have no reason to believe that students with limited English proficiency use full sets of monolingual English materials in addition to the materials furnished specifically for them.

Where possible, we separated development of materials from purchase of materials and equipment because of interest in start-up cost. Our data probably understate the initial cost of obtaining materials and equipment since most of these items were already in place in the districts we visited.

Table 5-12, which summarizes the total added cost of instruction per student to the nearest hundred dollars, includes these results. As expected, the cost of materials and equipment, although not negligible, is generally overshadowed by personnel cost. In district E, however, materials and equipment account for nearly 30 percent of the cost of instruction, largely because the added cost of instructional personnel is unusually low.

Estimated costs are shown to the nearest dollar not because the estimates are this accurate but to illustrate the computational procedures followed. Actually the cost estimates are probably accurate to only one significant figure, as shown in the last column of table 5-12.

Added Cost of Other Functions

The other functions on which we gathered data are student identification and assessment for program placement, staff development, program administration, and other support activities, including parental involvement. We used various sources and procedures to estimate the costs of these functions and generally assumed that the total cost of each is an added cost.

Student Identification and Assessment for Program Placement: It is our impression that this function is required solely for student placement in bilingual programs, so that all costs estimated for it are added costs. Nevertheless, students who are assessed and not subsequently placed in the program might benefit by being provided with more-appropriate instruction in the monolingual English classroom. Since no evidence showed that this was the case, we did not adjust the cost of identification and assessment accordingly.

Table 5-12
Total Added Cost of Instruction per Limited-English-Proficient Student

| District | Personnel | Materials and Equipment | | Total |
		Development	Purchase	
A	$159	$15	$21	$200
B	426	27	26	500
C	504	a	11	500
D	332	0	70	400
E	85	7	28	100
F	220	0	70	300

[a]Unavailable.

Although this function is integral to bilingual education, it is rarely identified separately in district budgets, and few data describing it are available. We used whatever strategies seemed appropriate to derive estimates of its cost.

District A, for example, identified personnel whose main assignment is the categorization of students with limited English proficiency for program placement. Estimates of the salaries of these persons provided the cost estimates for district A. In district B, the cost was separately identified in the budget. For districts C and D, we built costs from detailed descriptions of the identification and assessment procedures. District E, in which only personnel from the central office conduct this function, supplied detailed information on its cost. Budgetary figures for district F were supplemented with estimates of costs for training test administrators and for test administration by classroom teachers and instructional aides. (We subtracted the latter costs from the cost of instruction.)

Clearly this method is not altogether satisfactory with respect to completeness or consistency of approach. With these difficulties in mind, we present the results in table 5-13. As the table shows, the cost of this function is relatively low and varies by a factor of 5 among the districts. District D appeared to incur the highest cost partly because its testing program is relatively new.

Staff Development: This function includes in-service training, conferences, tuition, and other support provided by the school district to instructional staff to improve their bilingual-education skills. Unlike the identification and assessment function, staff-development activities are frequently identified separately in district budgets, partly because of the requirement to do so for receipt of categorical funds. Most of the data reported here came from such budgets; sometimes we supplemented this information by addition of salaries for personnel specifically identified for staff-development functions, such as in-service specialists. Staff-development activities paid

Table 5-13
Cost of Identification and Assessment, per Student

District	Cost per Student Served
A	$21
B	20
C	6
D	38
E	12
F	5

for by individual staff, such as attendance at relevant extension courses, were not included. These figures undoubtedly overstate added cost since many monolingual English instructional staff members participate in similar staff-development activities.

Program Administration: Included are the salaries of persons who administer bilingual programs and of secretarial and clerical personnel at central program offices and individual schools. Also included are the cost of office supplies, travel, communications, and conference attendance by administrative persons. Excluded are salaries of persons who administer multiple categorical programs, of which bilingual programs are only a part, largely because there was no defensible rationale for allocating fractions of these salaries among functions.[9] Except in the two smallest districts, this does not represent a significant omission. Costs of general district administration were excluded on the assumption that they would be removed in the computation of added cost.

Other Support Activities: This function includes medical aides identified as serving students with limited English proficiency, medical supplies for these persons, student counseling, remodeling and rental of facilities dedicated to bilingual instruction, and recruiting bilingual staff. By and large district and school budgets were used to derive these figures, which are more complete for some districts than for others.

Most districts allocated funds for parental-involvement activities, such as home liaison workers or baby-sitting services for parents attending school functions, but these funds were generally small. Data from district budgets were used to estimate the cost of this function. We assumed that all such funds represent added costs. The results, as well as estimates of the cost of the previous three functions, are presented in table 5-14.

Allocation of Costs among Functions

Table 5-14 summarizes the results of the preceding analyses. As the table shows, instruction accounts for 50 to 80 percent of the added cost at each of the districts in our sample. There also are large variations in percentages for some of the other functions, such as staff development and administration. We have less confidence in these figures than in those for instruction because we were less systematic and thorough in deriving them. Therefore the variations shown may reflect the true situation or may in part be artifacts of procedures for data reporting.

Total added cost per student with limited English proficiency appears to vary from about $200 to about $700, or by almost a factor of 4. Despite

Table 5-14
Added Cost of Bilingual Programs, by Function
(in thousands)

District	Instruction	Identification and Assessment	Parental Involvement	Staff Development	Administration	Other	Total[a]	Total Cost per Student with Limited English Proficiency
A	$2,000 (50%)	$200 (10%)	$100 [b]	$200 [b]	$900 (20%)	$600 (10%)	$4,000	$400
B	100 (70%)	10 [b]	20 (10%) [d]	[c]	20 (10%)	10 (10%)	200	700
C	1,000 (80%)	10 [b]	[b]	90 (10%)	200 (10%)	0	2,000	700
D	100 (60%)	10 (10%)	10 [b]	40 (20%)	20 (10%)	[b] [c]	200	700
E	1,000 (60%)	100 (10%)	0 [b]	300 (20%)	200 (10%)	200 (10%)	2,000	200
F	400 (60%)	10 [b]	30 [b]	100 (20%)	80 (10%)	0	600	500

Note: The last column is not in thousands.

[a] Rows may not add exactly to totals because of rounding.
[b] Less than 5 percent.
[c] Less than $5,000.
[d] Not available.

the problems in the data, the table appears to provide evidence that the added cost per student of bilingual education is at least as large as estimated by previous studies but not so large as asserted by some school districts.

Effects of Proposed Rules on Cost

In each sample district, we solicited reactions to the proposed rules and asked what the effects of the rules would be on the cost of education. In general even those who professed familiarity with the rules were not knowledgeable about them. This lack of familiarity existed at every level in the school system and often extended even to administrators of bilingual programs.

Therefore it was not surprising to find that in only two of the districts had someone estimated the numbers of students that would fall into the newly proposed categories. A person in one of these districts had estimated that the proposed rules, by making more students eligible for services, would impose the cost of additional ESL teachers on the district. This person felt, however, that the cost of additional language-assessment activities and other functions that would have to be expanded under the new rules could not be estimated.

Conclusions

Delivery of Services

Bilingual programs are delivered in many ways at the sample sites. These variations are important because they affect the amount and cost of language-assistance services the students receive. In particular, self-contained classrooms at the elementary level deliver more language-assistance services than do pull-out programs.

There was little formal instruction about primary languages in the sample sites. Elementary students in self-contained classes receive approximately one class period of instruction about their primary languages, but elementary students in pull-out programs and secondary-school students generally receive little or none.[10]

In the sample districts, elementary students receive more language-assistance services than do secondary students. At the secondary level, services can vary widely among schools within the same district. Whether a bilingual course is offered often depends on the availability of teachers willing and able to teach the class, not just on district policy.

The procedure or combination of procedures a district uses to deliver language-assistance services is affected by district policy, as well as by other factors such as availability of qualified staff. In fact, all districts need more qualified personnel willing to work with students with limited English proficiency, although the severity of the need varies. In districts A and E, for example, the shortage is less severe than in the other districts, perhaps because A and E have large populations that speak the target languages and because their programs are older.

Districts with declining enrollments, such as A and C, face conflicting demands to reduce the total number of teachers and, at the same time, to hire additional teachers who can meet a growing need for bilingual programs. These districts are under pressure to provide services for students with limited English proficiency by using excess teachers from the existing staff, teachers who are usually unqualified to fill these needs. Similarly, in districts experiencing dramatic increases in such students, whatever their primary languages, staffs state they are unable to acquire enough teachers and materials for their language-assistance programs.

The number of students who have the same primary language and the rarity of the language affect the way in which bilingual education is provided. Small numbers of students with limited English proficiency within a given school, or students speaking a relatively uncommon language, such as Afghan or Russian, are likely to receive part-time bilingual instruction from a pull-out teacher, an itinerant tutor, or an instructional aide.

Finally, different problems attend provision of services to Asian and Hispanic students in the sample districts. Staffs noted that tests of language proficiency, as well as achievement tests, need to be developed for Asian students and that Asian bilingual teachers are in shorter supply than are Spanish bilingual teachers.

Added Cost of Bilingual Education

In the districts visited, the added cost of language-assistance instruction ranges from $100 to $500 per student with limited English proficiency. We derived these numbers from detailed data describing the resources used to deliver language-assistance instruction in about sixty schools. The results provide a measure of the economic cost of such instruction and are different from results that would be obtained by dividing district budgets for language-assistance instruction by the numbers of students taught. The latter type of computation often does not provide a realistic measure of the cost of added resources delivered to students.

Variations in the added cost of instruction among the sampled districts reflect variations in average teacher salaries and in the mode of delivery of instruction. Within a given district, a self-contained classroom usually adds less cost than does a pull-out teacher. In the visited districts, self-contained classrooms deliver language-assistance services to individual students for a greater part of the school day than do pull-out programs. Thus, federal regulations that prohibit the use of categorical funds for support of classroom teachers but allow their use for support of bilingual coordinators and other noninstructional personnel may offer the wrong incentive to districts, whatever the legality of their rationale.

Other costs should be added to the cost of instruction to compute the total added cost of bilingual programs. Program administration and staff development can add significantly to cost. Other functions, such as student identification and assessment for program placement, add relatively little to cost.

We estimate that total added cost ranges from $200 to $700 per student with limited English proficiency in the districts visited. These figures are at least as high as those estimated in previous studies but not so high as some districts have claimed on the basis of their budgets for bilingual education. Since we were unable to reduce the budget cost for several functions by their cost without the bilingual program, our numbers may slightly overstate the true added cost of bilingual education.

The added cost of bilingual programs depends strongly on the procedures that districts use to deliver services. These procedures depend, in turn, on many factors specific to the district, including district policy, number of students with limited English proficiency to be served, the primary languages of these students, availability of qualified instructional personnel, and enrollment trends. Because of these complications, considerably more information is needed to establish the cost of bilingual programs nationwide.

First we would need to know the numbers of students in each district and in each language group that will require bilingual programs and the intensity and extent of such instruction. *Extent* refers to the range of subjects involved in the instruction, and *intensity* refers to the fraction of the instructional day involved. To determine extent and intensity would require making assumptions about policies for provision of bilingual programs. With the recent shelving of the proposed rules, state and local policies would be of overriding concern in making this determination.

This information could then be combined with information on the availability in each district of persons qualified to provide instruction at the desired levels of extent and intensity. If such data were available, they might suggest which modes of delivery would be most appropriate for which groups of students in each district.

We also would need to obtain nationally representative estimates of average added cost per student, by mode and by level. Using these figures, adjusted to nationwide averages, we could then produce a rough estimate of the added economic cost to the nation of providing bilingual education under various state and local policies.

Notes

1. Informal communications to the authors.

2. Most of the existing information relates to the cost of only a single hypothetical program in a restricted geographic area. See Carpenter-Huffman (1980).

3. See the full report (Carpenter-Huffman and Samulon 1981) for a description of the characteristics of language-assistance services provided by the school districts visited. The instruments used to guide on-site interviews are also presented in the appendix to that report.

4. Table 5-4 shows averages across all students. Actually, elementary students in district E in pull-out groups receive either ESL or instruction about their primary language, but not both.

5. District A provides bilingual aides in a few monolingual English classrooms that contain students with limited English proficiency. The cost of these aides was included in the computation of added cost per student for district A.

6. This number seems out of line with district A's contract with the teacher union, which gives thirty as the maximum class size at the elementary level. Put another way, we would expect to see a relatively low average class size in schools where bilingual teachers were added to, rather than replacing, staff. This was not the case in school 4.

7. If addition of teachers for pull-out programs were to result in larger classes for classroom teachers (which it does not, perhaps because of the complexities in scheduling that would arise if it did), the added cost of instruction would have to be computed on the basis of the entire school.

8. There were also variations in added cost among schools at a given level for a given delivery mode. These variations generally arose from variations in class size but tended to deviate from the mean less than did variations arising from the use of different delivery modes at different levels.

9. Undoubtedly, given time, we could have developed reasonable allocations on the basis of the numbers of teachers and students in each program.

10. In one district, most elementary students with limited English proficiency not in bilingual, self-contained classrooms are pulled out for instruction in their primary language.

References

Alston, H. 1977. *Title IV-C Pilot Program: An Educational Needs Projection Model. Estimates of Personnel Needed and Costs of HISD Bilingual Education Programs.* Houston Independent School District, Houston, Tex., March 4.

Cardenas, J.A.; Bernal, J.J.; and Kean, W. 1976a. *Bilingual Education Cost Analysis*. San Antonio, Tex.: Intercultural Development Research Association.

———. 1976b. *Bilingual Education Cost Analysis: A Summary*. San Antonio, Tex.: Intercultural Development Research Association.

Carpenter-Huffman, P. [Margaret]. 1980. *Findings of a Seminar on the Cost of Bilingual Education*. N-1504-ED. Santa Monica, Calif.: Rand Corporation, July.

Carpenter-Huffman, M., and Samulon, M. 1981. *Case Studies of Delivery and Cost of Bilingual Education*. Santa Monica, Calif.: Rand Corporation.

Fisher, G.H. 1970. *Cost Considerations in Systems Analysis*. R-490-ASD. Santa Monica, Calif.: Rand Corporation, December.

Garcia, J.O. 1977. "Analyzing Bilingual Education Costs." In G. Blanco et al., *Bilingual Education: Current Perspectives*. Vol. 4. Arlington, Va.: Center for Applied Linguistics, November.

Guss Zamora, M.; Zarate, R.; Robledo, M.; Cardenas, J.A. 1979. *Bilingual Education Cost Analysis: Utah*. San Antonio, Tex.: Intercultural Development Research Association.

Robledo, M.; Zarate, R.; Guss Zamora, M.; and Cardenas, J.A. 1978. *Bilingual Education Cost Analysis: Colorado*. San Antonio, Tex.: Intercultural Development Research Association.

U.S. Congress, Senate Committee on Human Resources. 1978. *Education Amendments of 1978, Report to Accompany S. 1953*, S. Report 95-856. 95th Cong., 2d sess., May 15.

U.S. Department of Education. 1980a. "Proposed Rules." *Federal Register*, August 5, pp. 52052-52076.

———. 1980b. *Preliminary Cost Estimates of Title VI Language Minority Rulemaking*. August 11.

The Availability of Bilingual-Education Teachers

Elizabeth R. Reisner

This chapter describes the extent to which qualified bilingual-education teachers are available to provide special education services to students whose English-language proficiency is limited.[1] The chapter also considers how the need for bilingual teachers might change under varying assumptions about the types of instructional services required to be delivered to students with limited English proficiency. The analysis reported here indicates that although too few qualified bilingual-education teachers are now providing bilingual instruction, there are a significant number of such teachers who are not now working in bilingual classrooms. By attracting these teachers into bilingual classrooms, local school districts might well be able to reduce or eliminate local shortages of bilingual teachers.

The information presented here was derived in part from a review of national studies that address the need for and availability of bilingual-education teachers. To supplement these statistical data, I also interviewed bilingual-education directors and other personnel in six state educational agencies and in four local school districts.

From a national perspective, the availability of bilingual-education teachers can have four types of educational policy effects, aside from issues in the design of a federal requirement for services to these students:

1. The difficulty that local school districts experience in acquiring qualified teachers (whether through recruitment outside the district, training of current staff, or reassignment of current staff) may significantly affect local start-up costs for special programs serving students with limited English proficiency and hence may affect local needs for federal and state financial assistance.
2. The availability of qualified teachers will affect decisions about the instructional approach that school systems can reasonably be expected to adopt for the delivery of services to these students.
3. The time needed for acquiring bilingual teachers will affect the rate at which school districts can fully comply with any legal requirement for special services. The probable lag time between promulgation of federal rules and full local compliance will affect federal civil-rights monitoring activities and the provision of federally sponsored technical assistance.

This chapter is based on research conducted under Contract Number 300-79-0421, U.S. Department of Education.

4. Because problems with the hiring of bilingual teachers are likely to vary from place to place, information on the pattern and seriousness of local difficulties will be important in determining the extent to which special targeted efforts are needed to assist school districts in hiring and training bilingual-education teachers.

Qualifications for Bilingual-Education Teachers

No single set of qualifications has been consistently used as the basis for describing the essential qualifications of a bilingual-education teacher. A useful model, however, is the set of qualifications in the regulations for ESEA Title VII, the Bilingual Education Act. Other models are the teacher-certification requirements for bilingual-education teachers that have been adopted by seventeen states and the District of Columbia.

Requirements in the Title VII Regulations

The Bilingual Education Act states that bilingual instruction is to be provided by "the most qualified available personnel, including only those personnel who are proficient in the language of instruction and in English" (sec. 721 (b) (3) (C) (i) of the act). Qualified bilingual personnel are defined as persons who:

(1) . . . are qualified under state and local law to teach the subjects and grades to which they are assigned;

(2) . . . have successfully completed a course of study or the equivalent in-service training in the use of classroom materials and instructional practices for bilingual education;

(3) . . . are able to converse with proficiency in English and in the native language of the students, both on general topics and in their assigned areas of instruction. This includes the ability to understand, speak, read, and write the language; it neither implies nor precludes an extensive vocabulary which might be necessary to converse with native speakers on complicated matters not related to the subjects which they are required to teach; and

(4) . . . are able to communicate effectively with parents in their native language and in English about school matters. [§123.4 in 45 CFR Part 123]

This set of qualifications relies largely on state standards for teacher qualification, except that bilingual teachers are explicitly required to be trained in the use of bilingual classroom materials and instructional practices. The regulations also require qualified bilingual personnel to meet standards of conversational proficiency in English and the appropriate second language. These standards are largely reflected in current state-certification requirements.

Current State Requirements

The basis for the development of bilingual-certification requirements in some states has been the *Guidelines for the Preparation and Certification of Teachers of Bilingual/Bicultural Education,* issued by the Center for Applied Linguistics (CAL) in 1974. Developed by a panel of thirteen bilingual educators and linguists, the *Guidelines* list eight skills recommended for attention in the training and certification of bilingual teachers:

1. Proficiency in English and in the home language of children participating in the bilingual program.
2. Knowledge of basic concepts of linguistics, including the nature of bilingualism.
3. Ability to promote awareness and understanding of students' cultural backgrounds and the cultural backgrounds of others.
4. Ability to use appropriate instructional methods to assist students in achieving their full academic potential in the home language and culture and in English.
5. Ability to use, adapt, develop, and evaluate instructional materials.
6. Ability to conduct comprehensive assessments of students' achievement and growth.
7. Knowledge of techniques for promoting parent and community involvement.
8. Practical teaching experience in a bilingual-bicultural classroom.

As of 1980, seventeen states and the District of Columbia had certification requirements for bilingual-education teachers, according to the National Clearinghouse for Bilingual Education (1980). Another state, New York, has issued bilingual certification requirements that are to become effective in 1983. Table 6-1 summarizes the requirements of each of these states by indicating whether each of CAL's eight competency areas is addressed in some way by the certification requirements of the state.

Implications of Bilingual-Teacher Requirements
for Program Effectiveness

States vary significantly in the amount of specialized pedagogical preparation they require for bilingual certification. According to the texts of

Table 6-1
Extent to Which State-Certification Requirements Meet 1974 CAL Guidelines for Preparation and Certification of Bilingual Teachers

State	Language Proficiency	Linguistics	Culture	Instructional Methods	Curriculum Use and Adaptation	Assessment	School-Community Relations	Supervised Teaching[b]
Arizona	Yes	No	Yes	Yes	No	No	No	No
California	Yes	Yes	Yes	No	No	No	No	No
Colorado	Yes	Yes	Yes	Yes	No	Yes	Yes	No
Delaware	Yes	No	Yes	Yes[a]	No	No	No	Yes
Illinois	Yes	No	No	No	No	No	No	No
Indiana	Yes	No	Yes	Yes	No	No	No	No
Louisiana	Yes	No	Yes	Yes	No	No	No	No
Massachusetts	Yes	No	Yes	Yes	No	No	No	Yes
Michigan	Yes	Yes	Yes	Yes	No	No	No	No
New Hampshire	Yes	Yes	Yes	Yes	No	No	Yes	No
New Jersey	Yes	Yes	Yes	Yes[a]	No	No	No	Yes
New Mexico	Yes	Yes	Yes	Yes	No	No	No	Yes
New York[c]	Yes	Yes	Yes	Yes	No	Yes	No	Yes
Pennsylvania	Yes	No	Yes	No	No	No	No	No
Rhode Island	Yes	No	Yes	Yes[a]	No	No	No	No
Texas	Yes	Yes	Yes	Yes[a]	No	No	No	Yes
Washington	Yes	Yes	Yes	Yes[a]	No	Yes	Yes	No
Wisconsin	Yes	Yes	Yes	Yes	No	No	No	Yes
District of Columbia	Yes	Yes	Yes	Yes	No	No	No	Yes

Note: A "yes" in this table indicates only that the state requires some type of training or demonstration of competency in the area shown. "Yes" does not necessarily indicate that the state meets the full scope of CAL's description of competency.

[a] Training or competencies explicitly required for the English-as-a-second-language program.

[b] A "yes" in this column indicates supervised teaching or comparable teaching experience explicitly required in a bilingual classroom.

[c] Bilingual-certification requirements will become effective in 1983.

various state requirements, some states require as many as twenty-four semester hours of bilingual-education methods for certification, while others include only a generalized statement that bilingual-education teachers must be familiar with instructional methods appropriate to bilingual-bicultural classrooms. Despite the variation, each state requires that bilingual teachers be proficient in both English and the primary language of their students with limited English proficiency.[2] Most states also require training in the culture of the students and knowledge of bilingual-instructional methods. Four states explicitly require training in English-as-a-second-language (ESL) methods.

Examination of these standards suggests that the state-certification requirements in almost all the states would be adequate to meet Title VII standards. Bilingual teachers in other states may typically acquire training (either preservice or inservice) in the areas identified in the Title VII regulations, but data are not available from certification standards to make that determination. Whether these entry-level requirements are actually reflected in higher levels of teacher competency, however, is almost impossible to determine without actual observations of bilingual teachers at work.

Estimates of the Need for Bilingual-Education Teachers Nationwide

To establish the number of bilingual-education teachers who are needed to serve the population with limited English proficiency, it is necessary to develop an estimation technique based on the population characteristics of students with limited English proficiency. First, the number of school-age children who are considered to have limited proficiency in English must be determined, but determining the total number does not provide enough information. The instructional services appropriate for concentrated groups of these students differ from the instructional services appropriate for less-concentrated, or more-isolated, students. Therefore it is necessary to divide the total number of students with limited English proficiency into two subsets: those who are sufficiently concentrated in numbers to permit class-size instructional groups and those who are enrolled in only very small numbers within a school. The latter group is likely to require individual or small-group instruction on a pull-out basis.

To some extent, instructional requirements will dictate the criteria used to establish the nationwide number of students in each subset. For example, if the student's primary home language is to be used extensively in the provision of instruction, as in bilingual education, it will be necessary to limit permissible classroom groupings to children speaking the same primary home language. If no instruction in the primary home language is required (for example, if intensive ESL is the primary instructional strategy) or if only a limited amount of conversation between student and teacher is expected to be conducted in the student's primary home language, it will be reasonable to base the class-size groupings on only similar age and enrollment in the same school, thus excluding primary home language as a limiting criterion. For estimation purposes, we will assume the bilingual-education option.

Derivation of the number of needed bilingual teachers can then be determined by the following calculation: (Number of students who have limited English proficiency and the same primary home language in schools with concentration of similar students divided by average number of students who have limited English proficiency and can be served by one bilingual-education teacher in a regular class-size grouping) plus (Number of students who have limited English proficiency but are not attending schools with concentrations on similar students divided by average number of students who have limited English proficiency and can be served by one bilingual teacher on a pull-out basis). The first half of the calculation will show the number of bilingual teachers needed nationally to provide instruction to students with limited English proficiency in situations in which the bilingual teacher serves as the regular classroom teacher providing bilingual education. The second half of the calculation will indicate the number of bilingual teachers needed nationally to provide pull-out instruction on an individual or small-group basis. This information must then be compared with data on teacher supply.

Demographic Characteristics of Students
with Limited English Proficiency

For purposes of this assessment, two demographic measures are particularly important: (1) How many students with limited English proficiency are there nationwide? (2) To what extent are they concentrated in class-size groupings?

Estimates of Total Student Population with Limited English Proficiency: Several different data sets are now available for use in estimating the total number of students who may need bilingual education. Chapter 1 in this book describes these data sets in detail, discussing alternative population estimates derived from each data source. Table 6-2 indicates the current range of population estimates for students with limited English proficiency based on these data sets. The size of the population estimates shown in the table varies with the differences in the assumptions and methodology used in collecting and analyzing the data. For purposes of estimation, however, two population estimates have been selected to define the probable range of numbers of children; the InterAmerica estimate and the Office of Planning and Budget estimate of children who are "primary-language superior" or

Table 6-2

Estimates of Number of Students with Limited English Proficiency Who Are Eligible for Bilingual Education

Source	Age	Population Counted	Year	Estimate (000s)
Children's English and Services Study	5-14	Entire United States	1978	2,409
Dubois	5-14	Entire United States	1978	2,631
InterAmerica	5-18	Entire United States	1980	2,927
Office of Planning and Budget, U.S. Department of Education	5-18	Primary-language superior[a]	1980	1,018
	5-18	Primary-language superior or comparable[a]	1980	1,388
Office for Civil Rights, U.S. Department of Education, as analyzed by AUI Policy Research	5-18	Public school only	1978	934

Source: Kaskowitz, Binkley, and Johnson (1981).

[a]Proficiency in a language other than English is higher than proficiency in English.

[b]Proficiency in a language other than English is comparable to or higher than proficiency in English.

comparable (see definition accompanying the table).[3] These estimates place the likely number of students with limited English proficiency at 2.927 million and 1.388 million, respectively.

To assess the national need for bilingual teachers, national aggregate counts of children with limited English proficiency should be broken down both geographically and by language group. The Office for Civil Rights data, as reanalyzed by Milne and Gombert (1980) and reported in chapter 4, indicate that as of the fall of 1978, students with limited English proficiency tended to be concentrated in a few states, in school districts with high enrollments, and in central cities. Neither the Office for Civil Rights data nor other data sources, however, permit reasonably accurate estimates to be made of the geographical and language-group distribution of students with limited English proficiency.

The Concentration of Students with Limited English Proficiency in Schools: Estimates of the extent to which students of the same language group are concentrated in particular schools are important for purposes of determining teacher need. A single bilingual teacher can serve different numbers of students depending on whether the students are concentrated in a single grade, language, and school or dispersed among several different grades, languages, and schools. This fact is reflected to some extent in current state laws.

States with laws requiring the provision of bilingual education to students with limited English proficiency generally also have statewide criteria identifying the concentration of these students who must be enrolled in a school or district in order to meet the threshold for local provision of a bilingual-education program. Table 6-3 shows the range of current state variation in concentration criteria. Another concentration criterion is the standard proposed in the Title VI Civil Rights Act draft regulations but withdrawn before becoming final: that bilingual education (or an alternative approved program) must be provided if twenty-five limited-English-proficient students with the same primary home language are enrolled in two consecutive grades below the ninth grade within a single school.

None of the data sets now available permits a precise estimation of the numbers of students with limited English proficiency in the various concentrated and nonconcentrated categories, so it is necessary for our purposes to develop our own estimate. The proposed Title VI criterion is the standard used here because of its simple intuitive appeal. It is reasonable to expect that twenty-five students with the same primary home language in two consecutive grades in a school can be grouped into a classroom and provided bilingual instruction by a single bilingual teacher. In addition, the limit at the eighth grade accords with my own observations of high-school programs serving students with limited English proficiency and the reports of other observers.[4] These sources indicate that students in grades 9 through 12

Table 6-3
State Concentration Criteria for Provision of Bilingual Education

Criterion	State
At least 10 students per grade, school, and language	California
At least 20 students per school and language	Connecticut
At least 20 students per grade, district, and language	Texas
At least 20 students per district and language	Illinois, Massachusetts, New Jersey, Rhode Island

Source: Kaskowitz, Binkley, and Johnson (1981).

tend to have such diverse skills, backgrounds, and interests that generally it is not feasible to require that they be served by classroom bilingual instruction. They are usually served by a combination of ESL classes and pull-out instruction.

From calculations performed by Kaskowitz and Binkley (1981), it is possible to estimate the number of students with limited English proficiency who meet the proposed Title VI concentration criterion. These estimates are presented in table 6-4. These figures indicate that the number of these students who are enrolled in schools where they meet the Title VI concentration criterion probably ranges between 608,000 and 1.147 million. The number of students who do not meet this criterion probably ranges between 780,000 and 1.780 million.

Number of Students Who May be Taught
by a Single Bilingual Teacher

Bilingual Teachers in Concentrated Schools: Although low pupil-teacher ratios are generally thought to be educationally desirable, there is no evidence to suggest that students with limited English proficiency are more favorably affected by low pupil-teacher ratios than are other students. Hence there is no basis for requiring that these students be permitted to enjoy a lower pupil-teacher ratio than other students. Still, equity considerations dictate that these students be treated at least the same as students who are proficient in English with respect to numbers of students per teacher. The National Education Association estimates that the current pupil-teacher ratio in the United States is twenty-four pupils per teacher. If each

Table 6-4

Application of Proposed Title VI Concentration Criterion to Estimates of Total Numbers of Students with Limited English Proficiency

Estimated Size of Population, Grades K-12 (in 000s)	Concentrated Students (000s)	Nonconcentrated Students (000s)
1,388[a]	608	780
2,927[b]	1,147	1,780

Source: Kaskowitz, Binkley, and Johnson (1981).

Note: Under this criterion students are considered to be concentrated if they are attending a public school below the ninth grade and are members of a group of at least twenty-five such students having the same primary home language and enrolled in two consecutive grades.

[a]Estimate of the Office of Planning and Budget in the Department of Education.

[b]Estimate of InterAmerica.

bilingual teacher were to be responsible for all activities of a single, self-contained classroom and if each class were made up only of students with limited English proficiency, each bilingual teacher would thus provide instruction to about twenty-four such students.[5]

A full day of bilingual instruction in a self-contained classroom is not necessarily desirable for students, however. To prevent unnecessary segregation from other students, it is generally thought to be important for students with limited English proficiency to interact with other students during the nonacademic parts of the school day. Since academic subjects generally consume only about half of a normal school day, a bilingual teacher under certain conditions—for example, a high concentration of students with the same primary language—might be expected to provide bilingual instruction in academic subjects to as many as two classes of students with limited English proficiency, which would total as many as fourty-eight such students.

According to a number of persons interviewed for this study, however, bilingual teachers in situations in which there are enough students with limited English proficiency to form classes do not ordinarily provide instruction to more students than regular teachers do. That is, bilingual teachers supervise self-contained classrooms or work in team-teaching arrangements, depending on the school's regular program, and do not necessarily deliver instruction to a larger number of students than is normal practice for other teachers in the school. The reason most often cited for this arrangement is that union contracts (or less-formal agreements) generally limit the instructional responsibilities that can be imposed on any one teacher and often require that certain noninstructional duties, such as playground and lunchroom supervision, be shared equally among teachers, thus precluding special treatment for bilingual teachers. In other words, school districts tend to treat bilingual teachers like other teachers to the extent that there are enough children with limited English proficiency to provide classes directed specifically to their educational needs.

An exception to this rule is noteworthy. Illinois (and possibly other states as well) requires that each student with limited English proficiency receive at least ninety minutes of daily instruction in the primary home language. This requirement, coupled with the serious shortage of bilingual teachers reported in Illinois, has meant that many bilingual teachers in that state are required to provide bilingual instruction each day to very high numbers of students with limited English proficiency. (In an interview for this study, the state bilingual office said it is common for a bilingual teacher to provide instruction to ninty to one-hundred students a day.)

For purposes of estimating the average number of students with limited English proficiency who may be served by a single bilingual teacher in a concentrated school, I hypothesize the following, based on the preceding factors:

1. That for 75 percent of all students with limited English proficiency, each bilingual teacher serves the same number of students as the national average (twenty-four students per teacher).
2. That for 25 percent of all such students, each bilingual teacher provides instruction to a significantly larger number of students with limited English proficiency. In these instances, let us assume that each bilingual teacher serves forty-eight students.
3. Therefore, the average number of students with limited English proficiency who can be served by a single bilingual teacher in a regular class-size grouping is 24 students × 75 percent plus 48 students × 25 percent, which equals 18 students + 12 students, or 30 students.

Bilingual Teachers in Nonconcentrated Schools: Where there are not enough students with the same primary home language to warrant the assignment of a regular classroom teacher to a class of students with limited English proficiency, services are generally provided on a pull-out basis by bilingual aides and volunteers working under the formal or informal supervision of a qualified bilingual-education teacher. Because these arrangements vary in each school district, there is no simple method for estimating the number of students who may be served by a single bilingual teacher under these circumstances.[6]

For purposes of deriving an estimate of the number of students with limited English proficiency who may be served by a bilingual teacher in these circumstances, the following assumptions will be made:

1. In school districts where students have some familiarity with English, well-trained bilingual aides are employed, appropriate instructional materials are available, and good cooperation exists between the regular teaching staff and the bilingual teaching staff, each bilingual teacher will be able to serve a large number of children with limited English proficiency, estimated here to be forty to forty-five.
2. In school districts where those conditions do not exist and where bilingual teachers must spend part of their work day driving from school to school, each bilingual teacher will be able to serve far fewer students, estimated at ten to fifteen.
3. Therefore, if conditions somewhere in the middle of these two extremes prevail on the average, one bilingual teacher would be required for the average of these two extremes. Or

Average number of
students who can be served   = $\dfrac{40 \text{ to } 45 \text{ students plus}}{2}$
by a single bilingual   10 to 15 students
teacher on a pull-out basis

$$= \quad \frac{42.5 \text{ plus } 12.5 \text{ students}}{2}$$

$$= \quad \frac{55 \text{ students}}{2}$$

$$= \quad 27.5 \text{ students}$$

Application of Estimates to Determine Total
Current Need for Bilingual Teachers

Using the estimates just generated, we have calculated a range of total need for bilingual-education teachers. The calculation is based on the formula described at the beginning of this section.

Number of bilingual
teachers needed $=$ $\dfrac{\text{608,000 to 1,147,000 students in ``concentrated'' schools}}{\text{30 students with limited English proficiency served by each bilingual teacher in a regular class-size group}}$

plus

$\dfrac{\text{780,000 to 1,780,000 students with limited English proficiency not in ``concentrated'' schools}}{\text{27.5 students with limited English proficiency served by each bilingual teacher on a pull-out basis}}$

$=$ (20,300 to 38,200) + (28,400 to 64,700) bilingual teachers

$=$ 48,700 to 102,900 bilingual teachers

Estimates of Current Availability of
Bilingual Teachers

Because of characteristics of the current data on bilingual teachers, the estimates of available bilingual teachers are based on two components: the number of minimally qualified bilingual teachers providing bilingual-education services in 1976-1977 and the number of new bilingual teachers who have taken bilingual teaching positions since that time. In addition, an estimate is made of the number of teachers trained specifically in English as a second language now providing ESL instruction. To set these estimates in the most-useful context, other data also are presented to answer these questions:

1. How many qualified bilingual teachers are not now teaching in special programs serving students with limited English proficiency?
2. Of that number, how many are teaching in regular, English-only classrooms, and how many are not teaching at all?
3. Of all teachers currently teaching, how many have most of the skills required to teach in a bilingual program but are not now fully qualified to provide such instruction?
4. What is the attrition rate for bilingual teachers?
5. What training and teaching experience typically have been acquired by ESL teachers?

Answers to the second and third questions are important in identifying alternatives for increasing the number of bilingual teachers at the minimum national cost. These alternatives might include incentives to local school districts for reassigning qualified bilingual teachers who are working in school systems but not now teaching students with limited English proficiency, incentives to attract persons qualified as bilingual-education teachers to assignments in bilingual classrooms, and training opportunities for teachers who possess most but not all the skills needed to provide bilingual instruction.

None of the data presented next on teacher availability include any information on geographical regions or urban-rural locations of teachers. No data to permit such analyses are currently available from any source.

Number of Teachers Providing Bilingual
or ESL Instruction in 1976-1977

In the 1976-1977 school year, the Teacher Language Skills Survey (TLSS) gathered information from a nationally representative sample of public-school teachers on the extent to which they were qualified to provide instruction to students with limited English proficiency, either through bilingual-education or ESL programs. The survey included questions on whether each responding teacher was using a language other than English, as well as English, in instruction and whether he or she taught ESL. Findings of the TLSS, presented in table 6-5 (and reported in Waggoner 1979), indicate that approximately 42,000 teachers provided instruction using a language other than English during that school year. This figure did not include the number of teachers providing foreign-language instruction to English-speaking students. Of the 42,000 teachers, 22,000 of them also taught ESL. Only 29 percent of these teachers used the second language more than a quarter of their time (Waggoner 1979:54). Many of them were

Table 6-5
Public-School Teachers Teaching through a Language other than English and/or Teaching ESL, 1976-1977
(*in thousands*)

Ability and Training to Teach through a Language Other Than English	(A) Total	(B) Total	Taught through a Language Other Than English or Taught ESL 1976-1977			(F) Before 1976-1977	(G) No Experience Teaching Through a 2d Language or Teaching ESL
			(C) Through a 2d Language plus ESL	(D) Through a 2d Language Only	(E) Through ESL Only		
1. Total teachers	2,182	120	22	20	77	137	1,925
2. With reported ability to teach language arts and/or other subject areas in language other than English	141	40	16	12	12	35	65
2a. With training to do so[a]	34	18	8	5	5	9	7
2b. With basic bilingual-education training[b]	11	8	4	2	2	3	1
3. With reported ability to teach a second language as a foreign language	174	12	2	3	8	25	137
3a. With training in teaching language arts and/or other subject areas in a second language[a]	7	2	*	*	1	3	3
4. With speaking skills but no teaching ability in second language	310	16	2	2	11	19	275

4a. With training in teaching language arts, etc., in second language[a]	6	2	*	2	1	4
5. Without speaking skills in a second language	1,557	52	2	46	57	1,448
5a. with training in teaching language arts, etc., in a second language[a]	14	4	*	4	2	8
6. With training in teaching ESL[c]	66	27	10	14	19	20

*Fewer than an estimated 1,000 teachers.

Source: Teacher Language Skills Survey, National Center for Education Statistics, 1976-1977, unpublished data.

Note: Detail may not add to totals because of overlapping categories.

[a]Teachers who reported taking courses specifically to teach the language arts of a language other than English to its speakers, or courses to teach other subject areas through a non-English language, or both.

[b]Teachers who reported taking courses to teach the language arts of a language other than English to teach other subject areas in a language other than English and to teach ESL, as well as courses in history, culture, or ethnic studies associated with the background of the students whose language is other than English.

[c]Teachers who reported taking at least one course in teaching ESL; all but 16,000 of these teachers had also taken courses in teaching the language arts of a second language, teaching other subject areas in a second language, or bilingualism or the theory of bilingual education.

not, therefore, full-time teachers of bilingual education, but information is not available to indicate exactly how many were full-time bilingual teachers.

Of the 42,000 teachers using a second language in instruction, only 13,000 could be considered minimally qualified in bilingual education. These were teachers who had taken courses in teaching the language arts of the second language, or taken courses in teaching other subject areas in the language, or both, and reported that they had necessary language skills in English and the second language required to teach in the second language.

Number of Persons Qualified to Provide Bilingual
Instruction But Not Doing So

The 1976-1977 survey indicated that 34,000 minimally qualified bilingual teachers were then working as teachers. However, only 13,000 were using a second language in instruction and thus could in any way be considered to be teaching in a bilingual program. Another 5,000 of the minimally qualified pool of bilingual teachers were teaching ESL but were not using a second language. The remaining 16,000 minimally qualified bilingual teachers were not using their bilingual or ESL skills in their teaching.[7] Of this number 7,000 had never taught using a second language or provided ESL instruction.

Number of Teachers Who Have Most Skills
Required to Provide Bilingual Instruction

In 1976-1977, approximately 27,000 teachers had taken the appropriate methodology courses for bilingual teaching but did not feel confident of their language skills. In table 6-5, this number is the sum of the numbers in column A at line 3a (7,000 teachers with appropriate training but with sufficient language skills only to teach the second language as a foreign language), line 4a (6,000 teachers with appropriate coursework training and necessary speaking skills, but inadequate teaching ability in the second language), and line 5a (14,000 teachers with appropriate training but no speaking skills in the second language). In addition to these teachers with methodological skills but limited language skills, another 107,000 teachers who had had no formal training in bilingual teaching methodologies rated their skills in a second language as adequate for use in teaching. (This number is the remainder of line 2a, column A subtracted from line 2, column A.) These teachers are obvious candidates for additional training to qualify them as bilingual-education teachers.

Many of the minimally qualified teachers need additional training in order to be able to deliver high-quality instruction. As the table shows, the TLSS found that only 11,000 teachers had had training in four of the areas often considered essential to bilingual teaching (courses in teaching the language arts of a second language, in teaching other subjects in a second language, in ESL, and in the history, culture, or ethnic studies associated with the second language).

Number of ESL Teachers in 1976-1977

In 1976-1977, approximately 77,000 teachers were providing ESL instruction to students. Of that number, however, only 14,000 had had at least one course in teaching ESL. This number does not include any of the minimally qualified bilingual teachers reported by the survey. No data are available to indicate how many of the 14,000 qualified ESL teachers also held the necessary qualifications to provide bilingual instruction. We do know, however, that 50,000 teachers, or 76 percent, of the total 66,000 teachers trained to teach ESL had received training as bilingual teachers. We can surmise, therefore, that a portion of the trained ESL teachers were also qualified to provide bilingual instruction.

Number of Persons Recently Trained as
Bilingual or ESL Teachers

Because of continuing shortages of bilingual teachers reported in many areas of the country, Congress has included a number of provisions in ESEA Title VII that provide federal funding for the training of bilingual teachers. Some of these training activities are intended to improve the bilingual teaching skills of current bilingual teachers, thus affecting competency levels but not necessarily the number of bilingual teachers available. Other training activities, however, have had a significant impact on the preparation of newly qualified bilingual teachers, including both new teachers who have not taught previously and regular classroom teachers who have received supplementary training in bilingual education.[8]

Number of New Bilingual Teachers Who Have Recently Completed Bilingual-Education Training: As part of their recent study, Kaskowitz, Binkley, and Johnson (1981) estimated the number of persons graduating from all bilingual training programs in colleges and universities in the United States in 1977, 1978, 1979, and 1980. Table 6-6 presents estimates of gradutes produced by bilingual-education teacher-training programs. (The

Table 6-6
Estimates of Number of New Graduates Entering National Supply of
Bilingual-Education Teachers between 1976 and 1980

	New Graduates Accepting Positions as Bilingual Teachers, by Type of Degree		
Numbers of Total Graduates[a]	Bachelor's/Credential	Master's	Total
8,737	2,887	1,269	4,156
11,624	3,715	1,758	5,473

Source: Kaskowitz, Binkley, and Johnson (1981).

[a]The lower of the two figures in this column is the original estimate of Kaskowitz, Binkley, and Johnson. However, because of indications that their estimate was unrealistically low, they recommended that the upper bound of the 95 percent confidence interval for their estimate be used as an alternative.

estimates are presented in terms of a range.) According to these data, between 4,200 and 5,500 new bilingual teachers entered the bilingual-education teaching pool between school years 1976-1977 and 1979-1980 (inclusive). This range represents less than half the total teacher-training graduates of the same period. Despite that relatively low proportion, however, these new teachers represent an increase of 32 to 42 percent over the number of minimally qualified teachers providing instruction using a language other than English in 1976-1977.

The occupational choices of these bilingual-training graduates are presented in table 6-7. The data indicate that a high proportion of these graduates now are employed in education in some way. Of all recent graduates of bilingual teacher-training programs, 89 percent are now employed in education. The figure for those trained as bilingual teachers is 97 percent.

The proportion of these persons who are actually employed in bilingual education is much smaller. Of all recent bilingual-education graduates, only 52 percent are now working directly in bilingual education. The corresponding proportion of bilingual teacher-training graduates is 62 percent; even that figure is remarkably low given the investment made in the professional training of these individuals. The inclusion of those persons working in educational programs that serve students with limited English proficiency though not through bilingual education increases the total proportion of graduates serving such students to 70 percent for recent bilingual-education graduates and 82 percent for recent bilingual teacher-training graduates.

Number of New Bilingual Teachers Entering the Bilingual Teacher Supply from Sources other than Traditional Preservice Programs: Each year an

Table 6-7
Positions Held by Recently Trained Bilingual Teachers and Teacher Trainers

Job Category	Percentage of Persons Trained as Bilingual Teachers	Percentage of Persons Trained as Bilingual Teacher Trainers
Bilingual education	52	62
Educational programs that serve population with limited English proficiency	18	20
Eduational programs that serve minority population	3	3
General education	14	11
Education related	3	2
Outside education	2	1
Not employed	9	2

Source: Kaskowitz, Binkley, and Johnson (1981).
Note: Figures do not total 100 because of rounding.

unknown number of new bilingual teachers become qualified without completing formal collegiate preservice training in bilingual education. These teachers include regular curriculum teachers who acquire skills in bilingual education through in-service training or self-directed study. They also include teachers trained outside the United States and bilingual teachers who have been out of the teaching labor market for some period of time. Given the national shortage of bilingual teachers, it is reasonable to expect that some of these qualified bilingual teachers assume bilingual teaching positions each year.

Because there is no way of counting these new teachers, it is necessary to estimate their number. For purposes of establishing a lower bound estimate of these new bilingual teachers, we have assumed that a number of teachers equivalent to 20 percent of the new teachers from traditional preservice programs have entered bilingual classrooms by this route. On that basis, about 800 to 1,100 such teachers should be added to the overall estimate of the bilingual teacher supply.

Number of New ESL Teachers: No data exist with which to estimate the number of ESL teachers who have taken ESL teaching positions since 1977. That number would be considerably lower than the 4,200 to 5,500 new bilingual teachers, due to the heavy Title VII investment in bilingual teacher training but not in the training of persons to be ESL teachers only. Assuming that the number of trained ESL teachers has increased by 15 percent since 1977, a total of 2,000 teachers would have been added to the ESL teacher supply since the time of the 1976-1977 survey.

Revision of TLSS Estimates to Reflect Teacher Attrition

Anecdotal reports suggest that bilingual teachers are particularly likely to leave bilingual teaching positions in pursuit of other professional opportunities. No data are available at present to verify these reports, however.

Using national data on teacher attrition rates overall, we can estimate how the TLSS teacher figures would have to be decreased to reflect the number of minimally qualified bilingual teachers who were teaching at the time of the survey and are still teaching in comparable positions. According to William Graybeal of the National Education Association, annual teacher turnover averages 5.9 percent. When rounded to 6 percent, this rate suggests that 78 percent of the teachers surveyed in 1976-1977 are still teaching in comparable positions. Thus, the figure of 13,000 minimally qualified bilingual teachers in 1976-1977 is reduced to 10,100 teachers in school year 1980-1981. Similarly, the figure of 14,000 minimally qualified ESL teachers is reduced to 10,900 teachers in 1980-1981. We have assumed no attrition in the numbers of bilingual teachers entering bilingual classrooms for the first time since 1976-1977 because they entered these positions so recently.

Application of Estimates to
Determine Total Current Teacher Supply

The total current supply of bilingual teachers includes those identified by the 1976-1977 TLSS, as corrected to reflect probable attrition, plus those teachers entering bilingual classrooms since that time. The TLSS data corrected for attrition suggest that 10,100 teachers counted at that time are now providing instruction using a second language for at least part of the school day and at least minimally qualified to provide bilingual instruction. In addition, 4,200 to 5,500 newly trained bilingual teachers have entered bilingual classrooms since the earlier survey was administered. Finally, 800 to 1,100 teachers have entered bilingual classrooms from sources other than traditional preservice programs. The 10,100 teachers in 1976-1977 plus 4,200 to 5,500 newly trained teachers plus an additional 800 to 1,100 teachers equal between 15,100 and 16,700 current bilingual teachers.

The total number of qualified ESL teachers in 1976-1977 corrected for attrition, or 10,900 teachers, plus newly trained ESL teachers numbering approximately 2,000 teachers, yields a current total of 12,900 ESL teachers.

Adding bilingual and ESL teachers yields a current total of between 28,000 and 29,600 teachers who are now providing services to students with limited English proficiency and have received training to qualify them to provide these services.

This figure however, must, be seen in the context of the large number of qualified bilingual teachers who are now teaching but not in bilingual or

ESL programs. In 1976-1977; these teachers were estimated to number 16,000. Assuming 6 percent annual attrition from the national pool of teachers, these teachers would now number 12,500. Another 3,100 to 4,100 bilingual teachers have been trained since the survey and have taken teaching jobs, but not in bilingual education. On the basis of these figures, an estimated 15,600 to 16,600 bilingual teachers are now teaching but not in bilingual education or ESL.

Comparison of Number of Teachers Needed and Those Available

The estimates developed in this study indicate a serious national shortage of minimally qualified bilingual teachers. The estimated need for approximately 48,700 to 102,900 bilingual-education teachers is being met by approximately 15,100 to 16,700 minimally qualified bilingual teachers now providing instructional services using a second language in some way. Data do not indicate clearly how many of these teachers could be considered full-time bilingual teachers. The shortage of qualified bilingual teachers is, therefore, estimated to number at least 33,600 to 86,200 teachers. If the 12,900 qualified ESL teachers are counted in estimating total teacher supply, the estimated teacher shortage is somewhat reduced. Also, the shortage could be significantly alleviated if the 15,600 to 16,600 teachers who are qualified to provide bilingual education but are not now doing so were brought into bilingual classrooms.

The totals that are cited, however, are nationally aggregated figures. Shortages of bilingual teachers vary significantly by language, region, and urban or rural location. The actual shortage of qualified teachers—the sum of all the regional shortages—is thus likely to be considerably higher than the shortages I have been able to estimate on a nationally aggregated basis.

Local Employment Conditions and Other Factors Affecting Bilingual-Education Teachers

One of the data-collection methods used in this study was telephone interviews with state and local bilingual-education personnel. In the six states with the largest populations of students with limited English proficiency, as identified by the National Center for Education Statistics: California, Florida, Illinois, New Jersey, New York, and Texas. Together these states account for 77 percent of all children ages 5 to 14 with limited English proficiency in the nation. Bilingual directors in four school districts—one each in California, Illinois, New Jersey, and Texas—were also interviewed by telephone. The four districts were suggested by their respective state bilingual offices.

From the telephone interviews with state and local bilingual-education directors as well as from other sources of information, a rough picture emerges of the problems local school districts face in bringing qualified bilingual teachers into bilingual-education classrooms and the circumstances those teachers encounter once they are there.

Bilingual Teacher Characteristics

No data are available nationally that compare the characterisitics and qualifications of bilingual teachers with those of regular classroom teachers. Reports from interviews for this study were consistent, however, with observations made by Carpenter-Huffman and Samulon (see chapter 5). That is, bilingual teachers on the whole are somewhat younger and more likely to hold graduate degrees than are regular teachers. Interview respondents consistently reported that their bilingual teaching staff was relatively young. They attributed this phenomenon to the relative newness of the field. Although Carpenter-Huffman and Samulon did not collect data on teachers' ages, they did determine that in their sample districts, regular teachers had an average of fifteen years of teaching experience and bilingual teachers had only ten years of experience. A predictable result of that disparity is that in their sample districts, the average salary earned by bilingual teachers was 75 to 80 percent of the average teaching salary earned by all teachers in their respective school districts.

Carpenter-Huffman and Samulon also found that 43 percent of the bilingual teachers in the districts studied had earned a master's degree, and only 20 percent of the regular teachers had done so. This finding is consistent with observations of the relative youth of bilingual teachers, since opportunities for advanced degrees in bilingual education have blossomed only recently with substantial funding under the Bilingual Education Act. In addition, many states have instituted requirements for training beyond the bachelor's degree for all teachers only in recent years.

Bilingual Teacher Recruitment

Activities associated with the recruitment of bilingual-education teachers varied widely across the sampled states. Some states reported that almost all beginning bilingual teachers are recruited from in-state college-level programs of bilingual teacher preparation. Bilingual personnel in Florida, on the other hand, reported that a number of Cuban-American immigrants who had been teachers in Cuba have acquired enough U.S. schooling while working as bilingual aides to enter bilingual classrooms as fully credentialed teachers.

In at least one large school system examined for this study, large monetary bonuses are given to attract new bilingual teachers. In that system, any employee who brings a qualified bilingual teacher into the system receives a cash bonus of $500 if the new teacher serves in a bilingual classroom for at least one year. The bilingual teachers themselves receive a bonus of $1,000 each year that they teach in a bilingual classroom.

Several states reported that school districts often recruit from college-level bilingual-training programs outside their own states. The Texas state bilingual coordinator reported frequent complaints from Texas school districts that recruiters from California school districts had lured away top bilingual teachers with offers of better salary and benefits. Local personnel in Texas, on the other hand, reported that their own districts often advertised in publications as far away as Michigan and Indiana to hire bilingual teachers.

Only in California was a systematic state effort described for helping school districts find bilingual teachers. A state-level clearinghouse, operated by the state's Commission for Teacher Preparation and Licensing, lists bilingual teaching vacancies for teacher candidates.

An important variable in local recruiting success has been the ingenuity of individual school districts in seeking sources of possible new teachers, such as their efforts to obtain Title VII funds to provide training stipends for paraprofessionals who want to become credentialed bilingual teachers. No one type of school district appeared more likely than others to demonstrate special ingenuity and initiative.

Bilingual Teacher Shortages

In terms of teacher shortages, as in other matters related to the employment of bilingual teachers, a substantial amount of regional and local variation was found, although respondents in all parts of the United States generally reported serious shortages of bilingual teachers. Some states reported shortages to be most prevalent in urban areas (Chicago was cited as having the most pronounced shortages in Illinois), while other states reported that urban districts were experiencing less-serious shortages than nearby non-urban areas (Miami-Dade County was cited as having a less-serious bilingual teacher shortage than were the nonurban counties in southern Florida). Even within a state, patterns of supply were not always discernible (in California, Los Angeles was reported to have serious shortages of bilingual teachers in all languages, while San Francisco apparently has not experienced shortages of the same magnitude).

Patterns of shortages by language were somewhat more consistent. Virtually all bilingual directors who were interviewed spoke of shortages of Spanish-language bilingual teachers. Even so, in the six districts described in chapter 5, fewer shortages were observed in Spanish-speaking bilingual personnel than in other bilingual personnel. This observation is consistent with other reports provided for this study. Serious shortages also were noted for languages spoken by recent immigrants to the United States (Haitian Creole in Florida and Indochinese languages in California). Teacher shortages in languages spoken by recent immigrants were not fully consistent with numbers of immigrants speaking a language, however. For example, among the Indochinese immigrants, relatively more Vietnamese speakers were reported by interview respondents to have become qualified as bilingual teachers or teacher aides, thereby making the teacher shortages in that language somewhat less serious than in other Indochinese languages. Conversely, the shortages in Haitian Creole are particularly severe because that language does not have a common written form, and a large percentage of recent immigrants, both children and adults, have had no schooling in Haiti. For these and other reasons, very few Haitian adults have been able to obtain positions as bilingual teachers or teacher aides.

Bilingual teacher shortages are also related to factors beyond the demographic characteristics of children with limited English proficiency. For example, two federal court decisions in Texas have dramatically increased the need for bilingual teachers in that state. In the first decision, *Doe* v. *Plyler*, the Fifth Circuit Court of Appeals required that local school districts in Texas provide educational services to children who have illegally immigrated to this country. These educational services are to be provided on the same basis as services provided to children who are U.S. citizens or otherwise legally present in the United States. Prior to that decision, many school districts with large numbers of undocumented children had either refused to provide any services to them or had required special tuition payments by parents of the children. Not surprisingly, an effect of the decision has been to increase the number of children with limited English proficiency who are enrolled in Texas, thus increasing the need for bilingual teachers there.[9]

In its recent decision in *United States* v. *Texas*, the Federal District Court for the Eastern District of Texas ruled that Mexican-American school children had been subjected to "pervasive, invidious discrimination throughout the state of Texas." Moreover, "current language-based learning problems suffered by these children were caused, at least in part, by prior unlawful acts" by the Texas education authorities. Accordingly the court's first priority in any plan for relief is that "bilingual instruction must be provided to all Mexican-American children of limited English proficiency in the Texas public schools." To this end, "a suitable plan to train and recruit sufficient bilingual education teachers to meet this requirement and a suggested timetable for implementation should be devised by TEA [Texas Education Agency]." In contradiction to provisions of previous Texas law, which required bilingual services only through the third grade, such services are to be provided to students with limited English proficiency through grade 12, as needed. Pending the resolution of appeals, Texas education authorities and representatives of plaintiffs in this suit are required to design a plan for implementation of the court's order. It will undoubtedly require the hiring of many more bilingual teachers than are now employed in the state, thus exacerbating current reported shortages.

A final issue associated with bilingual teacher shortages is the effect of such shortages on the types of services provided children with limited English proficiency. In school districts that have too few bilingual teachers, pull-out programs are frequently chosen as the bilingual instructional method. As noted by Carpenter-Huffman and Samulon in chapter 5, pull-out programs sometimes enable school districts to use their bilingual staffs more extensively by making larger student loads possible through the extensive use of bilingual aides to help regular bilingual teachers. These researchers noted that pull-out programs were used to compensate for the difficulty of recruiting sufficient bilingual staffs in general and to make up for teacher shortages in particular language areas, such as Chinese and Vietnamese. Carpenter-Huffman and Samulon did not indicate how many students with limited English proficiency were typically being served by each bilingual pull-out teacher. They did note, however, the higher-than-average instructional costs associated with bilingual pull-out instruction, as compared with bilingual classroom instruction. They attributed these higher costs to their observation that, unlike teachers in bilingual self-contained classrooms, teachers in bilingual pull-out programs do not replace regular classroom teachers and probably cannot do so because of the complexities in scheduling that would arise if they did. Thus, while pull-out programs constitute one solution to the problems of teacher shortages, they tend to cost more than other solutions.

Retention of Bilingual Teachers in Programs
Serving Children with Limited English Proficiency

A serious, recurring problem reported by state and local bilingual directors is the difficulty of retaining bilingual teachers in schools and classrooms providing special services to children with limited English proficiency. Not surprisingly, the characteristics of this problem varied widely according to the circumstances in the local school districts. For example, where the schools are located in blighted, high-poverty neighborhoods, bilingual teachers face all the problems of crime, truancy, and transience noted frequently in connection with inner-city schools. In areas where many children come from families who are not part of a religious, ethnic, or neighborhood support system, bilingual teachers often find themselves called on to serve as family advisers in health and social services as well as education. Even when these stresses and demands are not present, bilingual teachers often are required to assume particularly heavy instructional responsibilities because of a shortage of appropriate curricular materials and assessment instruments, particularly in languages other than Spanish. Several bilingual directors described this general phenomenon as "bilingual teacher burn-out."

The result of these problems is that in some school districts, bilingual teachers view their initial bilingual placement as an entry point into the school system, from which they can move into regular teaching positions as opportunities open up. In districts that are implementing affirmative-action hiring plans, a bilingual teaching placement is often a stepping-stone to more-senior instructional positions and to administrative roles. Bilingual directors uniformly support the notion of dispersing former bilingual teachers throughout the local education hierarchy (to serve as role models for students with limited English proficiency and for other bilingual teachers). They also noted the problems created by high turnover rates within the bilingual programs themselves.

Another factor causing high turnover rates in some places is the recruitment of experienced bilingual teachers by other school districts. A bilingual director in a Texas school district said in an interview that he often feels that his area is being used as a "training ground" by the big-city districts in Texas. When recruiters approach his experienced bilingual teachers with offers of higher salary, he has nothing comparable to offer to keep them, and so he loses his best teachers to districts with active recruitment programs and higher salary scales.

Extent to Which Patterns Are Evident

A major finding that emerges from this review is the regional variation reported by the respondents who were sampled. For example, all the districts in which interviews were conducted for this study engaged in recruitment activities, but the nature and intensity of such activities were largely dictated by local exigencies. Perhaps more important, all respondents reported serious teacher shortages, but the shortages of bilingual teachers did not fall into clearly discernible patterns. Teacher shortages and high turnover could not be attributed to specific states or regions, school district characteristics, or population density.

Conclusions

Among the findings of this study, three stand out as particularly relevant for purposes of national-policy consideration:

1. There are significant national shortages of bilingual teachers who are qualfied and willing to provide bilingual education. Although the inclusion of ESL teachers in the teacher count reduces the size of the estimated shortage, it does not eliminate the shortage.
2. The bilingual-teacher shortage could be dramatically lessened if all the qualified bilingual teachers not teaching in bilingual projects could be persuaded to do so.
3. School systems report that they have a serious need for bilingual teachers and that they use many approaches to fill that need, including various recruitment and training activities.

Considering these three findings in combination suggests that it is not particularly easy to lure qualified bilingual teachers into bilingual classrooms once they have decided, for whatever reason, not to teach there. State agencies and school system personnel with whom we talked had found recruitment to be difficult. Their experiences indicate that qualified bilingual teachers are not simply waiting to be asked to assume bilingual teaching positions. What is more likely is that school systems will have to devise more-compelling incentives to persuade bilingual teachers to take bilingual teaching jobs. These incentives may have to include monetary bonuses and lighter teaching loads. Also current bilingual training programs for teachers must be maintained and expanded.

It is apparent from conversations with many bilingual directors that whatever federal requirements are imposed, school districts that want to provide high-quality instructional programs to students with limited English proficiency will generally choose to employ bilingual-education teachers to teach in those programs. The two qualifications of bilingual teachers that seem to be most important in a practical sense are the teachers' willingness and ability to use the students' home language and English and the teachers' special personal focus on the learning needs of children with limited English proficiency. To the extent that other teachers who are not qualified as bilingual teachers can bring these qualities to bear in classrooms enrolling children with limited English proficiency, it may not be necessary to employ only qualified bilingual-education teachers to serve these students. In general, however, school districts that seek to serve these students adequately—whether as a result of federal regulatory requirements, decisions of the courts, or local educational priorities—will also want to employ bilingual-education teachers.

Notes

1. The term *bilingual-education teachers* is used to identify teachers who have received special training in the provision of instructional services

to students with limited English proficiency, including training in the provision of instruction using the home language of the students. This terminology is consistent with state practices in establishing minimum standards for teachers providing comprehensive instruction to these students.

2. Several states do not explicitly require proof of English proficiency as a prerequisite to certification. Since all states require at least a bachelor's degree, however, it seems probable that all states with bilingual-certification provisions do in fact assume that candidates will be proficient in English. I have received verbal reports, however, that several states with stringent requirements for second-language proficiency do not fully implement those requirements. Although these reports could not be confirmed, it appears that the serious shortage of trained bilingual teachers sometimes leads certfication examiners to accept candidates who do not meet the full requirements for proficiency in the second language.

3. As was indicated in chapter 1 by Robert Barnes, considerable evidence suggests that the lower of these two estimates is more nearly correct. However, because of the problems confronting any attempt to estimate the size of this group of students, the higher InterAmerica figure is also used here to indicate the upper bound on the estimated size of the population under consideration.

4. Carpenter-Huffman and Samulon in chapter 5 reported that they observed relatively little classroom instruction using bilingual education in the high schools that they visited for their study. What little bilingual instruction was provided to high-school students was generally delivered on a pull-out basis or using bilingual instructional aides working with English-monolingual teachers.

5. No data exist with which to estimate the number of students who are proficient in English who typically receive bilingual instruction. Therefore, my estimates of the need for bilingual teachers will be low to the extent that bilingual teachers typically serve students who are proficient in English, as well as those who are not.

6. California, which has a state law requiring bilingual classrooms whenever there are 10 or more students with limited English proficiency in the same grade in a school who speak the same primary home language, reports that 80 percent of its Spanish-speaking children are sufficiently concentrated to trigger the requirement for bilingual classrooms, whereas only 13 percent of the state's Vietnamese-speaking students (the state's second largest group with limited English proficiency) are similarly concentrated. The latter, therefore, are more likely to receive bilingual instruction on a pull-out basis.

7. Chapter 5 by Carpenter-Huffman and Samulon indicates that 19 percent of the regular classroom teachers in their sample school districts held bilingual-teaching certificates even though they were not teaching in bilingual

classrooms. Thus, a large number of teachers in these districts could have been providing bilingual instruction but were not.

8. Bilingual teacher training is a major objective of the Title VII program. The 1978 House report on ESEA reauthorization stated that improved training activities were needed to alleviate a serious national shortage of trained bilingual teachers and to improve the competencies of current bilingual teachers (Committee on Education and Labor 1978:88-89) In response to that concern, the Title VII statute contains a number of authorizations for bilingual training. In fiscal year 1981, more than $32 million was spent directly on training activities. In addition, a significant portion of the $113 million in Title VII grants to local school districts is used for training.

9. A bilingual director in a small south Texas city reported in an interview conducted for this study that in the fall of 1980, his district enrolled 2,150 new students recently arrived from Mexico, most of whom spoke no English and had had little or no schooling in Mexico. This number of new students represented almost 10 percent of the local school district's total enrollment. The respondent said he believed that approximately one-third of the new students are present in this country illegally.

References

Guidelines for the Preparation and Certification of Teachers of Bilingual/ Bicultural Education. 1974. Arlington, Va.: Center for Applied Linguistics.

Kaskowitz, D.; Binkley, J., and Johnson, D. 1981. *A Study of Teacher Training Programs in Bilingual Education.* Vol. II. *The Supply of and Demand for Bilingual Education Teachers.* Los Altos, Calif.: RMC Research Corp.

National Clearinghouse for Bilingual Education. 1980. *Guide to State Education Agencies.* Resources in Bilingual Education. Rosslyn, Va.: InterAmerica Research Associates.

U.S. House of Representatives. Committee on Education and Labor. 1978. *A Report on the Education Amendments of 1978, H.R. 15.* House of Representatives document 95-1137. 95th Cong. 2d Sess.

Waggoner, D. 1979. "Teacher Resources in Bilingual Education: A National Survey." *National Association of Bilingual Education Journal* 3 (Winter):53-60.

Appendix A:
The *Lau* Decision

SUPREME COURT OF THE UNITED STATES

No. 72-6520

Kinney Kinmon Lau, a Minor by and Through Mrs. Kam Wai Lau, His Guardian ad litem, et al, Petitioners, v. Alan H. Nichols et al.	On Writ of Certiorari to the United States Court of Appeals for the Ninth Circuit

[January 21, 1974]

Mr. Justice Douglas delivered the opinion of the Court.

The San Francisco California school system was integrated in 1971 as a result of a federal court decree, 339 F. Supp. 1315. See *Lee* v. *Johnson,* 404 U.S. 1215. The District Court found that there are 2,856 students of Chinese ancestry in the school system who do not speak English. Of those who have that language deficiency, about 1,000 are given supplemental courses in the English language.[1] About 1,800 however do not receive that instruction.

This class suit brought by non-English speaking Chinese students against officials responsible for the operation of the San Francisco Unified School District seeks relief against the unequal educational opportunities which are alleged to violate the Fourteenth Amendment. No specific remedy is urged upon us. Teaching English to the students of Chinese ancestry who do not speak the language is one choice. Giving instructions to this group in Chinese is another. There may be others. Petitioner asks only that the Board of Education be directed to apply its expertise to the problem and rectify the situation.

The District Court denied relief. The Court of Appeals affirmed, holding that there was no violation of the Equal Protection Clause of the Fourteenth Amendment nor of §601 of the Civil Rights Act of 1964, which excludes from participation in federal financial assistance recipients of aid which discriminate against racial groups. 483 F.2d 791. One judge dissented. A hearing *en banc* was denied, two judges dissenting. Id., at 805.

We granted the petition for certiorari because of the public importance of the question presented, 412 U.S. 938.

The Court of Appeals reasoned that "every student brings to the starting line of his educational career different advantages and disadvantages caused in part by social, economic, and cultural background, created and continued completely apart from any contribution by the school system." 483 F.2d at 497. Yet in our view the case may not be so easily decided. This is a public school system of California and §571 of the California Education Code states that "English shall be the basic language of instruction in all schools." That section permits a school district to determine "when and under what circumstances instruction may be given bilingually." That section also states as "the policy of the state" to insure "the mastery of English by all pupils in the schools." And bilingual instruction is authorized "to the extent that it does not interfere with the systematic, sequential, and regular instruction of all pupils in the English language."

Moreover §8573 of the Education Code provides that no pupil shall receive a diploma of graduation from grade 12 who has not met the standards of proficiency in "English," as well as other prescribed subjects. Moreover by §12101 of the Education Code children between the ages of six and 16 years are (with exceptions not material here) "subject to compulsory full-time education."

Under these state-imposed standards there is no equality of treatment merely by providing students with the same facilities, text books, teachers, and curriculum; for students who do not understand English are effectively foreclosed from any meaningful education.

Basic English skills are at the very core of what these public schools teach. Imposition of a requirement that, before a child can effectively participate in the educational program, he must already have acquired those basic skills is to make a mockery of public education. We know that those who do not understand English are certain to find their classroom experiences wholly incomprehensible and in no way meaningful.

We do not reach the Equal Protect Clause argument which has been advanced but rely solely on §601 of the Civil Rights Act of 1964, 42 U.S.C. §2000(d) to reverse the Court of Appeals.

That section bans discrimination based "on the ground of race, color, or national origin," in "any program or activity receiving federal financial assistance." The school district involved in this litigation receives large amounts of federal financial assistance. HEW, which has authority to promulgate regulations prohibiting discrimination in federally assisted school systems. 42 U.S.C. §2000(d), in 1968 issued one guideline that "school systems are responsible for assuring that students of a particular race, color, or national origin are not denied the opportunity to obtain the education generally obtained by other students in the system." 33 CFR §4955. In 1970 HEW made the guidelines more specific, requiring school districts that were federally funded "to rectify the language deficiency in order to open" the instruction to students who had "linguistic deficiencies." 35 Fed.Reg. 11595.

By §602 of the Act HEW is authorized to issue rules, regulations, and orders[2] to make sure that recipients of federal aid under its jurisdiction conduct any federal financed projects consistently with §601. HEW's regulations specify, 45 CFR §80.3(b)(1), that the recipients may not:

> Provide any service, financial aid, or other benefit to an individual which is different, or is provided in a different manner, from that provided to others under the program;

> Restrict an individual in any way in the enjoyment of any advantage or privilege enjoyed by others receiving any service, financial aid, or other benefit under the program.

Discrimination among students on account of race or national origin that is prohibited includes "discrimination in the availability or use of any academic . . . or other facilities of the grantee or other recipients." *Id.*, 80.5(b).

Discrimination is barred which has that effect even though no purposeful design is present: a recipient "may not . . . utilize criteria or methods of administration which have the effect of subjecting individuals to discrimination" or has "the effect of defeating or substantially impairing accomplishment of the objectives of the program as respect individuals of a particular race, color, or national origin." *Id.*, 80.3(b)(2).

It seems obvious that the Chinese-speaking minority receives less benefits than the English-speaking majority from respondents' school system which denies them a meaningful opportunity to participate in the educational program—all earmarks of the discrimination banned by the Regulations.[3] In 1970 HEW issued clarifying guidelines (35 Fed. Reg. 11595) which include the following:

"Where inability to speak and understand the English language excludes national origin-minority group children from effective participation in the educational program offered by a school district, the district must take affirmative steps to rectify the language deficiency in order to open its instructional program to these students." (pet. Br. App. 1a).

"Any ability grouping or tracking system employed by the school system to deal with the special language skill needs of national origin-minority group children must be designed to meet such language skill needs as soon as possible and must not operate as an educational deadend or permanent track." (Pet. Br. p. 2a).

Respondent school district contractually agreed to "comply with title VI of the Civil Rights Act of 1964 . . . and all requirements imposed by or pursuant to the Regulations" of HEW (45 CFR Pt. 80) which are "issued pursuant to that title . . ." and also immediately to "take any measures necessary to effectuate this agreement." The Federal Government has power to fix the terms on which its money allotments to the States shall be disbursed. *Oklahoma* v. *Civil Service Commission,* 330 U.S. 127, 142-143. Whatever may be the limits of that power, *Steward Machine Co.* v. *Davis*, 301 U.S. 548, 590 et seq., they have not been reached here. Senator Humphrey, during the floor debates on the Civil Rights Act of 1965, said:[4]

"Simple justice requires that public funds, to which all taxpayers of all races contribute, not be spent in any fashion which encourages, entrenches, subsidizes, or results in racial discrimination."

We accordingly reverse the judgment of the Court of Appeals and remand the case for the fashioning of appropriate relief.

Reversed.

Mr. Justice White Concurs in the result.

Notes

1. A report adopted by the Human Rights Commission of San Francisco and submitted to the Court by respondent after oral argument shows that, as of April 1973, there were 3,457 Chinese students in the school system who spoke little or no English. The document further showed 2,136 students enrolled in Chinese special instruction classes, but at least 429 of the enrollees were not Chinese but were included for ethnic balance. Thus, as of April 1973, no more than 1,707 of the 3,457 Chinese students needing special English instruction were receiving it.

2. Section 602 provides: "Each Federal department and agency which is enpowered to extend Federal financial assistance to any program or activity, by way of grant, loan, or contract other than a contract of insurance or guaranty, is authorized and directed to effectuate the provisions of section 2000d of this title with respect to such program or activity by issuing rules, regulations, or orders of general applicability which shall be consistent with achievement of the objectives of the statute authorizing the financial assistance in connection with which action be taken . . ."

3. And see Report of the Human Rights Commission of San Francisco, Bilingual Education in the San Francisco Public Schools, Aug. 9, 1973.

4. 110 Cong. Rec. 6543 (Senator Humphrey quoting from President Kennedy's message to Congress, June 19, 1963).

SUPREME COURT OF THE UNITED STATES

No. 72-6520

<table>
<tr><td>Kinney Kinmon Lau, a Minor
by and Through Mrs. Kam Wai Lau,
His Guardian ad litem, et al.,
Petitioners,
v.
Alan H. Nichols et al.</td><td>On Writ of Certiorari
to the United States
Court of Appeals for
the Ninth Circuit</td></tr>
</table>

[January 21, 1974]

Mr. Justice Stewart, with whom The Chief Justice and Mr. Justice Blackmun join, concurring in the result.

It is uncontested that more than 2,800 school children of Chinese ancestry attend school in the San Francisco Unified School District system even though they do not speak, understand, read, or write the English language, and that as to some 1,800 of these pupils the respondent school authorities have taken no significant steps to deal with this language deficiency. The petitioners do not contend, however, that the respondents have affirmatively or intentionally contributed to this inadequacy, but only that they have failed to act in the face of changing social and linguistic patterns. Because of this laissez faire attitude on the part of the school administrators, it is not entirely clear that §601 of the Civil Rights Act of 1964, 42 U. S. C. §2000d, standing alone, would render illegal the expenditure of federal funds on these schools. For that section provides that "[n]o person in the United States shall, on the ground of race, color, or national origin be excluded from participation in, be denied the benefits of, or be subjected to discrimination under any program or activity receiving Federal financial assistance."

On the other hand, the interpretive guidelines published by the Office for Civil Rights of the Department of Health, Education, and Welfare in 1970, 35 Fed. Reg. 11595, clearly indicate that affirmative efforts to give special training for non-English speaking pupils are required by Tit. VI as a condition to receipt of federal aid to public schools:

Where inability to speak and understand the English language excludes national origin-minority group children from effective participation in the educational program offered by a school district, the district must take affirmative steps to rectify the language deficiency in order to open its instructional program to these students.[1]

The critical question is, therefore, whether the regulations and guidelines promulgated by HEW go beyond the authority of §601.[2] Last Term, in *Mourning* v. *Family Publications Services, Inc.*, 411 U.S. 356, 369, we held that the validity of a regulation promulgated under a general authorization provision such as §602 of Tit. VI[3] "will be sustained so long as it is 'reasonably related to the purposes of the enabling legislation.' *Thorpe* v. *Housing Authority of the City of Durham* 393 U.S. 268, 280-281 (1969)." I think the guidelines here fairly meet that test. Moreover, in assessing the purposes of remedial legislation we have found that departmental regulations and "consistent administrative construction" are "entitled to great weight." *Trafficante* v. *Metropolitan Life Insurance Co.*, 409 U.S. 205, 210; *Griggs* v. *Duke Power Co.,* 401 U.S. 424, 433-343; *Udall* v. *Tallman,* 380 U.S.1. The Department has reasonably and consistently interpreted §601 to require affirmative remedial efforts to give special attention to linguistically deprived children.

For these reasons I concur in the judgment of the Court.

Notes

1. These guidelines were issued in further clarification of the Department's position as stated in its regulations issued to implement Tit. VI, 45 CFR pt. 80. The regulations provide in part that no recipient of federal financial assistance administered by HEW may: "Provide any service, financial aid, or other benefit to an individual which is different, or is provided in a different manner, from that provided to others under the program: [or]

"Restrict an individual in any way in the enjoyment of an advantage or privilege enjoyed by others receiving any service, financial aid, or other benefit under the program." 45 CFR §80.3 (b)(1)(ii), (iv).

2. The respondents do not contest the standing of the petitioners to sue as beneficiaries of the federal funding contract between the Department of Health, Education, and Welfare and the San Francisco Unified School District.

3. Section 602 provides: "Each federal department and agency which is empowered to extend Federal financial assistance to any program or activity, by way of grant, loan, or contract other than a contract of insurance or guaranty, as authorized and directed to effectuate the provisions of §2000d of this title with respect to such program or activity by issuing rules, regulations, or orders of general applicability which shall be consistent with achievement of the objectives of the statute authorizing the financial assistance in connection with which the action is taken . . ."

The United States as *amicus curiae* asserts in its brief, and the respondents appear to concede, that the guidelines were issued pursuant to §602.

SUPREME COURT OF THE UNITED STATES

No. 72-6520

Kinney Kinmon Lau, a Minor by and Through Mrs. Kam Wai Lau, His Guardian ad litem, et al, Petitioners, v. Alan H. Nichols et al.	On Writ of Certiorari to the United States Court of Appeals for the Ninth Circuit

[January 21, 1974]

Mr. Justice Blackmun, with whom The Chief Justice joins, concurring in the result.

I join Mr. Justice Stewart's opinion and thus I, too, concur in the result. Against the possibility that the Court's judgment may be interpreted too broadly, I stress the fact that the children with whom we are concerned here number about 1,800. This is a very substantial group that is being deprived of any meaningful schooling because they cannot understand the language of the classroom. We may only guess as to why they have had no exposure to English in their preschool years. Earlier generations of American ethnic groups have overcome the language barrier by earnest parental endeavor or by the hard fact of being pushed out of the family or community nest and into the realities of broader experience.

I merely wish to make plain that when, in another case, we are concerned with a very few youngsters, or with just a single child who speaks only German or Polish or Spanish or any language other than English, I would not regard today's decision, or the separate concurrence, as conclusive upon the issue whether the statute and the guideline require the funded school district to provide special instruction. For me, numbers are at the heart of this case and my concurrence is to be understood accordingly.

Appendix B:
Task-Force Findings Specifying Remedies Available for Eliminating Past Educational Practices Ruled Unlawful under *Lau* v. *Nichols*

Office for Civil Rights

I. Identification of Student's Primary or Home Language

The first step to be included in a plan submitted by a district found to be in noncompliance with Title VI under *Lau* is the method by which the district will identify the student's primary or home language. A student's primary or home language, for the purpose of this report, is other than English if it meets at least one of the following descriptions:

A. The student's first acquired language is other than English.
B. The language most often spoken by the student is other than English.
C. The language most often spoken in the student's home is other than English, regardless of the language spoken by the student.

These assessments (A-C, above) must be made by persons who can speak and understand the necessary language(s). Then the district must assess the degree of linguistic function or ability of the student(s) so as to place the student(s) in one of the following categories by language.

A. Monolingual speaker of the language other than English (speaks the language other than English exclusively).
B. Predominantly speaks the language other than English (speaks mostly the language other than English, but speaks some English).
C. Bilingual (speaks both the language other than English and English with equal ease).
D. Predominantly speaks English (speaks mostly English, but some of the language other than English).
E. Monolingual speaker of English (speaks English exclusively).

213

In the event that the student is multilingual (is functional in more than two languages in addition to English), such assessment must be made in all the necessary languages.

In order to make the aforementioned assessments the *district must, at a minimum, determine the language most often spoken in the student's home,* regardless of the language spoken by the student, the language most often spoken by the student in the home and the language spoken by the student in the social setting (by observation).

These assessments must be made by persons who can speak and understand the necessary language(s). An example of the latter would be to determine by observation the language used by the student to communicate with peers between classes or in informal situations. These assessments must cross-validate one another (Example: student speaks Spanish at home and Spanish with classmates at lunch). Observers must estimate the frequency of use of each language spoken by the student in these situations.

In the event that the language determinations conflict (Example: student speaks Spanish at home, but English with classmates at lunch), *an additional* method must be employed by the district to make such a determination (for example the district may wish to employ a test of language dominance as a third criterion). In other words, two of the three criteria will cross-validate or the majority of criteria will cross-validate (yield the same language).

Due to staff limitations and priorities, we will require a plan under *Lau* during this initial stage of investigation when the district has 20 or more students of the same language group identified as having a primary or home language other than English. However, a district does have an obligation to serve any student whose primary or home language is other than English.

II. Diagnostic/Prescriptive Approach

The second part of a plan must describe the diagnostic/prescriptive measures to be used to identify the nature and extent of each student's educational needs and then prescribe an educational program utilizing the most effective teaching style to satisfy the diagnosed educational needs. The determination of which teaching style(s) are to be used will be based on a careful review of both the cognitive and affective domains and should include an assessment of the responsiveness of students to different types of cognitive learning styles and incentive motivational styles—e.g., competitive v. cooperative learning patterns. The diagnostic measures must include diagnoses of problems related to areas or subjects required of other students in the school program *and* prescriptive measures must serve to bring the linguistically/culturally different student(s) to the educational performance level that is expected by the Local Education Agency (LEA) and State of nonminority students. A program designed for students of limited English-speaking ability must not be operated in a manner so as to solely satisfy a set of objectives divorced or isolated from those educational objectives established for students in the regular school program.

III. Educational Program Selection

In the third step the district must implement the appropriate type(s) of educational program(s) listed in this Section (III, 1-5), dependent upon the degree of linguistic proficiency of the students in question. If none seem applicable check with your *Lau* coordinator for further action.
1. In the case of the monolingual speaker of the language other than English (speaks the language other than English exclusively).
    A. At the Elementary and Intermediaste Levels:
        Any one or combination of the following programs is acceptable.

        1. Transitional Bilingual Education Program (TBE).
        2. Bilingual/Bicultural Program.
        3. Multilingual/Multicultural Program.

        In the case of a TBE, the district must provide predictive data which show that such student(s) are ready to make the transition into English and will succeed educationally in content areas and in the educational program(s) in which he/she is to be placed. This is necessary so the district will not prematurely place the linguistically/culturally different student who is not ready to participate effectively in an English language curriculum in the regular school program (conducted exclusively in English).
        Because an ESL program does not consider the affective nor cognitive development of students in this category and time and maturation variables are different here than for students at the secondary level, an ESL program *is not* appropriate.
    B. At the Secondary Level:

        Option 1. Such students may receive instruction in subject matter (example: math, science) in the native language(s) and receive English as a Second Language (ESL) as a class component.

        Option 2. Such students may receive required and elective subject matter (examples: math, science, industrial arts) in the native language(s) and bridge into English while combining English with the native language as appropriate (learning English as a first language, in a natural setting).

Option 3. Such students may receive ESL or High Intensive Language Training (HILT) . . . in English until they are fully functional in English (can operate equally successfully in school in English) then bridge into the school program for all other students.

A district may wish to utilize a TBE, Bilingual/Bicultural or Multilingual/Multicultural program in lieu of the three options presented in this section (III.1.B.). This is permissible. However, if the necessary prerequisite skills in the native language(s) have not been taught to these students, some form of compensatory education in the native language must be provided.

In any case, students in this category (III.1.B.) must receive such instruction in a manner that is expeditiously carried out so that the student in question will be able to participate to the greatest extent possible in the regular school program as soon as possible. At no time can a program be selected in this category (III.1.B.) to place the students in situations where the method of instruction will result in a substantial delay in providing these students with the necessary English language skills needed by or required of other students at the time of graduation.

NOTE: You will generally find that students in this category are recent immigrants.

2. In the case of the predominant speaker of the language other than English (speaks mostly the language other than English, but speaks some English):

A. At the Elementary Level:
Any one or combination of the following programs is acceptable.

1. TBE
2. Bilingual/Bicultural Program
3. Multilingual/Multicultural Program

In the case of a TBE, the district must provide predictive data which show that such student(s) are ready to make the transition into English and will educationally succeed in content areas and the educational program in which he/she is to be placed.

Since an ESL program does not consider the affective nor cognitive development of the students in this category and the time and maturation variables are different here than for students at the secondary level, an ESL program *is not* appropriate.

B. At the Intermediate and High School Levels:
    The district must provide data relative to the student's academic achievement and identify those students who have been in the school system for less than a year. If the student(s) who have been in the school system for less than a year are achieving at grade level or better, the district is not required to provide additional educational programs. If, however, the students who have been in the school system for a year or more are underachieving (not achieving at grade level) . . .the district must submit a plan to remedy the situation. This may include smaller class size, enrichment materials, etc. In either this case or the case of students who are underachieving and have been in the school system for less than a year, the remedy must include any one or combination of the following (1) an ESL, (2) a TBE, (3) a Bilingual/Bicultural Program (4) a Multilingual/Multicultural Program. *But* such students may not be placed in situations where all instruction is conducted in the native language as may be prescribed for the monolingual speaker of a language other than English, if the necessary prerequisite skills in the native language have not been taught. In this case some form of compensatory education in the native language must be provided.
    NOTE: You will generally find that students in this category are not recent immigrants.
3. In the case of the bilingual speaker (speaks both the language other than English and English with equal ease) the district must provide data relative to the student(s) academic achievement.
    In this case the treatment is the same at the elementary, intermediate and secondary levels and differs only in terms of underachievers and those students achieving at grade level or better.
    A. For the students in this category who are underachieving, treatment corresponds to the regular program requirements for all racially/ethnically identifiable classes or tracks composed of students who are underachieving, regardless of their language background.
    B. For the students in this category who are achieving at grade level or better, the district is not required to provide additional educational programs.
4. In the case of the predominant speaker of English (speaks mostly English, but some of a language other than English) treatment for these students is the same as III, 3 above.
5. In the case of the monolingual speaker of English (speaks English exclusively) treat the same as III, 3 above.
    NOTE: ESL is a necessary component of all the aforementioned programs. However, an ESL program may not be sufficient as the *only*

program operated by a district to respond to the educational needs of all the types of students described in this document.

IV. Required and Elective Courses

In the fourth step of such plan the district must show that the required and elective courses are not designed to have a discriminatory effect

A. Required courses. Required courses (example: American History) must not be designed to exclude pertinent minority developments which have contributed to or influenced such subjects.

B. Elective Courses and Co-curricular Activities. Where a district has been found out of compliance and operates racially/ethnically identifiable elective courses or co-curricular activities, the plan must address this area by either educationally justifying the racial/ethnic identifiability of these courses or activities, eliminating them, or guaranteeing that these courses or co-curricular activities will not remain racially/ethnically identifiable.

There is a prima facie case of discrimination if courses are racially/ethnically identifiable.

Schools must develop strong incentives and encouragement for minority students to enroll in electives where minorities have not traditionally enrolled. In this regard, counselors, principals and teachers have a most important role. Title VI compliance questions are raised by any analysis of counseling practices which indicates that minorities are being advised in a manner which results in their being disproportionately channeled into certain subject areas or courses. The school district must see that all of its students are encouraged to fully participate and take advantage of all educational benefits.

Close monitoring is necessary to evaluate to what degree minorities are in essence being discouraged from taking certain electives and encouraged to take other elective courses and insist that to eliminate discrimination and to provide equal educational opportunities, districts must take affirmative duties to see that minority students are not excluded from any elective courses and over included in others.

All newly established elective courses cannot be designed to have a discriminatory effect. This means that a district cannot, for example, initiate a course in Spanish literature designed exclusively for Spanish-speaking students so that enrollment in that subject is designed to result in the exclusion of students whose native language is English but who could equally benefit from such a course and/or be designed to result in the removal of the minority students in question from a general literature course which should be designed to be relevant for all the students served by the district.

V. Instructional Personnel Requirements

Instructional personnel teaching the students in question must be linguistically/culturally familiar with the background of the students to be affected.

The student/teacher ratio for such programs should equal or be less than (fewer students per teacher) the student/teacher ratio for the district. However, we will not require corrective action by the district if the number of students in such programs are no more than five greater per teacher than the student/teacher ratio for the district.

If instructional staffing is inadequate to implement program requirements, in-service training, directly related to improving student performance is acceptable as an immediate and temporary response. Plans for providing this training must include at least the following:

1. Objectives of training (must be directly related to ultimately improving student performance)
2. Methods by which the objective(s) will be achieved
3. Method for selection of teachers to receive training
4. Names of personnel doing the training and location of training
5. Content of training
6. Evaluation design of training and performance criteria for individuals receiving the training
7. Proposed timetables

This temporary in-service training must continue until staff performance criteria has been met.

Another temporary alternative is utilizing para professional persons with the necessary language(s) and cultural background(s). Specific instructional roles of such personnel *must* be included in the plan. Such plan must show that this personnel will aid in teaching and not be restricted to those areas unrelated to the teaching process (checking roll, issuing tardy cards, etc.)

In addition, the district must include a plan for securing the number of qualified teachers necessary to fully implement the instructional program. Development and training of para professionals may be an important source for the development of bilingual/bicultural teachers.

VI. Racial/Ethnic Isolation and/or Identifiability
of Schools and Classes

    A. Racially/Ethnically Isolated and/or Identifiable Schools—
        It is not educationally necessary nor legally permissible to

create racially/ethnically identifiable schools in order to respond to
student language characteristics as specified in the programs
described herein.
   B.   Racially/Ethnically Isolated and/or Identifiable Classes—
      The implementation of the aforementioned educational models
do not justify the existence of racially/ethnically isolated or identifiable classes, per se. Since there is no conflict in this area as
related to the application of the Emergency School Aid Act
(ESAA) and existing Title VI regulations, standard application of
those regulations is effective.

VII. Notification to Parents of Students Whose Primary or Home Language Is Other Than English

   A. School districts have the responsibility to effectively notify the
parents of the students identified as having a primary or home language other
than English of all school activities or notices which are called to the attention
of other parents. Such notice, in order to be adequate, must be provided in
English and in the necessary language(s) comprehensively paralleling the exact content in English. Be aware that a literal translation may not be sufficient.
   B. The district must inform all minority and nonminority parents of all
aspects of the programs designed for students of limited English-speaking
ability and that these programs constitute an integral part of the total school
program.

VIII. Evaluation

A "Product and Process" evaluation is to be submitted in the plan. This
type of evaluation, in addition to stating the "product" (end result), must
include "process evaluation" (periodic evaluation throughout the implementation stage). A description of the *evaluation design* is required.
Time-lines (target for completion of steps) is an essential component.
   For the *first three years,* following the implementation of a plan, the
district must submit to the OCR Regional Office at the close of sixty days
after school starts, a "progress report" which will show the steps which
have been completed. For those steps which have not been completed, a
narrative from the district is necessary to explain why the targeted completion dates were not met. Another "progress report" is also due at the close
of 30 days after the last day of the school year in question.

IX. Definition of Terms:

1. Bilingual/Bicultural Program

    A program which utilizes the student's native language (example: Navajo) and cultural factors in instructing, maintaining and further developing all the necessary skills in the student's native language and culture while introducing, maintaining, and developing all the necessary skills in the second language and culture (example: English). The end result is a student who can function, totally, in both language and cultures.

2. English as a Second Language (ESL)

    A structured language acquisition program designed to teach English to students whose native language is not English.

3. High Intensive Language Training (HILT)

    A total immersion program designed to teach students a new language.

4. Multilingual/Multicultural Program

    A program operated under the same principles as a Bilingual/Bicultural Program (X,1) *except* that more than one language and culture, in addition to English language and culture is treated. The end result is a student who can function, totally, in more than two languages and cultures.

5. Transitional Bilingual Education Program (TBE)

    A program operated in the same manner as a Bilingual/Bicultural Program, except that once the student is fully functional in the second language (English), further instruction in the native language is no longer required.

6. Underachievement

    Underachievement is defined as performance in each subject area (e.g. reading, problem solving) at one or more standard deviations below district norms as determined by some objective measures for nonethnic/racial minority students. Mental ability scores cannot be utilized for determining grade expectancy.

7. Instructional Personnel

    Persons involved in teaching activities. Such personnel includes, but is not limited to, certified, credentialized teachers, para professionals, teacher aides, parents, community volunteers, youth tutors, etc.

Appendix C:
The Proposed
Regulations,
August 1980

**Part 100 Nondiscrimination under Programs
Receiving Federal Assistance through the Department
of Education, Effectuation of Title VI of the Civil
Rights Act of 1964.**

The Secretary proposes to amend 34 CFR, Part 100 as follows:

1. Designate current regulations (§100.1-100.13) as Subpart A—Prohibited Discrimination.
2. Add a new Subpart B.

**Subpart B—National Origin Discrimination in Elementary
and Secondary Education**

§100.30 What is the purpose of this subpart?
The purpose of this subpart is—
  (a) To ensure that students will not be excluded from participation in, be denied the benefits of, or be subjected to discrimination in education programs and activities because they have a primary language other than English; and
  (b) To ensure that a student's limited proficiency in the English language will not bar the student from equal and effective opportunities to participate in Federally assisted education programs and activities.
(42 U.S.C. 2000d *et seq.*)

§100.31 To whom does this subpart apply?
This subpart applies to all recipients of Federal financial assistance who use this assistance to aid programs and activities of elementary and secondary education serving students from the beginning of school through twelfth grade.
(42 U.S.C. 2000d *et seq.*)

§100.32 What is the effect of violating this subpart?
A recipient's failure to identify students having a primary language other than English, to assess their language skills, to provide appropriate services,

or to undertake the other requirements of this subpart constitutes noncompliance with Title VI of the Civil Rights Act of 1964.
(42 U.S.C. 2000d *et seq.*)

§100.33 What definitions apply specifically to this subpart?
"Bilingual education" means instruction given through two languages, one of which is English.

"Bilingual individuals" refers to persons who are able to converse in English and in the appropriate primary language with considerable proficiency in those areas of instruction to which they are assigned. This ability includes the ability to speak and understand both languages and, where necessary to the duties assigned, the ability to read both languages. It neither implies nor precludes an extensive vocabulary that might be necessary to converse in the appropriate primary language with speakers on complicated matters not related to the duties to which they are assigned. However, bilingual individuals who are expected to communicate with parents on school matters must be able to do so in the appropriate primary language.

"Comparably limited in English and in the primary language" refers to limited-English-proficient students who are neither English-superior nor primary-language-superior.

"English-superior" refers to limited-English-proficient students whose ability to speak and understand English is clearly superior to their ability to speak and understand their primary language.

"Guardian" means the legal guardian or other person responsible for the welfare of the student.

"Limited-English-proficient" refers to students with a primary langage other than English who have sufficient difficulty with the English language that the opportunity to participate effectively in school is denied when English is the exclusive language of instruction.

"Minority" refers to students—

(a) Who are ordinarily identified by others, or who identify themselves, as either Black, Hispanic, Native American, of Asian origin; or
(b) Who have a primary language other than English.

"Primary-language-superior" refers to limited-English-proficient students whose ability to speak and understand their primary language is clearly superior to their ability to speak and understand English:

"Primary language other than English" means a language other than English that is—

(a) The first language the student acquired; or
(b) A language the student normally uses.

"Qualified bilingual education teacher" means a teacher who meets all of the following requirements:

(a) The teacher is qualified under State law to teach the subject and grade to which he or she is assigned.
(b) The teacher has successfully met appropriate standards for teaching in more than one language and for teaching English to speakers of other languages. These standards may be established by the State, recipient, or other lawful authority responsible for establishing such standards.
(c) The teacher is able to converse in English and in the appropriate primary language with considerable proficiency in those areas of instruction to which he or she is assigned. This ability includes the ability to speak, understand, read, and write both languages. It neither implies nor precludes an extensive vocabulary which might be necessary to converse in the appropriate primary language on complicated matters not related to the subjects which he or she is required to teach.
(d) The teacher is able to communicate with parents on school matters in the appropriate primary language.

"Relative language proficiency" refers to whether the student is primary-language-superior, English-superior, or comparably limited in English and in the primary language.

"Required subjects" means required courses, their officially approved alternatives, or other subject matter which the recipient expects all students to master. Art, music, and physical education are not required subjects for purposes of this subpart.

"Small student population" means a group of twenty-five or fewer students in a school—

(a) Who are entitled to bilingual instruction;
(b) Who are enrolled in two consecutive grades in the school;
(c) Who have a common primary language other than English; and
(d) Whose parents or guardians have not elected to withdraw them from the bilingual instruction described in §100.39(c).

(42 U.S.C. 2000d *et seq.*)

§100.34 What other definitions apply to this subpart?
The following terms, defined in 34 CFR 100.13, also apply to this subpart:

Department	Recipient	State
Federal financial assistance	Secretary	

(42 U.S.C. 2000d *et seq.*)

§100.35 How are students with a primary language other than English identified?

(a) (1) A recipient must identify the primary language of each student unless it determines that the student is not limited-English-proficient according to assessment procedures described in §100.36 or §100.37.

    (2) Students need not be identified if the assessment described in §100.36 or §100.37 indicates that they are not entitled to the services described in §100.38(b) or (c).

(b) Subject to paragraph (a) of this section, a recipient must use the following identification procedures:

    (1) In kindergarten through eighth grade the identification must be made either by an interview of the student's parent or guardian or by a questionnaire completed by the parent or guardian. The interview must be conducted or the questionnaire written in a language the parent or guardian fully understands. If the parent or guardian is unable to read a questionnaire, or if a questionnaire is not available in an appropriate language, an interview must be conducted.

    (2) For students in grades nine through twelve, a recipient may—

        (i) Use the identification methods described in paragraph (b)(1) of this section; or

        (ii) Interview the student or have the student complete the identification questionnaire.

    (3) If the questionnaire is not returned and an interview cannot be conducted, the recipient shall make every reasonable effort to contact the parent, guardian, or student to obtain the necessary information.

    (4) If, within four weeks of enrollment, the information required in paragraph (a) of this section cannot be obtained for a particular student, the student must be considered unidentified. These students must be assessed, as described in §100.36 and §100.37.

(42 U.S.C. 2000d *et seq.*)

§100.36 How must a recipient assess students to determine if they are limited-English-proficient?

(a) Each student who is unidentified, as defined in §100.35(b)(4), and each student having a primary language other than English, must be assessed to determine whether the student is limited-English-proficient.

(b) A student is limited-English-proficient if the assessment reveals either of the following circumstances:

    (1) The student's ability in English is so limited that the assessment procedure cannot be administered.

(2) The student's score, either on a test of proficiency in speaking and understanding English or, in grade two or above, on a test of reading comprehension achievement, is below the fortieth percentile of the norm established—

    (i) By the recipient's students (other than minority students) enrolled in the grade to which students of the same age are ordinarily assigned;

    (ii) Statewide, by students enrolled in the grade to which students of the same age are ordinarily assigned; or

    (iii) Nationally, by students enrolled in the grade to which students of the same age are ordinarily assigned.

(3) (i) For students below grade two, the recipient may omit the tests otherwise required by this section, temporarily classify the student as limited-English-proficient, and determine the student's instructional program after assessing the student's relative language proficiency according to the assessment procedures described in §100.37.

    (ii) At or before the beginning of grade two, these students must be assessed to determine whether they are limited-English-proficient using the procedures described in this section.

(42 U.S.C. 2000d *et seq.*)

§100.37 How does a recipient assess students' relative language proficiency?

(a) Each student classified as limited-English-proficient must be assessed to determine the student's relative language proficiency using an assessment procedure that independently measures proficiency both in English and in the student's primary language in such a way that the results can be compared.

(b) If no such assessment procedure is available in the student's primary language, recipients may develop or use a structured interview in English and in the student's primary language or some other documented procedure.

(42 U.S.C. 2000d *et seq.*)

§100.38 What standards of validity and reliability must assessment procedures meet?

An assessment procedure used to determine a student's limited English proficiency or relative language proficiency must be one that would be generally regarded by experts in the assessment or analysis of language proficiency as capable of—

(a) Measuring the language skills necessary to make instructional or other educational decisions about these students; and

(b) Producing consistent results.

    (42 U.S.C. 2000d *et seq.*)

§100.39 What services must be provided to limited-English-proficient students?

(a) *Equal access to compensatory education.* English-superior students shall receive equal access to services and classes designed to improve the speaking, undertaking, reading, and writing of English. For purposes of this paragraph, equal access means access on the same basis as students who do not have a primary language other than English.

(b) *Improving English language skills.* Students who are primary-language-superior or comparably limited in English and the primary language shall receive help designed to develop full proficiency in speaking, understanding, reading, and writing English.

(c) *Bilingual Instruction.*

ALTERNATIVE A

(1) *Instruction given in required subjects through both English and the primary language shall be provided to primary-language-superior students.*

ALTERNATIVE B

(1) *Instruction given in required subjects through both English and the primary language shall be provided to primary-language-superior students and to students who are comparably limited in English and the primary language.*

(2) (i) Except as otherwise provided by this subpart, this instruction must be given by a qualified bilingual teacher and shall be comparable in content, quality, objectives, and instructional materials to that offered students whose primary language is English.

   (ii) The pupil-teacher ratio for classes or instructional groups taught bilingually must be at least comparable (i.e. within two students per teacher) to that of similar classes taught through English. Nothing in this section prohibits a recipient from providing a lower pupil-teacher ratio for classes or instructional groups taught bilingually.

   (iii) English may be introduced as a means of instruction commensurate with the student's progress in acquiring skill in English.

(42 U.S.C. 2000d *et seq.*)

§100.40 When and how may required bilingual instruction be modified?

(a) For small student populations or students enrolled in or above grade nine, a recipient may provide instruction in required subjects through English and the primary language using any of the following methods:

(1) Magnet schools offering instruction through the primary language or itinerant qualified bilingual education teachers serving several schools.

(2) Any other method of using bilingual individuals (including student or parental tutors) or providing bilingual instruction (including the use of bilingual tapes and materials), if the method is offered in good faith and is monitored by the recipient to ensure that it is within the constraints imposed by the location or number of students, as effective as possible in serving these students.

(b) A recipient adopting a modified program must—

(1) Develop a detailed written plan describing the steps it will take to provide services to students receiving a modified program;

(2) Document efforts to meet the objectives of the plan; and

(3) Review its efforts at least annually, and modify the plan to improve upon the program provided to these students as necessary.

(42 U.S.C. 2000d, *et seq.*)

§*100.41 When may a recipient stop providing services to individual students?*

(a) *Bilingual instruction.* A recipient may stop providing the bilingual instruction described in §100.39(c) or §100.40 to a student who meets any of the following criteria:

(1) The student is no longer limited-English-proficient.

(2) The student has received the services for two years and the student—

(i) Is no longer entitled to bilingual instruction by virtue of relative language proficiency; or

(ii) Scores at or above the thirtieth percentile using an assessment procedure to determine whether a student is limited-English-proficient.

Cross-reference: See 34 CFR 100.36(b)(2)

(b) *Improving English language skill.* A recipient may stop providing the assistance in improving English language skills described in §100.39(b) to a student who meets any of the following criteria:

(1) The student is no longer limited-English-proficient.

(2) The student has received the services for two years and the student—

(i) Is no longer primary-language-superior or comparably limited in English and the primary language; or

(ii) Scores at or above the thirtieth percentile using an assessment procedure to determine whether a student is limited-English-proficient.

Cross-reference: See 34 CFR 100.36(b)(2)
    (3) The student has received the services for 5 years.
(42 U.S.C. 2000d *et. seq.*)

§100.42 How often must a student receiving required services be reassessed?

(a) Students receiving the bilingual instruction described in §100.39(c) must be reassessed for both limited English proficiency and relative language proficiency within two years of first receiving these services, and annually thereafter.

(b) (1) To reassess a limited-English-proficient student a recipient may use an assessment procedure that was different from the one used to assess the student initially. The reassessment procedure must meet the standards required for initial assessment described in §100.38.

    (2) However, the reassessment procedure must meet the standards required for initial assessment procedures.

Cross-reference: See 34 CFR 100.36, 100.37, 100.38.
(42 U.S.C. 2000d *et seq.*)

§100.43 What must a recipient do to avoid racial or ethnic isolation?

(a) Subject to the requirements in paragraphs (b), (c), and (d) of this section, the assignment of students to classes or instructional groups in a manner necessary to comply with the provisions of this subpart is not a violation of Title VI of the 1964 Civil Rights Act.

(b) Recipients must be able to show that they are using the least segregative method of meeting the requirements of this subpart.

(c) Limited-English-proficient students may not be assigned to separate classes in art, music, physical education, or extra-curricular activities nor given separate locations or times for meals and recess.

(d) No student having a primary language other than English may be assigned to a racially or ethnically identifiable class for more than one-half of the student's regular school day unless the recipient demonstrates that no other available, less segregative method of instruction is effective for that student. For purposes of this subpart, students' regular school day refers to the period beginning when the students in the same grade formally assemble to begin regular instruction and ends when these students are dismissed from such instruction.

(42 U.S.C. 2000d *et seq.*)

§100.44 What are minimum staff requirements?

(a) School districts must make every reasonable effort to identify, recruit, and employ a sufficient number of qualified bilingual education teachers to provide eligible students with required services.

(1) A sufficient number of qualified bilingual education teachers is the number necessary to ensure that the pupil-teacher ratio in classrooms offering this type of instruction will be at least comparable (i.e., within two students per teacher) to that for the same grade and for similar subjects taught in English.

(2) Employment of qualified bilingual education teachers who are not used to provide required services does not satisfy the requirements of this section.

(b) A recipient will be in compliance with the personnel requirements of this subpart even if it has been unable to obtain sufficient numbers of qualified bilingual education teachers when the following conditions are met:

(1) The recipient is assisting and encouraging its present staff to become qualified.

(2) If the recipient is obtaining a qualified bilingual education teacher through the additional training of an employee, the recipient can reasonably anticipate that the employee will become qualified within 5 years of the start of training if he or she is already a teacher, or within 6 years if he or she was not a teacher when training began.

(3) The recipient uses other bilingual individuals to provide services in the interim.

(4) (i) The recipient develops a detailed written plan describing the steps it will take to obtain qualified bilingual education teachers and to provide required services on an emergency basis.

(ii) The recipient documents its efforts to meet the objectives of its plan, reviews the plan annually, and improves upon it whenever possible.

(42 U.S.C. 2000d *et. seq.*)

§100.45 Must educational programs consider the cultural backgrounds of eligible students?

(a) Subject to paragraph (b) of this section, a recipient's educational programs and activities shall be operated with respect for the culture and cultural heritage of the recipient's limited-English-proficient students.

(b) A recipient is not required to make any changes in its educational programs and activities unless they have the effect of excluding students from effective participation in the recipient's programs on the basis of race or national origin.

(42 U.S.C. 2000d *et seq.*)

§100.46 Is a parent or guardian required to permit his or her child to participate?

A parent or guardian of a limited-English-proficient student may refuse

Bilingual Education

placement in, or withdraw the student from, any program to which the student is entitled under this subpart.
(42 U.S.C. 2000d *et seq.*)

§100.47 What are the parental notification requirements?
(a) Recipients must accurately, fully, and fairly inform parents or guardians within five days of any placement decisions made concerning their child.
(b) A responsible school official must inform parents or guardians of—
    (1) The purpose and nature of the services to which their child is entitled;
    (2) The reasons for their child's placement in classes providing the service;
    (3) Their right to refuse placement in, or withdraw the student from, any program to which the student is entitled and choose placement in an educational program generally provided to students who are not limited-English-proficient; and
    (4) The educational consequences that could result from failure to receive this assistance.
(c) The information required under paragraph (b) of this section must be provided in a language that the parent or guardian fully understands.
(42 U.S.C. 2000d *et seq.*)

§100.48 Can additional instruction be provided?
This subpart does not limit a recipient's right to offer instruction in or through a language other than English or to provide instruction in the literature, history, or culture of groups with a language other than English.
(42 U.S.C. 2000d *et seq.*)

§100.49 To what services are limited-English-proficient handicapped students entitled?
(a) Procedures to identify, evaluate, and place limited-English-proficient students who may be handicapped and eligible for special education and related services must take into account their language characteristics so that language background does not affect the outcome of these procedures.
(b) Where such a student is entitled to instruction through a language other than English, such instruction or appropriate equivalent instruction must be provided.
(c) The procedures to identify, evaluate, and place handicapped limited-English-proficient students must otherwise adhere to the requirements of 34 CFR 104, Subpart D, pertaining to nondiscrimination on the basis of handicap.
(42 U.S.C. 2000d *et seq.*)

§*100.50 When may the Secretary waive or modify the requirements of this subpart?*

The Secretary may waive or modify the requirements of this subpart under the following circumstances;

(a) *Enrollment increase.*

    (1) The recipient requests in writing a waiver for a limited period because of a substantial, rapid, unforeseen increase in the enrollment of limited-English-proficient students.

    (2) The recipient submits a proposal for the development of a plan that will show how and when the recipient will return to compliance with the requirements of this subpart.

    (3) The request is accompanied by appropriate evidence that documents the recipient's enrollment and inability to meet the requirements of this subpart.

(b) *Pilot programs.*

    (1) The recipient requests in writing a partial waiver of the requirements of this subpart in order to conduct a limited pilot program using other approaches designed to fulfill the purpose of this subject. The Secretary may approve programs that—

        (i) Are designed to demonstrate a more cost-effective approach to meeting the purpose of this subject;

        (ii) Are designed to demonstrate improved approaches to meeting the purpose of this subject that are capable of adaptation or adoption by other recipients; or

        (iii) Implement an innovative project conducted under an approved grant or contract with any agency of the Federal Government.

    (2) The request is accompanied by the following:

        (i) Evidence showing a substantial likelihood that the effort will be effective in fulfilling the stated purpose of this subpart.

        (ii) A description of procedures that will be used to evaluate the effectiveness of the pilot program. The first evaluation results must be available within two years of the date the waiver was granted.

        (iii) A description of the personnel, program of instruction, tests, and materials that will be used in the pilot program.

        (iv) A statement of the terms and conditions under which the recipient will discontinue the pilot program.

        (v) Should the program prove successful, a plan for expansion and, if the recipient chooses, a plan for replication of this program.

        (vi) Evidence that the recipient is in compliance with the requirements of this subpart.

(c) *Existing Alternative Programs.*

(1) The recipient requests in writing a waiver of personnel and services requirements of this subpart in order to operate an alternative program designed to meet the purpose of this subpart.

(2) The program for which a waiver is sought was in existence during the school year prior to the year in which these regulations become effective.

(3) The request is accompanied by evidence comparing students who have received assistance under the existing program with otherwise comparable students who are not entitled to bilingual instruction under this subpart and are enrolled in the same grade. The comparison group may be either local, state-wide, or national and must show similar results on the following factors:

(i) Achievement in reading and mathematics.

(ii) Dropout rate.

(iii) Attendance rate.

(iv) Average age in each grade.

(4) The recipient provides information about school matters to parents in a language the parents understand.

(5) The recipient describes the personnel, program of instruction, tests, and materials specifically used in the program.

(6) The recipient agrees to reevaluate its program every two years and to discontinue the program if the results of the evaluation show that the program is no longer achieving the results described in paragraph (c)(3) of this section.

(42 U.S.C. 2000d *et seq.*)

§100.51 What action is required to remedy a violation of the requirements of this support?

(a) (1) When a recipient is found to have violated the provisions of this subpart, the recipient must take such remedial action as the Secretary may require to correct the violation and to overcome its effects.

(2) If another recipient exercises control over the noncomplying recipient, both recipients may be required to take action to correct the violation and to overcome its effects.

(3) A recipient who has violated the provisions of this subpart must submit a plan, describing in detail how the recipient will eliminate the violation and overcome the effects of the violation on its students. This may include remedial instruction in the required subjects in which a student has been denied the services required by this subpart.

(i) Plans may be amended at any time with the mutual consent of the Secretary or his or her designee and the recipient.

(ii) Failure to comply with the terms and conditions of this plan constitutes a violation of Title VI of the 1964 Civil Rights Act.

(42 U.S.C. 2000d *et seq.*)

§100.52 What records must a recipient keep?

(a) Each recipient shall maintain adequate records to establish that it is in compliance with this subpart.

(b) The records shall show the following:

(1) The number, grade level, and relative language proficiency of limited-English-proficient students in each school.

(2) A summary description of the programs being offered these students.

(3) The number of qualified bilingual education teachers, and the number of other bilingual individuals by language in each school who are providing required bilingual instruction.

(4) The number of qualified bilingual education teachers, by language, necessary to provide required bilingual instruction.

(5) Representative samples of information sent to parents or guardians in a language other than English.

(6) A record of assessment procedures and results or other documentation to show that the assessment procedures being used to determine eligibility for services meet the requirements of this subpart.

(42 U.S.C. 2000d *et seq.*)

§100.53 What requirements apply to recipients using other languages for instruction?

(a) The provisions of this subpart shall apply to recipients whose primary language of instruction is not English.

(b) In the case of recipients of this type, the language the recipient ordinarily uses to provide instruction shall be deemed substituted for "English" wherever this word is used in this subpart.

(42 U.S.C. 2000d *et seq.*)

IDENTIFICATION STAGE	All students with a primary language other than English must be identified.

English Proficiency

All students with a primary language other than English must be assessed to determine whether they are limited-English-proficient.

ASSESSMENT STAGE	*Relative Language Proficiency*

All limited-English-proficient students must be further assessed using a measure of relative language proficiency to determine whether they are (1) primary-language-superior; (2) comparably limited in both languages; or (3) English-superior. The type of service (or services) that must be provided to a student depends on the student's relative language proficiency.

	What students must receive bilingual instruction?	What students must receive special English instruction?	What students must receive equal access to compensatory education?
THREE TYPES OF REQUIRED SERVICES	Students who are *primary language-superior* must receive bilingual instruction (Note: Depending on the alternative selected, students who are *comparably limited* may also be entitled to bilingual instruction).	Students who are either *primary-language-superior* or *comparably limited* must receive special instruction to improve English skills.	Students who are *English-superior* receive access to compensatory education on the same basis as students who do not have a primary language other than English.

Instruction continues until the student is no longer limited-English-proficient, *OR*	Instruction continues until student is no longer eligible to participate on the same basis as students who do not have a primary language other than English.

TERMINATING SERVICES	Instruction has been provided for at least two (2) years and the student is English-superior, (or comparably limited if ALTERNATIVE A IN §100.39(c) is selected).	Instruction has been provided for at least two (2) years and the student is English-superior, *OR*
		Instruction has been provided to the student for a maximum of five (5) years.

Figure C-1. Summary of Requirements in the Proposed Rules

Table C-1
Summary of Estimated Average Annual Cost for Start-Up Period (5 Years) and Alternative Options Considered and Rejected
(*Dollars in Thousands*)

Option	Cost above Current Services[a]	Cost over Full Compliance with the Lau Remedies	
Lau Remedies	$186,425 to $359,437		
Proposed rules			
40th percentile			
Alternative A	$175,989 to $389,361	− $ 10,436 to	$ 29,924
Alternative B	$288,513 to $591,774	$102,088 to	$232,337
25th percentile			
Alternative A	$142,055 to $312,972	− $ 44,370 to	− $ 46,465
Alternative B	$232,760 to $475,951	$ 46,335 to	$116,514
50th percentile			
Alternative A	$189,199 to $418,270	$ 2,774 to	$ 58,833
Alternative B	$308,412 to $632,748	$121,987 to	$273,311

[a]The estimates in this column represent the costs of providing services to eligible students who are currently unserved. No figures of actual expenditures for current services are available. However, if we assume that expenditures for each student presently served are equivalent to per pupil start-up costs under the *Lau Remedies* then we can estimate a maximum current expenditure level. On the basis of the 1978 Office for Civil Rights survey, we estimate that there are currently 831,000 PLS [Primary Language Superior] children receiving some special language instruction. This includes an allowance of 10 percent improvement in compliance for 1979 and 1980. Using our estimates of per pupil costs under the *Lau Remedies*, we obtain:

Low ($203 per pupil). Cost is $169 million
High ($391 per pupil). Cost is $325 million

Index

About the Contributors

Robert E. Barnes is a policy analyst in the Office of the Deputy Under Secretary for Planning, Budget, and Evaluation, U.S. Department of Education. Between 1977 and 1980 he was a member of the education planning group in the Office of the Assistant Secretary for Planning and Evaluation at the Department of Health, Education and Welfare. He has also directed data-user training and education programs at DUALabs and the Bureau of the Census. Before moving to Washington in 1968, he taught sociology and social psychology at the University of Michigan, Tulane University, and Louisiana State University.

Beatrice F. Birman is a policy analyst in the Office of the Deputy Under Secretary for Planning, Budget, and Evaluation, U.S. Department of Education. Dr. Birman completed her undergraduate work in sociology at Barnard College and graduate work in sociology of education at Stanford University. Her publications and papers have focused on the federal role in education, especially problems in the local implementation of federal education programs. She was instrumental in writing the Education Department's Regulatory Impact Analysis of the proposed Title VI rule for language-minority children. In addition to participating on the Title VII Part C Committee that determines research priorities for the Department of Education's bilingual-education program, she has recently been working on programs for handicapped children, educational technology, and issues of teacher quality.

Margaret Carpenter-Huffman began her research at the Rand Corporation and now develops training systems at Northrop Corporation. She has directed research on education and training for more than fifteen years, during which time she has addressed a broad range of topics from evaluation of alcohol-abuse-prevention programs to the design of military training. She has written more than thirty books and papers documenting her research findings. She received the B.A. in education and the M.S. in mathematics from Ohio State University.

Fran M. Ellman is a senior research analyst at Decision Resources in Washington, D.C., specializing in policy analysis and evaluation and program management. She has participated in policy studies of compensatory, special bilingual, and vocational education. She is now studying state approaches to programs for populations with special needs, including economically and educationally disadvantaged, handicapped, and language-minority students. She received the B.S. in early-childhood education from the University of Maryland and the M.A. in educational psychology and evaluation from Catholic University.

241

Alan L. Ginsburg is Director of Planning and Technical Support in the Office of the Deputy Under Secretary for Planning, Budget, and Evaluation, U.S. Department of Education. He received the Ph.D. in economics from the University of Michigan. Dr. Ginsburg was previously employed at the City University of New York and the Brookings Institution. He has published numerous articles on federal policy, school-finance reform, and educational evaluation. He has worked on the design of education legislative initiatives under Presidents Nixon, Ford, Carter, and Reagan.

Jan M. Gombert received the B.A. in mathematics from Princeton University and the M.A. in mathematics from the University of Virginia. He has taught secondary-school mathematics in Virginia, England, and Hawaii. As a computer analyst for AUI Policy Research, he has worked on numerous demographic and economic analyses of elementary, secondary, and higher education for the Department of Health, Education and Welfare and its successor agency.

Ann M. Milne, a senior research associate at Decision Resources, has been analyzing and evaluating federal education programs and policy since 1975. She is currently studying the operation of and future prospects for bilingual and other special-needs programs offered by a number of states. While at the National Institute of Education in the late 1970s, Dr. Milne was a senior member of the staff of the Compensatory Education Study, from which Congress drew during the 1978 reauthorization of the Elementary and Secondary Education Act. She has also done research on such topics as selection of air-traffic controllers and cigarette smoking among adolescents.

Elizabeth R. Reisner is director of the Washington office of NTS Research Corporation. Her professional work has consisted mainly of the examination of federal-policy issues in elementary and secondary education. In addition to her work on bilingual education, she has written about federal policy in desegregation, compensatory education, and vocational education. She has also examined policy issues in educational evaluation and the effects of federal regulatory activities in education.

Alvin S. Rosenthal is a statistician and analyst for Decision Resources in Washington, D.C. He has participated in educational-policy studies concerning language services for needy students, the equity of distribution of public-school funding across and within states, and the equity of distribution of educational resources among school districts within a state. He is now studying the stability of student achievement across grades and the socioeconomic and school-based influences on student learning. He received the Ph.D. in sociology from the Pennsylvania State University.

Marta K. Samulon joined the Rand Corporation in 1973 where she has conducted program evaluations and policy analyses relating to bilingual education, school desegregation, criminal justice, and women's equity. She is a consultant to both the Los Angeles Unified School District's Commission for Sex Equity, and Research and Evaluation Branch; and Orange County's Immigrant and Refugee Planning Center. She received the B.A. in political science and the M.A. in public policy from the University of California at Berkeley.

About the Editors

Keith A. Baker is a social-science analyst in the Office of the Deputy Under Secretary for Planning, Budget, and Evaluation, U.S. Department of Education. He received the B.A. from Miami University and the M.A. and Ph.D. in sociology from the University of Wisconsin. He has worked on the evaluation staff at the Office of Economic Opportunity and has taught at the Pennsylvania State University. In addition to publishing articles in several journals, he is coauthor of *Prison Education, Comprehensive Services to Rural Poor Families, Year-Round Schools,* and *Violence and Crime in the Schools.*

Adriana A. de Kanter, currently working for the U.S. Senate Subcommittee on Education, Arts and Humanities, held a Presidential Management Internship with the U.S. Department of Education in 1980. She received the B.A. from Mount Holyoke College and the M.P.A. from the Lyndon Baines Johnson School of Public Affairs at the University of Texas at Austin. Before working on the subcommittee, she coordinated all bilingual-education research efforts in the Office of Technical and Analytic Services, Office of the Deputy Under Secretary for Planning, Budget, and Evaluation. Most of her research and publications have focused on bilingual education and nutrition education.